Katherine Mansfield and Children

KATHERINE MANSFIELD STUDIES

Katherine Mansfield Studies is the peer-reviewed, annual publication of the Katherine Mansfield Society. It offers opportunities for collaborations among the significant numbers of researchers with interests in modernism in literature and the arts, as well as those in postcolonial studies. Because Mansfield is a writer who has inspired successors from Elizabeth Bowen to Ali Smith, as well as numerous artists in other media, *Katherine Mansfield Studies* encourages interdisciplinary scholarship and also allows for a proportion of creative submissions.

Katherine Mansfield and Children

Edited by
Gerri Kimber and Todd Martin

EDINBURGH
University Press

Edinburgh University Press is one of the leading university presses in the UK. We publish academic books and journals in our selected subject areas across the humanities and social sciences, combining cutting-edge scholarship with high editorial and production values to produce academic works of lasting importance. For more information visit our website: edinburghuniversitypress.com

Edinburgh University Press Ltd
The Tun – Holyrood Road
12(2f) Jackson's Entry
Edinburgh EH8 8PJ

Typeset in 10.5/12.5 New Baskerville by
Servis Filmsetting Ltd, Stockport, Cheshire

A CIP record for this book is available from the British Library

ISBN 978 1 4744 9190 7 (hardback)
ISBN 978 1 4744 9191 4 (paperback)
ISBN 978 1 4744 9192 1 (webready PDF)
ISBN 978 1 4744 9193 8 (epub)

Contents

Illustrations

Frontispiece

Plates

Figures

Acknowledgements

The editors would like to extend particular thanks to the judging panel for this year's Katherine Mansfield Society Essay Prize: Associate Professor Anna Jackson, Victoria University of Wellington, New Zealand, who served as Chair of the Judging Panel; Donna Couto, Assistant Editor at Juvenilia Press, University of New South Wales, Australia; and Dr Gerri Kimber, Visiting Professor, University of Northampton, UK. The winning essay, 'Casting "a haunting light": Katherine Mansfield's Modernist Vision of Childhood' by Tracy Miao, is featured in this volume.

The editors would also like to thank the following organisations and individuals: the Alexander Turnbull Library, Wellington, New Zealand, for permission to reproduce the following material: two illustrations by Edith Robison (*née* Bendall), a letter from Patrick White, an illustrated advertisement, and photographs of Mansfield's paper knife and typewriter. The Alexander Turnbull Library also kindly sponsored the colour reproductions of the latter. We are also grateful to the National Library of Australia for permission to publish the photograph of Patrick White, and to the Newberry Library, Chicago, USA, for providing the image by Edith Robison which adorns the cover. We also appreciate the kind correspondence we had with Lindy Erskine, granddaughter of Edith Robison. We would like to thank New Zealand's *Pantograph Punch* for permission to reprint Monica Macansantos's 'The Life-Affirming Words of Katherine Mansfield in a Time of Pandemic'.

As always, our thanks go to the entire team at Edinburgh University Press for facilitating the publication of the yearbook, especially Dr Jackie Jones, Ersev Ersoy, Fiona Conn and our diligent copy editor, Wendy Lee. Finally, we would like to thank our indexer, Ralph Kimber, for his professionalism and scrupulous eye for detail.

Abbreviations

Unless otherwise indicated, all references to Katherine Mansfield's works are to the editions listed below and abbreviated as follows. Letters, diary and notebook entries are quoted verbatim without the use of editorial '[*sic*]'.

CL1
The Edinburgh Edition of the Collected Letters of Katherine Mansfield: Vol. 1 – *Letters to Correspondents A–J*, eds Claire Davison and Gerri Kimber (Edinburgh: Edinburgh University Press, 2020).

CP
The Collected Poems of Katherine Mansfield, eds Gerri Kimber and Claire Davison (Edinburgh: Edinburgh University Press, 2016).

CW1 and CW2
The Edinburgh Edition of the Collected Works of Katherine Mansfield: Vols 1 and 2 – *The Collected Fiction*, eds Gerri Kimber and Vincent O'Sullivan (Edinburgh: Edinburgh University Press, 2012).

CW3
The Edinburgh Edition of the Collected Works of Katherine Mansfield: Vol. 3 – *The Poetry and Critical Writings*, eds Gerri Kimber and Angela Smith (Edinburgh: Edinburgh University Press, 2014).

CW4
The Edinburgh Edition of the Collected Works of Katherine Mansfield: Vol. 4 – *The Diaries of Katherine Mansfield, including Miscellaneous Works*, eds Gerri Kimber and Claire Davison (Edinburgh: Edinburgh University Press, 2016).

***Letters* 1–5**
The Collected Letters of Katherine Mansfield, 5 vols, eds Vincent O'Sullivan and Margaret Scott (Oxford: Clarendon Press, 1984–2008).

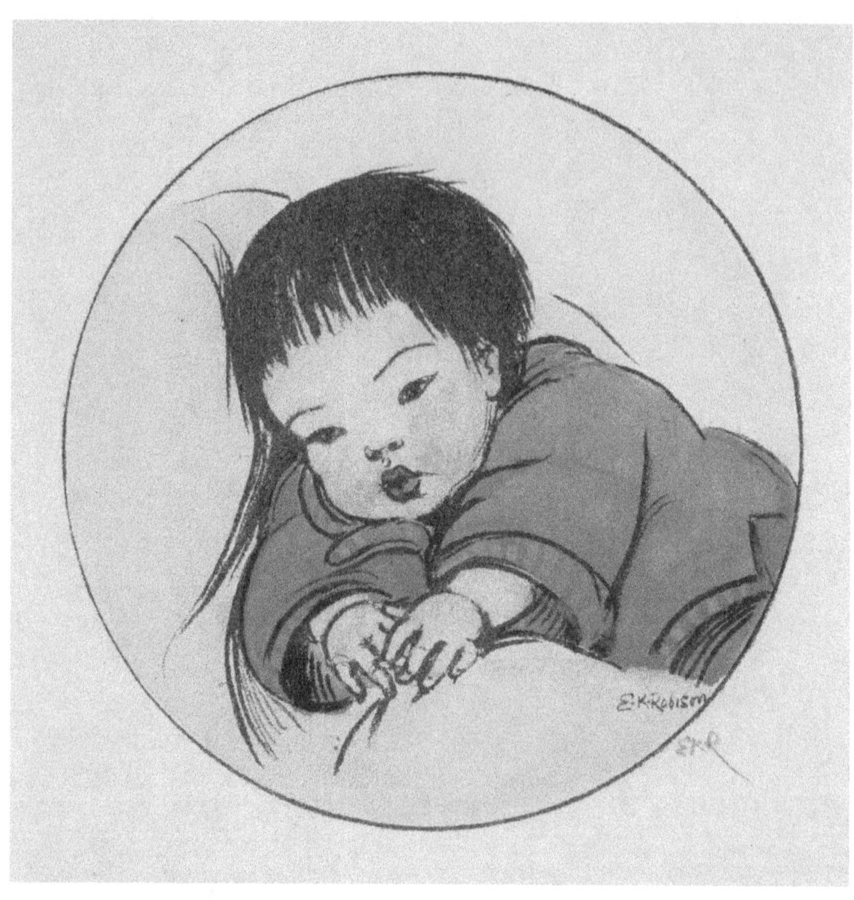

Frontispiece. Calendar illustrated by Edith Kathleen Robison (*née* Bendall), ink and watercolour on board, MS-Papers-11923-19, Brownlee Jean Kirkpatrick Papers, Alexander Turnbull Library, Wellington, New Zealand.

Introduction
'A kind of childlikeness' – Katherine Mansfield and Children

Gerri Kimber

Katherine Mansfield

Many years ago, when still a PhD student, I went to a conference where I found myself chatting in a coffee break to a senior academic whose field of expertise was entirely different to my own research. When I told her I was working on Katherine Mansfield, she responded: 'Oh yes, I've heard of her. Didn't she mainly write stories for children?' Indeed, this used to be quite a common misperception: the children Mansfield depicts are so vividly presented, so finely portrayed and thus so memorable, that they appear to monopolise the stories in which they appear, which explains why, in the past, many critics chose to dwell almost exclusively on them. When combined with the beauty of her natural descriptions and unusual images, the general effect of many of Mansfield's stories can have an almost fairy-tale-like quality and appear 'childlike'. Discussing the English short story, Anthea Trodd points out how, in the early years of the twentieth century, 'the brevity and relative marginality of this still, in English, fairly new form, offered [Mansfield] a refuge analogous to that of children's fiction'.[1] And as noted in my anecdote above, for many readers and critics, the perception was that she *was* almost writing children's fiction.

Mansfield criticism remained in the doldrums for many decades after her death, in part because of this misperception and the fact that her stories are deceptively easy to read, which unjustifiably led to a dismissal of her œuvre as slight. Negativity towards her in general was also, to a large degree, brought on by her husband, John Middleton Murry, whose overwhelming hagiography and falsification of his dead wife's life and works, in numerous posthumous publications, tainted his reputation as well as hers, especially in England, for many years. Murry most certainly had an agenda in promoting Mansfield's work, seeing himself as the sole guardian of her literary legacy. As Jenny McDonnell notes, 'Sylvia Lynd described his generation of a Mansfield industry as "boiling Katherine's bones to make soup", while Lawrence claimed he "made capital out of her death".'[2]

Happily, in the last couple of decades the tide has turned in Mansfield studies, in part due to the formation of the international Katherine Mansfield Society and its prestigious annual publication, Katherine Mansfield Studies, so that now Mansfield is viewed as one of the most exciting and cutting-edge exponents of the modernist short story. Indeed, Peter Childs goes so far as to state that she is 'the most important Modernist author who wrote only short stories'.[3] Today, New Zealand recognises Mansfield as one of its greatest literary icons and her birthplace in Wellington is one of the country's most visited tourist attractions, where schoolchildren especially love to see where Kezia – the little fictional girl in whom Mansfield imbued so much of herself in her New Zealand 'Burnell' cycle of stories – had her origins. Kezia had been an old family name, and several generations of Beauchamp women could lay claim to it, a fact well known to Mansfield. It was a name she underlined in her schoolgirl Bible: 'And he called the name of the first, Jemima; and the name of the second, Kezia; and the name of the third, Kerenhappuch.'[4] Years later, as a professional writer, she would draw on her rich memories of her childhood to fashion some of the most memorable stories ever written by a New Zealand author, using innovative, experimental techniques that we now associate with literary modernism. Yet, as I shall explain, though children may be depicted in many of her most famous stories, her subject-matter is entirely adult in both form and content.

The theme of this volume, Katherine Mansfield and Children, is a deliberately broad one, intended to encompass far more than just the child characters in her short stories. Virginia Woolf once remarked that Mansfield had 'a kind of childlikeness somewhere which has been much disfigured, but still exists'.[5] This 'childlikeness' is, indeed, a facet of Mansfield's personality which permeates every aspect of her personal and creative life. It is present in her mature fiction, where some of her most well-known and accomplished stories, such as 'Prelude' and 'At the Bay', have children as protagonists; it is present in her early poetry, which includes a collection of poems for children intended for publication; it is also present in her juvenilia, where many of the stories she wrote from an early age, for school magazines and other publications, feature children. As Tracy Miao notes of her mature fiction, 'in Mansfield's modelling of her child artists, and their relationship with seeing and representation, there is more than a simple "childlikeness" [. . .] but a serious thought process on art and the artist'.[6] Even as an adult, Mansfield's love of the miniature, her delight in children in general, her fascination with dolls, all feature in her personal writing. Her two Japanese dolls, O Hara San and Ribni, are anthropomorphised into living little beings, as here in a letter to Murry, written on Christmas Day, 1915:

> We are still quite babies enough to play with dolls and I'd much rather pretend about [O] Hara [San] than about a real person. I would so see her, with her little hands in her kimono sleeves, very pale and wanting her hair brushed.[7]

Mansfield's attraction to Japonisme continued throughout her adult life and was even a feature of her own physical appearance. A childhood friend, Sylvia Lynd, claimed she looked 'not unlike one of those little dolls [. . . from] Japan's less commercial days',[8] and Woolf, reminiscing after Mansfield's death about a visit she had paid to her in 1919, wrote: 'She had her look of a Japanese doll, with the fringe combed quite straight across her forehead.'[9] J. Lawrence Mitchell comments on her deep affection for her Japanese dolls as being a symbol of 'her aesthetic of the miniature',[10] which is clearly present in all her writing, and adds to its childlike quality.

Childbirth

Mansfield herself never had children, though most biographers agree that she almost certainly underwent at least two abortions and an ectopic pregnancy. In addition, in late June 1909, in probably the most traumatic – and bleakest – moment of her life, alone in Bavaria, she suffered the horror of a stillbirth.[11] Just a few days before, Mansfield had written a diary entry addressed to Garnet Trowell, the baby's father:

> The only adorable thing I can imagine is for my Grandmother to put me to bed – & bring me a bowl of hot bread & milk & standing, her hands folded – the left thumb over the right – and say in her adorable voice:– 'There darling – isn't that nice'. Oh, what a miracle of happiness that would be. To wake later to find her turning down the bedclothes to see if your feet were cold – & wrapping them up in a little pink singlet softer than a cat's fur . . . Alas![12]

Remembering her own precious childhood became the only comfort she sought. Indeed, Mansfield seemingly never forgot the pain – both physical and emotional – of this period. Thereafter in her fiction, childbirth would become associated with anguish, drudgery and exhaustion, as well as the condemnation of voracious male sexual appetites.

Nowhere is this more pronounced than in her first collection of stories, *In a German Pension,* published in 1911, but mostly written in Bavaria in the second half of 1909, following the delivery of her own dead baby. Three of the stories, 'At Lehmann's', 'A Birthday' and 'The Child-Who-Was-Tired', are different from the others, in that they take childbirth as their most overt theme. In 'At Lehmann's', an innocent young servant is left traumatised, both by the terrifying realities of her mistress's pregnancy and labour, and the sexual advances of a predatory male. The physical pain of childbirth is also revealed in 'A Birthday', where a selfish husband considers his own mental strain during the process of childbirth rather than his wife's physical pain. In the most depressing story of them all, 'The Child-Who-Was-Tired', a very young, overworked and underfed servant girl resorts to the suffocation of one of the babies in her charge when she finds out her mistress is pregnant again. In a fourth story, 'Frau Brechenmacher Attends a Wedding', the constant assertion of conjugal rights leaves the titular character, Frau Brechenmacher, at the mercy of her husband's sexual appetites. Here Mansfield sends out a clear message about the general unhappiness, subjugation and physical suffering of the female, in contrast to the selfishness, greed and sexual appetites of the male. In this cycle of stories, set in a Bavarian spa town, the setting is semi-autobiographical, as are a number of the themes. The horrific experiences Mansfield underwent during 1909 are covertly interwoven, with an insightful mockery, into her tales of the hypochondriac 'cure' residents in the German pension.

Almost ten years later, in both 'Prelude' and 'At the Bay', an uneasy sexual awareness still penetrates and colours Mansfield's writing. In 'Prelude', the sexual undertone centres firstly on the mother, Linda Burnell, and the narrator's intent is to show how three births in close succession have reduced a wife to near-frigidity. In Linda's eyes, her husband is a 'Newfoundland dog [. . .] that I'm so fond of in the daytime',[13] but at night the good-natured buffoon of a man, Stanley Burnell, so amusingly portrayed in both stories, seems an entirely different character:

> There were times when he was frightening – really frightening. When she just had not screamed at the top of her voice: 'You are killing me'. And at those times she had longed to say the most coarse hateful things. Yes, yes it was true. [. . .] For all her love and respect and admiration she hated him.[14]

Linda Burnell is a strange, almost fleeting character, whose personality and innermost thoughts are revealed by Mansfield in a series of thinly veiled interior monologues during the course of the 'Burnell' cycle of stories. She is a dreamer, a solitary person, a woman with no urgent sexual desire, yet who has had to give herself up to her husband as duty compels her to do. The despair she feels in 'Prelude' carries through to 'At the Bay':

> And what was left of her time was spent in the dread of having children. Yes, that was her real grudge against life; that was what she could not understand. [. . .] It was all very well to say it was the common lot of women to bear children. It wasn't true. She for one could prove that wrong. She was broken, made weak, her courage was gone, through child-bearing. And what made it doubly hard to bear was, she did not love her children.[15]

In this extract, Mansfield is seen fighting for a woman's right to do as she sees fit with her own body. Dominic Head concurs generally with this notion and sees in 'Prelude' 'the evocation of male sexual predacity and female victimisation'[16] in a story superficially centred on a simple house move, where the main characters appear to be little children, absorbed in their world of make-believe and play. Such outbursts as expressed above by Linda Burnell are blistering attacks on the then commonly held view of women as mere child-bearers. The same is true of Ma Parker, the protagonist in 'Life of Ma Parker'. Though she does not have the verbal means to express it, we see her, alone, in a society that places no value on her, except as a child-bearing machine:

> 'A baker, Mrs Parker!' the literary gentleman would say. For occasionally he laid aside his tomes and lent an ear, at least, to this product called Life. 'It must be rather nice to be married to a baker!'
>
> Mrs Parker didn't look so sure.
>
> 'Such a clean trade,' said the gentleman.
>
> Mrs Parker didn't look convinced.
>
> 'And didn't you like handing the new loaves to the customers?'
>
> 'Well, sir,' said Mrs Parker, 'I wasn't in the shop above a great deal. We had thirteen little ones and buried seven of them. If it wasn't the 'ospital it was the infirmary, you might say!'
>
> 'You might, *indeed*, Mrs Parker!' said the gentleman, shuddering, and taking up his pen again.[17]

In fact, the story 'Life of Ma Parker' is, for Susan Lohafer, a 'Feminist Exemplum':

> In the short, declarative statement that ends this story, Ma states what she needs [. . .], an urgency is developing, an I is emerging. From a feminist perspective, this is a tragically meagre, yet relatively great achievement for a woman like Ma.[18]

Strikingly, we see in the character of Ma Parker the potency of Mansfield's narrow focus, which, while individualising one person's suffering, is in fact representative of an entire sociological group.

Once her relationship with Murry had been established, Mansfield clearly longed for a child of her own, but the damage inflicted on her body by her past affairs and subsequent ill health made this dream an impossibility. Angela Smith goes so far as to speculate that in the case of both Mansfield and Virginia Woolf, 'it is possible to wonder whether the unfulfilled desire to experience motherhood led to the creation of fictional children: Kezia, the Sheridan children, the young Ramseys. [. . .] Certainly both writers see their work as a refuge from sterility and despair.'[19] Even in Mansfield's personal writing, occasional glimpses of regret at her past actions, which have resulted in her childless state, are evident. At the beginning of 1920, in Ospedaletti, at the height of a severe bout of loneliness and depression, she writes:

> Very tired. The sea howled and boomed and roared away. When will this cup pass from me? Oh misery! I cannot sleep. I lie retracing my steps – going over all the old life before. . . . The baby of Garnet's love.[20]

Childlike Relationships

In 1911, in a diary entry, Mansfield described herself in childlike terms: 'I am become a little child again. [. . .] I live only, only in my imagination. All my feelings are there and my desires and my ambitions.'[21] This would almost appear to be a credo for Mansfield's subsequent writing technique: becoming a child, in the sense of retreating into the world of the imagination. It prefigures her subsequently much-quoted letter to Murry, dating from almost ten years later, on 3 November 1920, when she would write:

> Ive *been* this man *been* this woman. Ive stood for hours on the Auckland wharf. Ive been out in the stream waiting to be berthed. Ive been a seagull hovering at the stern and a hotel porter whistling through his teeth. It isn't as though one sits and watches the spectacle. That would be thrilling enough, god knows. But one IS the spectacle for a time. If one remained oneself all the time like some writers can it would be a bit less exhausting. Its a lightning change affair, tho.[22]

Her imagination is so vivid that she can almost become *any*one and *any*thing.

Mansfield's relationship with Murry was characterised by their mutual descriptions of themselves as little children fighting against a corrupt world. Alluding to their innocence, she once wrote to him:

> My grown up self sees us like two little children who have been turned out into the garden. There we are hand in hand, while my G.U.S [grown-up self] looks on through the window. And she sees us stop – & touch the gummy bark of the tree, or lean over a flower & try to blow it open by breathing very close – or pick up a pebble and give it a rub & then hold it up to the sun & see if there's any gold in it.[23]

It is the intensity of the detail, as if Mansfield is remembering a specific scene from her childhood, with Murry now added as an extra persona, which renders the description so lifelike and so memorable. Two years later, in 1920, speaking of Murry's writing, she notes, 'Take care of yourself – my beloved child with all these wild men about throwing stones and striking. Make yourself small – fold yourself up.'[24] Here she takes on a more motherly tone, comforting and cosseting Murry as if he were a small, frightened boy. Her maternal feelings, in the absence of a child of her own, are now projected onto her relationship with Murry. Elsewhere, she herself is the child, and Murry the wicked, cruel, unfeeling grown-up, as in a poem she sent to him in 1919, called 'The New Husband', the first stanza of which reads:

> Some one came to me and said
> Forget, forget that you've been wed
> Who's your man to leave you be
> Ill and cold in a far country
> Who's the husband – who's the stone
> Could leave a child like you alone.

The poem is a bitter attack on Murry, for his perceived abandonment of her in Ospedaletti, as she voices her inner fears and despair at his cruelty. Analysing her feelings in a diary entry written on 17 December 1919, the day after Murry finally arrived to be with her, she writes:

> We had been for 2 years drifting into a relationship different to anything I'd ever known – we'd been children to each other, openly confessed children, telling each other everything, each <u>depending</u> equally upon the other. Before that I'd been the man and he had been the woman & he had been called upon to make no real efforts. He'd never really 'supported' me. When we first met, in fact, it was I who kept him and afterwards we'd always acted (more or less) like men friends. Then this illness – getting worse & worse & turning me into a woman and asking him to put himself away & to <u>bear</u> things for me. He stood it marvellously. It helped very much because it was a 'romantic' disease (his love of a 'romantic appearance' is <u>immensely</u> real) and also being 'children' together gave us a practically unlimited chance to play at life – not to live. It was child love.[25]

This psychological comprehension of the true state of her relationship with Murry would eventually also feed into her fiction, in stories such as 'Psychology' and 'The Man Without a Temperament', where the male figure is a two-dimensional cardboard cut-out, oblivious to the reality of the situation in which he finds himself.

Child Characters

As noted above, it is, of course, for her depiction of children that Mansfield is particularly renowned. Children are of paramount importance in every story in which they appear – and they appear very frequently – in 'Prelude', 'At the Bay', 'Sun and Moon', 'The Doll's House' and many others. But these stories are *not* children's stories (which they are sometimes mistaken for). Instead, children are used as pawns in Mansfield's symbolist narrative. Mansfield portrays them in their own world but also trying to survive in the adult world with all its inherent difficulties.

The New Zealand stories in particular are the most autobiographical in content and are dominated by the portrayal of children and the relationships they have with their parents and the adult world in general. Anne Holden Rønning states that 'a child's attempt to understand grown-up behaviour should [. . .] be a key issue in any interpretation of "The Garden Party"'.[26] I would agree, and extend this notion to cover every story of Mansfield's where children play a prominent role, and where her social conscience and finely tuned sense of injustice is particularly evident.

Nowhere is this better demonstrated than in 'The Doll's House'. Here again are the Burnell children, and the title invites the reader to settle back and enjoy a light-hearted children's story, but the title is only the outward visual presence hinting at a more significant, if hidden, reality. The little girl, Kezia, whose mind the reader inhabits, shows the shock children suffer when confronted with the adult world. It is a child's-eye view of the world, portrayed through such images and child-speak as 'spinach green',[27] 'the door was like a little slab of toffee' (p. 415), 'why don't all houses open like that?' (p. 415). Adults intrude only briefly into the narrative. Instead, they are presented through the speech and thoughts of the children, achieved by exploiting the way children mimic their elders: 'Emmie swallowed in a very meaning way and nodded to Isabel as she'd seen her mother do on these occasions' (p. 418). The unbending, awkward attitudes of the adult world are portrayed in the image of the stiffly sprawled father and mother dolls who do not really fit, either in the doll's house itself, or in the innocent world of the children. Head notes how

> The children [. . .] absorb and use adult discourse not specifically designed for their own consumption, and this, again, raises the issues of ideological power and conditioning. When Mansfield has the children play at being adults a serious investigation along these lines lies beneath the humorous vignette of childish mores.[28]

The children imitate their parents in the world of social rules and regulations. They follow their parents' lead in despising the Kelvey family for their poverty. Mrs Kelvey is described as a 'spry, hardworking washerwoman' (pp. 416–17). Spry and hardworking are praiseworthy attributes, yet this description is followed by the ironical statement, 'This was awful enough' (p. 417). What is awful is that she is a washerwoman; it is merely her situation in life that lets Mrs Kelvey down. The unfounded rumour that Mr Kelvey is in prison soon becomes a 'fact'. The whole episode is a penetrating insight into the sometimes bigoted and narrow-minded attitudes of provincial life, together with its ritualistic behaviour.

The little lamp in the doll's house is the centrepiece of the story, making a symbolic reappearance from the original real-life lamp that Kezia carries in 'Prelude'. Kezia (and her lamp) hold out a ray of hope to the ostracised Kelveys, with her childlike, innocent attempt to include them in the fold. Yukiko Kinoshita asserts that 'Kezia (as well as Mrs Fairfield) is characterised ideally; she represents conscience and humanity in the story. [. . .] The lamp in "Prelude" is given the same symbolical meaning as in "The Doll's House"; it represents truth, beauty and morality.'[29] For Clare Hanson and Andrew Gurr, too, '[t]he little lamp is not only light but art, the central reality amidst the material splendours of the doll's house'.[30]

As is clear, even a brief examination of this story reveals the deeper undercurrents that pervade all Mansfield's writing, completely overlooked by some early English critics, such as Kay Boyle, who, in 1937, wrote:

> There are blue skies with soft puffs of cloud in them, quaint houses, shimmering seas in pastel colours, Frenchmen invariably with big mustaches; doll's tea sets, incredibly cute children, pretty names such as Pearl Button, pretty places and not enough, for what the intent must have been, hot love and comprehension for the persecuted young or old, or satire bitter enough for those she would condemn.[31]

Yet even Jack Garlington, who, in 1956, condemned the above opinion as 'warped', goes on to state that 'it is true that little of Katherine Mansfield's work has a sociological basis'.[32] I contend that *all* of Mansfield's narrative art has a sociological basis, more overt in some stories than in others, and especially true in the stories where children are present.

As I have noted elsewhere,[33] understanding Mansfield the child is the key to unlocking Mansfield the adult. No amount of biographical research can compete with Mansfield's own portrait of herself in the guise of Kezia in the Burnell stories. If you want to understand the essence of her much-loved uncle, Val Waters, his spirit is to be found in Jonathan Trout. All the characters from Mansfield's childhood – even walk-on parts for outsiders, such as 'Old Tar' – are present in her fiction. In particular, the delineation in her fiction of children and young adults reveals a remarkable ability to enter into the mind of her subject, where the smallest details illuminate the bigger picture, as here in 'Prelude' (1917):

> Kezia liked to stand so before the window. She liked the feeling of the cold shining glass against her hot palms, and she liked to watch the funny white tops that came on her fingers when she pressed them hard against the pane. As she stood there, the day flickered out and dark came. With the dark crept the wind snuffling and howling. The windows of the empty house shook, a creaking came from the walls and floors, a piece of loose iron on the roof banged forlornly. Kezia was suddenly quite, quite still, with wide open eyes and knees pressed together. She was frightened.[34]

A universal childhood experience – staring through a window, hands pressed against the glass – is turned into a particularly New Zealand one, where the passage from day to night is a far swifter process than in the northern hemisphere. And thus, an empty room, an empty house and darkness become the symbols of the Beauchamp family's actual move from 11 Tinakori Road to Chesney Wold, Karori, as described through the eyes, and in the unique language, of Kezia. Mansfield's particular ability to live in the imagination, to be able to conjure up impressions from her childhood, no matter how small or seemingly insignificant the details, becomes the hallmark of her mature, modernist technique. Mansfield never provides her reader with comprehensive description; from an early stage in her writing career, her preference was always for a style associated with the vignette, providing her reader with fleeting glimpses of people and places, a preoccupation with colour and an emphasis on surfaces and reflections.

Katherine Mansfield and Children

In this volume, numerous aspects on the theme of Katherine Mansfield and Children are analysed in seven ground-breaking essays. Tracy

Miao's prize-winning essay, 'Casting "a haunting light": Katherine Mansfield's Modernist Vision of Childhood', begins the volume. In its discussion of characters who pretend to be children, yet who, in fact, are placed on the threshold of adulthood and refuse to enter, this assured and beautifully argued essay offers tantalising new connections between Mansfield's fiction and *Peter Pan* which have not been made before. The arguments are contextualised via a notion of Mansfield's writing transitioning from the Edwardian period to the modern, which also offers numerous innovative readings. In 'Mansfield and Murry: Two Children Holding Hands', internationally renowned Mansfield biographer Kathleen Jones takes a closer look at the childlike relationship between Mansfield and her husband, John Middleton Murry, ultimately concluding that 'It was a love that failed to grow into adulthood. Later, looking back on their relationship, Murry confided to his journal, "Probably I couldn't love anyone but a girl. I don't know what Woman is and never shall"' (p. 43). Todd Martin's absorbing essay, 'The Thoughtful Child: The Sentimental Origins of Katherine Mansfield's Children', takes a close look at a group of early stories written by Mansfield under the general title 'Thoughtful Child', which have been more or less overlooked by scholars until now. Martin suggests that 'understanding Mansfield's early perspective on and portrayal of children in both her "baby stories" and Thoughtful Child stories can enrich our readings of Mansfield's later child-focused fiction' (pp. 50–2). In 'Katherine Mansfield's Play Aesthetics', Imola Nagy-Seres offers a compelling critique of some of Mansfield's child characters via an educational lens, discussing them in relation to the Montessori education method of teaching small children. Focusing on the aesthetic, political and ecological role of play, the essay shows how, via the child characters in 'Prelude', 'At the Bay' and 'Marriage à la Mode', Mansfield advocates the importance of free-imaginative play instead of pedagogical play. Erika Baldt's sophisticated essay, 'Katherine Mansfield's Sleeping Boys', considers Mansfield's depictions of children via the history of literature, incorporating classical imagery from ancient Greek funerary rites. Innovative and exciting, the essay discusses little-known stories by Mansfield, as well as offering important new readings of 'The Garden Party', 'Psychology' and 'Six Years After', considering the notion of death via the trope of sleep. The focus of Janka Kascakova's delightful essay, 'Kezia a "ninseck", Kezia the Bee', is the moment in part IX of 'At the Bay', when the child character Kezia decides, against the implied rules of the game which is being played, to take on the character of a bee. Viewing this as a subversive declaration with many symbolist connotations, Kascakova makes a valuable contribution to our understanding of one of Mansfield's most important child characters – Kezia – an idealised version of her own youthful self. Last but not least, Ann Herndon Marshall's innovative essay discusses the connection between Mansfield and the writer Alice Meynell, and their depiction of child characters in their fiction, especially Meynell's notion of 'child's time' in her essay 'Real Childhood', and the temporal experiences of Mansfield's character, Pearl Button, as well as the children in 'At the Bay'. Marshall concludes by noting that if she had read her stories, 'Meynell would certainly have placed Mansfield in the same pantheon as Dickens and Stevenson, as a writer gifted with memory and authentic awareness of children and their vulnerability to forgetful or self-absorbed adults' (p. 121).

The rest of this volume offers equally absorbing contents to tempt the reader. Martin Griffiths has located what he believes to be a new story by Katherine Mansfield, called 'The Chorus Girl and the Tariff', first published in the USA in 1909, about a young woman who, exhausted and demoralised as she tries to make a living on Broadway, nevertheless appears to be a 'thick-skinned suffragette with fading illusions of fame and fortune' (p. 127). As Griffiths notes, the subject and the timing of the story's publication make Mansfield's authorship seem plausible, since she herself had been 'a chorus singer for a few weeks in March 1909 in the north of England and Scotland (with Garnet Trowell and the Moody Manners Opera Company)' (p. 127). The rest of Griffiths's essay offers further, tantalising evidence to link this story to Mansfield. A new short story, 'Mr. Brill', by Michael Hoover and Daniel Humberd, is loosely based on Mansfield's story, 'Miss Brill', which celebrated its publication centenary in 2020. The story is written as a 'modern' response to the original piece, centred on similar themes of solitude and sadness, but this time from a male perspective. The creative section of the volume concludes with a personal response to the COVID virus by Monica Macansantos, in her essay 'The Life-Affirming Words of Katherine Mansfield in a Time of Pandemic'. Forced to spend much of 2020 locked down in the Philippines, where the pace of daily life slows to a crawl, Macansantos's nostalgia for her former life in New Zealand leads her to pick up a second-hand copy of Mansfield's selected stories. There she finds endless delights and a new-found understanding of Mansfield's technique, concluding that her stories 'draw their narrative pacing from the normal, unhurried pulse of everyday life, and one must recalibrate one's sense of narrative time in order to appreciate the description of "a green wandering light playing over" a cup of coffee' (p. 154).

Two exciting essays in the Critical Miscellany section enhance our understanding of Mansfield's life – and afterlife. In 'The Paper Knife

– Patrick White and Katherine Mansfield', Oliver Stead examines the history and ownership of the little greenstone paper knife once belonging to Mansfield, which eventually ended up as the property of the Australian Nobel Prize-winning author, Patrick White, and which now forms part of the permanent Mansfield collection of memorabilia in the Alexander Turnbull Library in Wellington, where Stead is a curator. J. Lawrence Mitchell's essay, 'Appearances Matter: Katherine Mansfield and the Photographic Record', discusses the photographic portraits of Mansfield still extant, noting how many of them 'speak directly to her desire to control her self-image – how she wanted to appear to her distant family in New Zealand and Canada, to friends, to lovers and to the world at large' (p. 179). Mitchell's essay takes advantage of new biographical material which has come to light in recent years to resolve important aspects regarding these images. The volume concludes with a substantial and fascinating review essay by Jenny McDonnell, which examines five recently published books pertaining to Mansfield, all of which, in their different ways, present 'new approaches to Mansfield's writing that repeatedly generate points of connection, communication and dialogue across space and time' (p. 194).

As with every volume of Katherine Mansfield Studies, *Katherine Mansfield and Children* offers innovative and enticing ways to examine the writer's rich legacy. Happy reading!

Notes

1. Anthea Trodd, *A Reader's Guide to Edwardian Literature* (London: Harvester Wheatsheaf, 1991), p. 72.
2. Jenny McDonnell, *Katherine Mansfield and the Modernist Marketplace: At the Mercy of the Public* (Basingstoke: Palgrave Macmillan, 2010), p. 170.
3. Peter Childs, *Modernism* (London: Routledge, 2002), p. 95.
4. Job 42: 14.
5. Anne Olivier Bell, ed., *The Diary of Virginia Woolf, Volume I, 1915–1919* (London: Hogarth, 1977), p. 216.
6. Tracy Miao, 'Children as Artists: Katherine Mansfield's "Innocent Eye"', *Journal of New Zealand Literature*, 32: 2 (2014). Special Issue: *Katherine Mansfield Masked and Unmasked*, pp. 143–66 (p. 144).
7. *Letters* 1, p. 232. J. Lawrence Mitchell notes that 'the name O Hara San must be a misrecollection of O Hana San ("Miss Flower"), the title of a poem in Yone Noguchi's *From the Eastern Sea* (1903)'. See J. Lawrence Mitchell, 'Katherine Mansfield and the Aesthetic Object', *Journal of New Zealand Literature*, 22 (2004), pp. 31–54 (p. 48).
8. Guy Morris, 'In Memory of . . . Katherine Mansfield', *New Zealand Railways Magazine*, 13: 7 (1 October 1938), pp. 25–9 (p. 27).
9. Anne Olivier Bell, ed., *The Diary of Virginia Woolf, Volume II, 1920–1924* (London: Hogarth, 1978), p. 226.
10. Mitchell, p. 50.

11. See Kathleen Jones, *Katherine Mansfield: The Story-Teller* (Edinburgh: Edinburgh University Press, 2010), pp. 112–15.
12. CW4, p. 115.
13. CW2, p. 87.
14. CW2, p. 87.
15. CW2, p. 355.
16. Dominic Head, *The Modernist Short Story* (Cambridge: Cambridge University Press, 1992), p. 119.
17. CW2, p. 294.
18. Susan Lohafer, *Reading for Storyness: Preclosure Theory, Empirical Poetics and Culture in the Short Story* (Baltimore: Johns Hopkins University Press, 2003), p. 80.
19. Angela Smith, *Katherine Mansfield and Virginia Woolf: A Public of Two* (Oxford: Clarendon Press, 1999), p. 47.
20. CW4, p. 298.
21. CW4, p. 121.
22. *Letters* 4, p. 97.
23. *Letters* 2, p. 46.
24. *Letters* 4, p. 76.
25. CW4, p. 288.
26. Anne Holden Rønning, 'Katherine Mansfield, British or New Zealander – The Influence of Setting on Narrative Structure and Theme', in Paulette Michel and Michel Dupuis, eds, *The Fine Instrument: Essays on Katherine Mansfield* (Sydney: Dangaroo, 1989), pp. 126–33 (p. 131).
27. CW2, p. 415. Further references to this story are placed in the text.
28. Head, p. 120.
29. Yukiko Kinoshita, *Art and Society: A Consideration of the Relations Between Aesthetic Theories and Social Commitment with Reference to Katherine Mansfield and Oscar Wilde* (Chiba: Seiji Shobo, 1999), p. 134.
30. Clare Hanson and Andrew Gurr, *Katherine Mansfield* (Basingstoke: Macmillan, 1981), p. 128.
31. Kay Boyle, 'Katherine Mansfield: A Reconsideration', *New Republic*, 92 (20 October 1937), p. 309.
32. Jack Garlington, 'Katherine Mansfield: "The Critical Trend"', *Twentieth Century Literature*, 2: 2 (July 1956), pp. 51–61 (p. 56).
33. See Gerri Kimber, *Katherine Mansfield: The Early Years* (Edinburgh: Edinburgh University Press, 2016), p. 2.
34. CW2, p. 59.

CRITICISM

Casting 'a haunting light': Katherine Mansfield's Modernist Vision of Childhood

Tracy Miao

'Are you very fond of small children? They always will captivate me –.'[1] When Katherine Mansfield wrote to her cousin, Sylvia Payne, in December 1904, the same year that J. M. Barrie's play *Peter Pan* premiered in London, little did she know that this fascination with children would develop into one of her greatest hallmarks as a writer. Mansfield is a writer of children and childhood, and the spectrum of her literary representations of children stretches beyond the polar images of the Apollonian and the Dionysian child.[2] Although influenced by her Edwardian predecessors, Mansfield created more diverse and daring children and childlike characters. These range from the iconically innocent to the marginalised, desperate and murderous, or characters that are placed at the threshold of adulthood, yet refuse to enter.

Mansfield's literary vision of childhood did not generate from a vacuum. The topic must be contextualised within the transition from the Edwardian period to the modern. According to Adrienne Gavin, a fundamental change in portraying children in literature began in the early twentieth century: such 'literature depicts children as important not because they are heaven sent or set for heaven, but in and of themselves. Children's innocence remains a common trope but is also fissured by darker psychological and sexualized portrayals of the child.'[3] Mansfield's vision of childhood is, for the most part, consistent with this shift of focus, yet she recodes her literary legacy by amplifying the dark impulses of child psychology and blurring the borders between dream and reality. Both give her vision of childhood a more modern rather than Edwardian outlook.

The Edwardians were known for their cult of childhood, embodied by *Peter Pan*. As literary descendants of the Edwardians, the modernists largely disowned their *Peter Pan* legacy. Yet as a member of a new generation of literary *enfants terribles*, Mansfield never fully cut her ties with the idolisation of childhood. In her fiction and personal writings there is an explicit longing to revisit New Zealand – a *place* of childhood. Indeed, her very persona maintained a childlike quality that was famously remarked on by Virginia Woolf: 'I think [Mansfield] has a kind of childlikeness somewhere which has been much disfigured, but still exists.'[4] From her predecessors, Mansfield mainly inherited two traditions, upon which she redesigned her versions of literary childhood. The first is the *Peter Pan* myth. Mansfield recalibrated it to frame fictional metamorphosis and explore liminality between childhood and adulthood. The second is the Edwardian concept of children's play. Mansfield not only interrogates play as children's resistance against adult discipline or corruption in her fiction, but also re-enacts childhood with John Middleton Murry in her personal writings, thus further complicating her vision of literary childhood. As Michelle Beissel Heath observes, Edwardian fictions of childhood

> suggest [. . .] child's play refuses to remain outside the bounds of reality, and the very notion of fictions of childhood may be taken to mean that childhood itself is a fiction of adults at play, selfishly refusing to leave their own Neverlands.[5]

Mansfield and Murry's role-playing as children proves incompatible with reality, but provides fantastic creative material for her stories, especially when she splices play-acting with fairy-tale motifs redesigned with a modern shade of psychological intrigue.

Mansfield was an intensely autobiographical writer, but if she relied only on her intuition and memory she would have produced too many sentimental stories, though some of her writings are perceived as such. One of her clearest and most relevant theoretical musings on literary childhood is articulated in 'The Magic Door', a review published in the *Athenaeum* in 1920. In the review, Mansfield points out that literary recreations of childhood contain both dream and reality, and it 'must be more than a catalogue of infant pleasures and pangs', which is inadequate for expressing this dual quality.[6] Literary childhood is not only sentimental memory, but also a concoction of adult desires. By acknowledging childhood's intrinsic complexity, Mansfield illuminates her approach: in order to gratify 'our longing as well as our memory', literary representation of childhood 'must have, as it were, a haunting light upon it',[7] thus acknowledging adult fantasy to revisit childhood as a legitimate desire, on the one hand, and on the other, eliminating any trace of sentimentality in portraying childhood.

Peter Pan*'s Modernist Afterlife and Mansfield's 'cry against corruption'*

Although in Mansfield's stories and poems Peter Pan and Pan's presence are strongly felt, she recognises that childhood, like the ability to compose child verses, is not permanent. Her association of Pan with childhood as a place and time ephemeral in nature is expressed in her more sentimental stories and poems. In a 1908 poem titled 'To Pan', Mansfield imagines a mythical encounter with Pan.[8] The first stanza describes the narrator being cooped up indoors on a winter day with an unnamed partner, and they note particularly an image of their window bars 'heaped with snow', prefiguring a very similar setting for 'A Suburban Fairytale'.[9] Tension is created in the fifth stanza as the narrator describes not a permanent residence in Arcadia with Pan, but rather a state of being alienated from the world:

> So we would laugh, your arm round my shoulder
> Laugh at the world that was ours to keep
> Cry that we two could never grow older
> We were awake though the world lay asleep.[10]

'Cry' is an ambiguous term because of its emotional association with either joy or grief, thus casting doubt on the remainder of this line. '[C] ould never grow older' is synonymous with the same magic power of Neverland, yet it also suggests, as in *Peter Pan*, that permanent childhood can become entrapment. Such ambiguity in Mansfield's word choices betrays the narrator's psychological conundrum between choosing a life with Pan, or leaving this seductive vision behind and moving on to reality and adulthood. Indeed, the final lines offer no guaranteed residency: 'Well, my dear, we pass in this fashion | But Pan, God Pan, continues to play.'[11] The narrators are mere tourists passing through Pan's domain, whereas Pan's act of playing suffers no interruption. In this poem, Mansfield expresses, as early as 1908, a complex and conflicted belief in the redeeming powers of childhood, as personified by Pan. It questions the legitimacy of trapping children or childlike minds in an idealised childhood.

Mansfield's most memorable child character and the one closest to the Edwardian model of an ideal child is Kezia. George Shelton Hubbell viewed Kezia as 'the essential child'.[12] Indeed, Kezia embodies all the fundamental merits and faults of a child. But an undercurrent of darkness runs through her consciousness that she refers to as 'IT' – a capitalised menace too frightening to name. Hubbell also called Mansfield 'a prophet of children' without further clarification of what the 'prophecies' entailed. But what distinguishes her from other writers is that 'Mansfield *respects* children' by treating them as real 'human beings'.[13] Not only does she respect children, but she also accepts and represents their unspeakable fears. Acknowledging child characters' own rights to feel and fear in literary spaces exemplifies Mansfield's attitude that is aligned with a modern realism.

Like Peter Pan, Kezia is also an embodiment of childhood. The little girl's status as a child that is closest to Barrie's character is depicted in 'Prelude'. Linda Burnell acknowledges that 'Isabel is much more grown up than any of us,' while Mrs Fairfield replies, 'Yes, but Kezia is not,' as if underscoring Kezia's child identity as an innate and possibly permanent trait.[14] It is because of this not-fully-grown-up quality that Kezia is privileged with innocent vision and is an advocate of Mansfield's 'cry against corruption'.[15]

Kezia makes her debut in 'The Little Girl' (1912), which is often viewed as a sentimental story. Its central conflict begins with Kezia shredding her father's speech to stuff a cushion she had sewn for his birthday. Kezia is punished, and laments: 'Why did Jesus make fathers for?'[16] The story ends with Kezia waking up from a nightmare, and her father coming to her rescue. The little girl reconciles with her father as she lies next to him in the big bed: '"Oh," said the little girl, "my head's on your heart; I can hear it going. What a big heart you've got, Father dear."'[17] The ending is arguably the best line in the story. 'The Little Girl' ends on a dark fairy-tale note, ironically echoing Little Red Riding Hood's famous refrain. A question looms: is Kezia truly safe, or is she about to be devoured by the Big Bad Wolf, who only pretends to be her father? Mansfield subtly stirs the deceptively quiet waters of innocence that is mistaken for sentimentality by directing the reader's gaze towards shadows tucked away in the child's subconscious.

Just as innocence is associated with child characters like Kezia, corruption in Mansfield's writings is often associated with adulthood. The power of imagination unlocks the force behind her 'cry against corruption'. Mansfield develops the trope of Neverland for the privileged child Kezia, whose vision is enhanced by the power of imagination against adult corruption. In fiction, Mansfield lavishes this power upon her children, who transform reality into fantasy through imagining. 'This imaginative power is precisely what enables different realms of existence to overlap,' writes Delphine Soulhat.[18] Soulhat's argument echoes Mansfield's insight that '[i]t is implicit in the belief of the child that the dream exists side by side with reality; there are no barriers between.'[19] In 'See-Saw', the little girl teaches the little boy to collect imaginative sticks to build an imaginative fire. In 'Sun and Moon', childlike imagination blurs the line between 'real things and not real ones',[20] so that flowers become hats, and men in tuxedos look like 'beetles'.[21] The kernel of Sun and Moon's imaginative power is the beautifully fashioned little house made of ice – something that, in reality, is eaten – destroyed – by the adults, yet in Sun's memory and imagining should have remained untouched or permanent, or something he subconsciously wishes to protect. Sun's invented world crumbles only when adult power intrudes. On seeing the destruction, he wails, '"I think it's horrid – horrid – horrid!"'[22] His vehement protest cautions against the readers' stroll into the heart of darkness – adult corruption.

Soulhat analyses children's real, as well as imagined, adventures in Mansfield's fiction, saying that Mansfield 'qualifies such bright evocations of the mental landscape of childhood by considering this space as liminal, situated between bright naivety and darker prospects, and this gives her text a distinctly modernist tone'.[23] Often, this modernist tendency explores representations of childhood as manifold and complex. Mansfield's review of *The Bonfire* by Anthony Brendon (1919) contains a view of children and childhood which is different to that perceived by the Edwardians. Mansfield explains that

> [i]t is the devils who keep the schoolhouse in a glow, and not the angels. It is the sinfulness of those little boys, or their potential sinfulness, which is almost the whole concern of their masters. [. . .] We find this idea of the persistent viciousness of normal healthy children very hard to swallow. But, if we have read Mr. Brendon aright, the Jesuits do not believe there is such a person as a normal healthy boy; there is the coarse, cunning and dirty-minded boy, and the too soft, too gentle, almost idiotic boy. Both of them are defective; both stand an equally good chance of going to hell, an equally poor one of getting to heaven; [. . .] It is a sorry view of childhood.[24]

Mansfield rejects a binary definition of children, as well as an adult policing of childhood into a socio-psychological space of artificial purity. In Mansfield's own writings she acknowledges children's secret selves, allows them to breathe and to explore the world, in either the shadows or the light, transgressing the divide at will. This is the essence of her 'respect' for children by treating them as beings with their own rights. Although, at first glance, Mansfield's children appear indistinguishable from Edwardian children, their normality is marked by both their closeness to reality and their potential to be Otherised. Mansfieldian children can be frequently haunted by dark shadows, or seduced by fantastic imaginings from which they must wake.

All Little Boys Were Birds Once: Metamorphosis in 'A Suburban Fairytale'

Indulgence in the fantasy world destabilises the transition from childhood to adulthood. To Kezia's imaginative landscape Mansfield adds fairy-tale mechanisms and tropes to further her vision of childhood. With other child characters Mansfield sets metamorphosis in motion, paying homage to *Peter Pan,* yet simultaneously imparting a chilling caution against corruption, which manifests as indifference to or lack of imagination. Seeing the world through imaginative and sympathetic lenses, Little B. in 'A Suburban Fairytale' chooses to become the Other, rather than remaining complacent in his normative role as a child.[25] Transformation is the next step towards realising his vision of a better, if less cosy, world where he finds his real kin, who shapeshift between boy and bird forms.

Implicit references to *Peter Pan* abound in Mansfield's poems, but one in particular, titled 'When I Was a Bird' (1923), is most appropriate in a close examination of 'A Suburban Fairytale', as it mirrors Peter Pan's initial attempt to win the acceptance of fairies and animals. The narrator of the poem emulates birdlike behaviour, yet the natural world 'didn't believe [she] was a bird'. When her human status is further confirmed by 'Little Brother', who is, for a short moment, 'startled' and almost believes that she is a bird sitting in the tree, he quickly corrects his vision and says, 'Pooh, you're not a bird | I can see your legs.' Yet, regardless of this involuntary shedding of her pretence, the narrator feels '*just* like a bird'.[26] The child narrator in the poem is convinced that there is transformative power in prolonged pretence, which is the essence of play. The same magical power is amplified through Little B.'s crossing over to the world of the Other in 'A Suburban Fairytale', a story which bears a rather complex kinship with *Peter Pan,* not simply because it is a story about a boy's transformation or reversal back to a bird. (Barrie's premise for his childhood fairy tale was that all little boys and little girls were birds once, and children who no longer fly have simply forgotten that skill.)[27]

From the outset of 'A Suburban Fairytale', the central child character, Little B., is depicted in avian terms: 'He was undersized for his age, with legs like macaroni' that are hollow, just like birds' bone; he also has

> tiny claws, soft, soft hair that felt like mouse fur and big wide-open eyes. For some strange reason everything in life seemed the wrong size for Little B. – too big and too violent. Everything knocked him over, took the wind out of his feeble sails and left him gasping and frightened.[28]

The final description evokes associations of young birds testing the wind. Ignored by his parents, Little B.'s attention is drawn to a group of sparrows on the lawn. At first, the birds speak an unintelligible language that marks their Otherness: '*Cheek-a-cheep-cheep-cheek!*'[29] But metamorphosis occurs as Little B.'s gaze focuses more closely upon the birds, and 'they grew, they changed, still flapping and squeaking. They turned into tiny little boys, in brown coats, dancing, jigging outside.'[30] Immediately, Little B. begins to understand their language. When finally his parents notice his absence, they see 'the little boy's thin arms flapping like wings', saying 'Want something to eat, want something to eat.'[31] The end of the story harkens back to Peter Pan's decisive transformation in identity, if not in form: Little B., which may be short for Little Bird, morphs into a sparrow with all the other boys, and flies 'out of sight – out of call'.[32] Rather than a pretending child, as in Mansfield's poem, Little B. assumes his true identity as a bird.

The story parallels imagery in Barrie's *Peter Pan,* with subtle differences. Both boys experience a crossing into the fairy world, though Little B. shape-shifts while Peter Pan remains in boy form. The portal of escape for both boys is the unbarred window. While Peter Pan returns to find iron bars preventing him from roaming the real world, as well as the fairy world, there is no clear indication of Little B.'s intention to return. The bars, according to Gavin, originate from a folk belief that 'cold iron prevents the passage of ghosts and spirits'.[33] They can also block fairies and boys who choose fairy tale over reality.

Mansfield's critique of the representation of childhood in her 1920 *Athenaeum* review, 'The Magic Door', can be read as a comment on both her Peter Pan complex and 'A Suburban Fairytale'. According to Mansfield, children do not distinguish reality from fantasy.

> It is only after he has suffered the common fate of little children – after he has been stolen away by the fairies – that the changeling who usurps his heritage builds those great walls which confront him when he will return. But to return is not to be a child again. What the exile, the wanderer, desires is to be given the freedom of his two worlds again – that he may accept reality and live by the dream.[34]

Mansfield's review clearly refers to *Peter Pan,* especially when she analyses the incompatibility between adulthood and childhood. Children's stories are really told by adults who are aware of the existence of the dream world alongside the real world, and literary representation is the only magic that grants passage to both. In Mansfield's fiction, dream operates alongside reality, whereas Edwardian tropes of halcyon childhood are semi-eclipsed by the fairy-tale gothic.

Collapsing Neverland: The Mansfield–Murry Literary Role-Play and 'Something Childish but Very Natural'

Critics who pay attention to Mansfield's interactions with childhood often view her 'childishness' as a double-edged sword because 'childhood prolonged cannot remain a fairyland. It becomes a hell.'[35] The impression of Mansfield's childlikeness is represented satirically in Aldous Huxley's novel *Point Counter Point* (1928). Huxley depicts John Middleton Murry as a type of Peter Pan, who idolises his wife Susan – the Mansfield character – as a child-woman. Murry's curated image of her has, indeed, problematised Mansfield's all too personal connections with her work, while diminishing her critical power to review and represent complex pictures of childhood. It is not the child-woman image that tugs at our hearts, but her sympathetic portraits of children and depiction of childhood as a haunting space and time.

Cherry Hankin attributes Mansfield's taste for the childlike to her belief in Pan and her upbringing in the Edwardian era, yet also points out that 'Mansfield, like [Virginia] Woolf, broke decisively from Edwardian convention and in doing so assured herself a permanent place in English literature.'[36] But Hankin also calls Mansfield a 'female Peter Pan', implying that her break from the Edwardians is incomplete.[37] If Mansfield's former rejection of her predecessors was literary in nature, the latter identification with Peter Pan was more personal. Such an incomplete breaking away from Edwardian convention indicates Mansfield's complex and conflicted attitude towards childhood as a personal fantasy and a literary space. Mansfield's 'female Peter Pan' found her counterpart in Murry, an ideal partner at first to play the game of being children together, though gender is usually taken out of the equation. To unlock Mansfield's secret of maintaining equilibrium in representing children and childhood, we need to look at her successful, as well as failed, experimentations with the *Peter Pan* myth, especially when she chose to invite Murry to participate in her childlike play.

Mansfield was the initiator of childlike role-play with Murry. In a 1915 letter she issued her invitation of play to him in the form a picture: she described how she felt like 'a tiny little girl [. . .] standing on a chair looking into an aquarium'.[38] The description is reminiscent of one that she created for Kezia in 'Prelude', in which the little girl shifts her vision between two coloured windowpanes. Kezia is the 'innocent eye' personified; she embodies idealised seeing in Mansfield's stories. The child's way of seeing parallels other modernist aesthetic ideals, notably those heralded by the Fauves. Just as Fauvists imitated childlike use of lines and pure colours in painting, Mansfield emulates childlike seeing in her writings.[39] The parallels of childlike seeing in her letter to Murry and in 'Prelude' are descriptions of childlike vision and how memory and wonder preserve that sense of innocent fascination. By sharing such fascination, Mansfield and Murry construct, via literary role-play, their own version of Neverland.

Mansfield and Murry's literary role-playing as the little girl and the little boy is often enacted in their letters. The letter in which Mansfield casts herself as a 'tiny little girl' is the culmination of exchanging real and imagined images of childhood between them. In another letter, after Mansfield describes her childhood home to him, Murry responds by imagining their future home, Heronsgate, as an ideal playground:

> – you can run out naked in the long grass and roll, roll, right under the pine trees, and little winds creep about and pin your body all warm, and right over the wall on the right hand side is a deep place, all white nettle and convolvulus, and you don't dare jump down because there must be creepy things in the water, so you wriggle back under the tummocky grass right back to the Cherry Tree, and then you cry just out of pure joy because you know the world is made for you and you can do anything with it.[40]

Murry's empathetic use of 'you' ties his imaginary world and Mansfield's together. His description, the size of surrounding objects, and the exultation in an imaginary place and time all indicate that he is assuming a child's perspective. By deliberately matching Mansfield's tone and descriptive preferences, Murry makes himself a collaborator with Mansfield's literary act of being children together.

Their literary play-acting does not end here. Murry's imaginary scene of a child taking perfect delight in nature is mirrored in Mansfield's Kezia. In Chapter VI of 'Prelude', Kezia explores the Burnell's garden in a fashion that recalls the quintessential Edwardian child who explores circumferenced nature within the safe boundaries of a garden. Yet different from the Edwardian specimens, Mansfield's little New Zealander is licensed to explore all of the wild territory that extends from the new house. Kezia the modern child enjoys the privilege of a borderless garden. Standing 'at the top of the rolling grassy slope that led down to the orchard. . . . She looked down at the slope a moment; then she lay down on her back, gave a squeak and rolled over and over into the thick flowery orchard grass.'[41] Kezia truly fulfils Murry's vision of an ideal child who knows the world is 'made for [her]', so that she 'can do anything with it' and *within* it.[42] This is Mansfield's response to Murry's imagining of a version of Neverland that belongs exclusively to them.

Both Murry and Mansfield took their play-acting as children to the next level when Murry published 'The Little Boy', and Mansfield followed with 'The Little Girl', in two issues of *Rhythm* in 1912. When read alone, Mansfield's story, also featuring Kezia, is a sentimental story at best. Yet when juxtaposed with Murry's, the story makes more sense, as it signifies the desire to be children together in a literary space they carved for themselves. 'The Little Boy' is a story about an unnamed child who suffers constant abuse from his employer and caretaker, Mother Thompson. One day, he picks up some coloured Christmas paper, used to wrap meat, and is fascinated with the pattern of '[r]ed and yellow and green devils with pitchforks danc[ing] all over it'.[43] This is an odd image for Christmas. An explanation is found when Murry recalls a relevant autobiographical detail in *Between Two Worlds*. As a child, he read a Christmas issue of *The Graphic* that included similar images of 'a pack of little devils with tails and toasting forks dancing round a curmudgeonly old man'.[44] The image later gave Murry nightmares that led to a comforting end of being 'taken into the big bed beside [his] mother',[45] an ending that echoes that of 'The Little Girl'. It is possible that Mansfield made use of Murry's biographical information for 'The Little Girl', except that she reversed the genders of the characters in Murry's memory.

In Murry's story 'The Little Boy', the image of dancing devils provides comfort to the little boy, so much so that it is the first time in a while that the boy 'did not cry quietly for Lily his doll'.[46] It is no coincidence that the child's doll is named Lily because when Mansfield published 'The Little Girl' in the subsequent issue of *Rhythm*, she used the pseudonym Lili Heron. This behaviour further deepens Mansfield and Murry's entanglement with their literary play, so that they are imparting fictive details such as pseudonyms to the reality of their writing. Deliberate mixing of reality and fiction occurs in their interactive playing as the little girl and the little boy. To this, they also added numerous references to each other as children in their letters, initiating Japanese dolls and cats as family members in their own fairy tale, taking such role-playing to even more slippery grounds that further remove them from reality. That reality was Mansfield's illness. The pattern of their role-playing escalated into a more desperate form after Mansfield's health deteriorated.[47]

Gender is a determining issue that at first constructs but later erodes their play. In another letter that Murry wrote in December 1915 to Mansfield, he reaffirms that the two of them 'belong to [their] own kingdom', apart from the known world. They create this 'kingdom' merely by holding hands and 'cross[ing] together like two little boys'.[48]

Crossing over to another world again recalls the Peter Pan experience of transporting to the world of fairies and permanent childhood. Yet Murry also takes gender out of the equation by comparing himself and Mansfield to 'two little boys'. His vision of their return to childhood as two boys betrays his own diffidence in having a carnal relationship with her, as he later confessed in *Between Two Worlds* concerning the early stages of his romance with Mansfield.[49] Mansfield, in turn, responds by using the same phrase, describing them as 'two little boys walking with our arms (which don't quite reach) round each other's shoulders & telling each other secrets & stopping to look at things'.[50] This shared fantasy permeates their actual and imagined spaces, eventually resulting in tension in their relationship because, like Peter Pan, they cannot constantly traverse between adulthood and childhood, even via fictional dialogue. Neither can they take gender out of the question.

As Mansfield's health continued to worsen in 1919, gender further underscores the unsustainability of the couple's childlike play. In December 1919, she wrote with a certain measure of determination and bitterness that the childish play-acting between her and Murry must end:

> We'd be children to each other, openly confessed children, telling each other everything, each depending equally upon the other. Before that I'd been the man and he had been the woman & he had been called upon to make no real efforts. [. . .] we'd always acted (more or less) like men-friends. Then this illness – getting worse & worse & turning me into a woman and asking him to put himself away & to bear things for me. He stood it marvelously. It helped very much because it was a 'romantic' disease [. . .] and also being 'children' together gave us a practically unlimited chance to play at life – not to live. It was child love.[51]

Their play-acting is essentially escapist. A detail in Mansfield's 1921 story 'At the Bay' reflects the falseness of such fanciful play as two little boys. Linda Burnell recalls a promise her father made in their Tasmanian home: 'As soon as you and I are old enough, Linny, we'll cut off somewhere, we'll escape. Two boys together.'[52] The promise is self-contradictory because Linda's father cannot be a boy again, and when Linda grows up, gender will matter. In the relationship between Mansfield and Murry, even though the 'two boys' can pretend to ignore gender and maintain a friendship like that between men, erasing gender, together with her very real and inescapable illness, makes further literary role-playing impossible.

A story that can best represent Mansfield's anxiety of returning to or reassuming adulthood is 'Something Childish but Very Natural'.

Hankin notes that an 'intensely autobiographical' feature appears in Mansfield's writing much earlier than the aforementioned journal entry, saying that the story, though written in 1914, 'prefigures remarkably the change that took place in her relationship in 1920. The idyllic – because childlike – companionship of a young couple, Henry and Edna, is ruined by Henry's desire for a more normal, adult relationship.'[53] Mansfield wrote, in a rather desperate notebook entry, of a foreboding sense of an end, using the child metaphor again: 'I'd say we had a child – a love-child, and it's dead. We may have other children, but this child can't be made to live again.'[54] The description of this 'love-child' dying, Hankin argues, is an accurate allegory of the 'withering of romantic love between her and Murry', and in the letters they exchange after this date, though the image of the child still exists, it is no longer Mansfield herself who is cast in the role but only Murry.[55] He is the child who refuses initiation into adulthood and truth.

Combining Mansfield's own confession and Hankin's analysis, it is not difficult to discern the parallels between 'Something Childish but Very Natural' and the Mansfield–Murry role-play. The story features a young couple who fall in love and plan to live together, yet Edna fails to show up in the end. The narrative begins with the obvious indication of Henry's maturity because, since last summer, his straw hat has become too small for him.[56] Yet the idea of childhood charms Henry as he reads Samuel Coleridge's poem, which is also the eponymous title of Mansfield's story. In Coleridge's poem there is another link to Peter Pan's notion of little children being birds and able to fly, but it also depicts a place that can be reached only via dreaming. Edna, on the other hand, takes residence in childhood more seriously. Her reluctance to proceed to adulthood is foiled when Henry desires more physical intimacy. Although she feels guilty for rejecting Henry, she confesses,

> 'Somehow I feel if once we did that – you know – held each other's hands and kissed it would be all changed – and I feel we wouldn't be free like we are – we'd be doing something secret. We wouldn't be children any more . . .' (p. 381)

It is this fear of losing her innocence that forces desire out of their relationship. Henry plays along with Edna's decision to remain children and 'London became their play-ground' for a while (p. 382). But Henry's desire is not extinguished: 'He wanted to kiss Edna, and to put his arms round her and press her to him and feel her cheek hot against his kiss and kiss her until he'd no breath left and so stifle the dream' (p. 384). The tension between consummating desire and maintaining virginity can no longer be sustained by pretending to be children. The

Edna–Henry relation mirrors that of Murry and Mansfield in reality, for at the early stage of their romance Mansfield was more sexually adventurous and experienced. Such biographical detail inspires the interpretation that Henry, rather than Edna, had been modelled upon Mansfield instead of Murry.

The story also has a darker layer of fairy-tale gothic under the veneer of prolonged childhood in fantasyland. Images of birds, butterflies and moths abound in the story, creating connections with fairy tales of transformation, as well as to Peter Pan. Once Henry and Edna decide to become children together, they '[find] their own shops' and 'their own tea-shop with their own table – their own streets', even their own village, structuring a Neverland just for the two of them (p. 382). The name of their village, explains Henry, has 'white geese' in it, which is really a thinly disguised reference to Heronsgate (p. 382). Henry and Edna's relationship is subtly profiled through confessional lines and imagery. Although Henry does not spread his wings and fly, his character is hauntingly associated with that of a bird. He works in an architect's office that is 'a funny little place up one hundred and thirty stairs', and he says that they 'ought to be building nests instead of houses' (p. 378). As he confesses his love for Edna, he uses the metaphor of having devoured a butterfly – food for birds – and putting his hand to his heart, says, 'it's fanning its wings just here' (p. 378). Edna, on the other hand, evokes association with a butterfly – Henry's predatory preference. When Henry first meets Edna, he notices her 'eyebrows like two gold feathers' and her marigold hair (p. 375). Edna's colouration resembles that of a monarch butterfly. Throughout the story, Henry is urged by a constant desire to devour Edna, but '[e]very time he tried to or even asked for her hand she shrank back and looked at him with pleading frightened eyes as though he wanted to hurt her' (p. 380).

In Mansfield's sexualised portrayals of her childlike characters, desire compels Henry to terminate childlike pretence. Equating desire to hunger, Henry sees 'himself and Edna as two very small children' conducting imaginary childlike activities, yet he suddenly 'rolled over and pressed his face in the leaves – faint with longing' (p. 384). Edna, on the other hand, is drawn to primroses, elated by their beauty or perhaps their early spring nectar (p. 385). Both primrose and marigold are nectar plants for monarch butterflies from spring into summer. 'I'm so frightfully happy!' cries Edna. She feels so light that she may be able to fly, and she makes Henry promise to catch her feet if she does (p. 385). For a moment, Mansfield seems to suggest that Edna's metamorphosis is about to happen. Yet Edna may also be on dangerous ground, for they 'came to a weird place, covered with heather' (p. 385). Ripe seeds of heather are food for many species of birds. Edna may very well have intruded upon risky territory.

In the final segment of the story, Henry again refers to Coleridge's poem: 'Had I two little wings | And were a little feathery bird | To you I'd fly, my dear –' (p. 387). This time the poem is interrupted by a dash, a sudden halt of thought, or maybe an indication pointing towards a name – Edna. But Edna fails to show up. Whether it is out of fear or a desire to fly away is made ambiguous, as Henry sees a mothlike little girl delivering a telegram from Edna. Henry feebly dismisses his disappointment by saying that it is just paper, or '"Perhaps it's only a make-believe one, and it's got one of those snakes inside it that fly up at you"' (p. 388). How accurate for a birdlike creature to be fearful of its own predator! Henry spreads open the paper regardless: 'The garden became full of shadows – they span a web of darkness over the cottage and the trees and Henry and the telegram. But Henry did not move' (p. 388). The boy may have been stung by poisonous love.

Henry's final immobility resembles an anaesthetised state. The whole experience may have been a dream for him: 'Ever since waking he had felt so strangely that he was not really awake at all, but just dreaming. The time before Edna was a dream [. . .] and somewhere in some dark place another dream waited for him' (p. 384). Henry's attitude towards his relationship with Edna reaches its zenith in terms of ambiguity and contradiction: he defines the time before and after Edna as dreams, but now they are 'dreaming together'; he embellishes their present and future with great detail, yet simultaneously questions, '"[A]re we a dream?"' (p. 384). He plays along with Edna's game of being children, yet longs to gratify his desire. The conflicting impulses heighten Henry's sense of limbo in the dream-reality state. If he chooses to remain a child with Edna, he must stay in a dream from which he frequently tries to awake. But if Henry remains a child with Edna, his identity will never transform from that of a child to an adult, or bird to man. 'Childhood then would appear to be the time when everything is possible, but also when subjects can only live on the edge of things. Such an attitude seems to suggest an identity crisis or identity transition.'[57] Soulhat's analysis applies to both Mansfield's story and her literary role-play with Murry. To live 'on the edge of things' can be a dangerous thing, just as it is for Peter Pan, who once roamed the territories of both reality and fantasy. Like Barrie's Peter Pan, Mansfield's childlike characters must face a decision between transformation or permanent entrapment in a land filled only with dreams.

Thus, in one story, Mansfield successfully casts a fairy-tale gothic light over the facile fantasy of pretending to be children together. This artful twist furthers Hankin's biographical reading that 'Something

Childish' foreshadows and reflects Mansfield and Murry's role-playing. Though written prior to Mansfield's complaint that she must resume her woman's role in her relationship with Murry, 'Something Childish' remarkably predicts the trajectory of their failed pretence in endlessly prolonging the Peter Pan game. But Mansfield is ultimately an artist of images, memory and words, distinguishing herself from Edwardian representations of children and childlike characters, for her vision of childhood is laced with a darker gothic undertone. Amalgamating the *Peter Pan* fairy tale and role-play makes for more complex and evolved versions of childhood that are distinctly modern. This is how Mansfield casts her 'haunting light'.

Notes

1. *Letters* 1, p. 15.
2. Chris Jenks, *Childhood* (New York: Routledge, 2005), p. 62. Jenks separates children into two kinds or two 'codes', which he calls the Dionysian child who loves pleasure and is closely associated with desire, and the Apollonian child, who is angelic and untainted by the world. But he emphasises that these are 'images' rather than categorisations that signify intrinsic differences between two types of children.
3. Adrienne E. Gavin, ed., *The Child in British Literature: Literary Constructions of Childhood, Medieval to Contemporary* (Basingstoke: Palgrave Macmillan, 2012), p. 11.
4. Anne Olivier Bell, ed., *The Diary of Virginia Woolf, Volume I, 1915–1919* (London: Hogarth, 1977), p. 216.
5. Michelle Beissel Heath, 'Playing at House and Playing at Home: The Domestic Discourse of Games in Edwardian Fictions of Childhood', in Adrienne E. Gavin and Andrew F. Humphries, eds, *Childhood in Edwardian Fiction: Worlds Enough and Time* (Basingstoke: Palgrave Macmillan, 2009), pp. 89–102 (p. 101).
6. CW3, p. 687.
7. CW3, p. 687.
8. CW3, pp. 60–1.
9. CW3, p. 60.
10. CW3, p. 61.
11. CW3, p. 61.
12. George Shelton Hubbell, 'Katherine Mansfield and Kezia', *Sewanee Review*, 35 (July 1927), pp. 325–35 (p. 326).
13. Hubbell, pp. 325–6.
14. CW2, p. 71.
15. *Letters* 2, p. 54.
16. CW1, p. 303.
17. CW1, p. 304.
18. Delphine Soulhat, 'Kezia in Wonderland', in Janet Wilson, Gerri Kimber and Susan Reid, eds, *Katherine Mansfield and Literary Modernism* (London: Continuum, 2011), pp. 101–11 (p. 106).
19. CW3, p. 687.
20. CW2, p. 136.
21. CW2, p. 139.
22. CW2, p. 141.

23. Soulhat, p. 104.
24. CW3, p. 483.
25. Gina Wisker argues that this story is 'a Gothic-influenced, reversed changeling tale that questions adult justifications for ignoring the child, rather than a traditional tale of infanticide'. See Gina Wisker, 'Katherine Mansfield's Suburban Fairy Tale Gothic', in Delia da Sousa Correa, Gerri Kimber, Susan Reid and Gina Wisker, eds, *Katherine Mansfield and the Fantastic* (Edinburgh: Edinburgh University Press, 2012), pp. 20–32 (p. 31).
26. CW3, p. 108.
27. J. M. Barrie, *Peter Pan in Kensington Gardens* (New York: Charles Scribner, 1910), pp. 14–15.
28. CW2, p. 170.
29. CW2, p. 171.
30. CW2, p. 172.
31. CW2, p. 172.
32. CW2, p. 173.
33. Adrienne E. Gavin, 'Intangible Children: Longing, Loss, and the Edwardian Dream Child in J. M. Barrie's *The Little White Bird* and Rudyard Kipling's "They"', in Gavin and Humphries, pp. 53–72 (p. 67).
34. CW3, p. 687.
35. Louise Bogan, 'Katherine Mansfield', *New Republic*, CII (1940), p. 415.
36. Cherry Hankin, 'Katherine Mansfield and the Cult of Childhood', in Roger Robinson, ed., *Katherine Mansfield: In from the Margin* (Baton Rouge: Louisiana State University Press, 1994), pp. 25–35 (p. 30).
37. Hankin, p. 30.
38. *Letters* 1, p. 157.
39. For more information on Mansfield and the 'innocent eye', see my article, 'Children as Artists: Katherine Mansfield's "Innocent Eye"', *Journal of New Zealand Literature: Katherine Mansfield Masked and Unmasked*, 32: 2 (2014), pp. 143–66.
40. Cherry A. Hankin, ed., *Letters Between Katherine Mansfield and John Middleton Murry* (London: Virago Press, 1988), pp. 12–13.
41. CW2, p. 72.
42. Hankin, *Letters*, p. 12.
43. John Middleton Murry, 'The Little Boy', *Rhythm* 2: 3 (1912), pp. 95–7 (p. 95).
44. John Middleton Murry, *Between Two Worlds: An Autobiography* (London: Constable, 1935), p. 15.
45. Murry, *Between Two Worlds*, p. 16.
46. Murry, 'The Little Boy', p. 96.
47. Hankin, 'Cult of Childhood', p. 32.
48. Hankin, *Letters*, p. 66.
49. Murry, *Between Two Worlds*, p. 205.
50. *Letters* 1, p. 220.
51. CW4, p. 288.
52. CW2, p. 354.
53. Hankin, 'Cult of Childhood', p. 33.
54. CW4, p. 290.
55. Hankin, 'Cult of Childhood', p. 33.
56. CW1, p. 373. Further references to this story are placed in the text.
57. Soulhat, p. 109.

Mansfield and Murry: Two Children Holding Hands

Kathleen Jones

The Boy-and-Girl Beatitude of First Love

Philip Larkin described Katherine Mansfield's relationship with John Middleton Murry as an 'all-for-love-two-children-holding-hands' charade, played out by both of them while they found 'actual cohabitation [. . .] a bit of a strain'.[1] Their unorthodox partnership, as lovers for seven years and then as husband and wife for a further five, often puzzled their contemporaries. There were infidelities on both sides and periods of estrangement.

They met in 1911, at the house of W. L. George, a literary figure and mutual friend. Mansfield had recently published her first collection of short stories, *In a German Pension*, which had attracted a lot of interest. She had submitted a story to Murry, who was the editor of a small magazine called *Rhythm.* He turned it down, but was impressed enough to ask for another, which he accepted, and there was a brief exchange of letters. W. L. George offered to introduce them. Murry found Mansfield fascinating. There was something androgynous about her that attracted him. He later wrote, 'I was not conscious of her as a woman.'[2] Murry was twenty-one, an undergraduate at Oxford, and described himself as 'terrified of life'.[3] He was over-sensitive and too aware of his own vulnerability. He wrote in his journal that he felt 'like an oyster without any shell', endangered by the 'hard rocks' of everyday life.[4] He had already run away from two young women who hoped to marry him, giving neither of them an explanation. There was something androgynous about Murry too, and several men, including Henri Gaudier-Brzeska and D. H. Lawrence, were sexually attracted to him at various times.

Despite mutual interest, it was several months before Mansfield and Murry met again, and a close friendship began to develop. Murry confided that he was very unhappy living with his parents in south London, having come down from Oxford after a crisis of confidence, and Mansfield offered him a room in her flat. As their relationship developed, Mansfield was puzzled that Murry did not attempt to seduce her. As they sat on the floor in front of the fire she asked, 'Why don't you make me your mistress?'[5] Murry's response to this difficult question was to wave his legs in the air 'like a little boy playing with his toys', while giving an evasive answer.[6] This was the defining moment of their relationship, which never changed. Whenever Murry was asked to be serious, he became evasive. Larkin, after reading Murry's letters to Mansfield, described him as 'a slippery emotional character'.[7]

There was something of the child about Murry – in a letter to Mansfield he described himself as having 'a very timid, girlish, love-seeking sort of soul'.[8] It was Mansfield who took the initiative sexually, something that continued throughout their relationship and which troubled her. Murry's immaturity was observed by friends, including Lawrence, who told him to stop being a child and advised him to throw away his 'rather childish charm'.[9] The idea of 'two-children-holding-hands' seems to have been Murry's view of his relationship with Katherine, and often those fantasy children were male. There is a curious passage in one of his letters to Mansfield, where he observes that 'sometimes we were born again in each other, tiny children, pure and shining, with large sad eyes and shocked hair, each to be the other's doll'.[10]

It was a fantasy that Mansfield willingly entered into for her own reasons, including, possibly, the illusion of a return to innocence. There are constant references in their letters to this aspect of their relationship. For Mansfield, Murry became her 'child playfellow', perhaps a version of her younger brother, Leslie Beauchamp, whose nickname, 'Bogey', she transferred to Murry.[11] In return, Murry referred to the 'secret child-ness' of Mansfield.[12] Looking at the photo of her in her black jacket with the marguerite in her buttonhole, Mansfield seemed 'so tiny, such a fairy child', and that was how he liked to think of her.[13]

They were in what Murry described as 'the boy-and-girl beatitude of first love',[14] but though it may have been Murry's first serious love affair, it was not Mansfield's. Although she was only ten months older, she had years more experience of life, and she kept the details of her past to herself. The story of her relationship with William Orton remained untold until he published his autobiographical novel, *The Last Romantic,* in 1937, which contained passages from one of Mansfield's lost journals. Murry knew nothing about the baby she had lost in Germany. She did not tell him the truth about her former lover, Floryan Sobieniowski, even when he unexpectedly came to stay with them at Runcton. Murry knew only the bare fact of her marriage to George Bowden, not the details. The full story of her previous relationships was revealed to him only when Antony Alpers began researching his biography of Mansfield in the early 1950s.

For Mansfield, after a series of disastrous and damaging relationships, including that abandoned marriage, her partnership with Murry was intended to be the shining, perfect thing that was going to make up for everything that had gone wrong in her life before. She had an image of the ideal life partner, everything that she imagined Murry would be, but she was doomed to be disappointed. In her notebooks she explained that:

> the mind I love must have wild places – a tangled orchard where dark damsons drop in the heavy grass, an overgrown little wood, the chance of a snake or two [. . .] a pool that nobody's fathomed the depth of, and paths threaded with those little flowers planted by the wind.[15]

Cultivated minds, she went on to say, almost always had a shrubbery: 'I loathe & detest shrubberies.'[16] Murry, a product of public school and an Oxford college, was the epitome of the cultivated mind. He was intellectually precocious, but also emotionally immature, sexually timid and, according to his family, possibly suffering from Asperger's syndrome.[17] Starved of love in childhood, physically ill-treated by his father, he soon became emotionally dependent on Mansfield, but was unable to give her the support she craved when her health deteriorated.

Murry took Mansfield to Paris in spring 1912, as a kind of honeymoon, and introduced her to his friends John Fergusson, Anne Rice and Francis Carco. Murry felt a curious peace in his life, as though there was no yesterday and no tomorrow, only today 'and to be child eternal'.[18] Mansfield wrote in a letter about the security and intimacy of a settled relationship: 'There is something so wonderfully sustaining and comforting to have another person with you, who goes to bed where you do and is there when you wake up – who turns to you, and to whom you turn.'[19] But the honeymoon ended on their return to London. Mansfield was a married woman with a past, regarded as sordid in the moral climate of the time. Murry was shocked when his mother and her sister came to the flat, assaulted Mansfield and attempted to drag him away. His family thought that she was ruining his academic prospects. Encouraged by Mansfield, Murry had now left Oxford in the middle of his final year.

In the beginning they stimulated each other; Murry opened up new literary directions for Mansfield, while she encouraged him to be bolder and believe in his own talents. They collaborated on editing *Rhythm*, the

Blue Review and *Signature.* But Mansfield soon found that supporting Murry in his literary career was detrimental to her own creative output. After the success of her *German Pension* stories in 1911, there was a seven-year gap until the publication of *Prelude* in 1918. Her best work was often done when they were apart. Mansfield sometimes blamed domestic chores, as their way of relating to each other slipped into traditional gender roles. She wrote him a letter expressing her frustration at the fact that he was free to talk about books and writing with the male friends who came to stay, while she washed dishes and walked about 'with a mind full of ghosts of saucepans & primus stoves & will there be enough to go round [. . .] & you calling (whatever I'm doing) Tig – isn't there going to be tea?'[20]

The couple attempted to live in Paris, where Mansfield felt most at home, but Murry discovered it was impossible to work without his network of male colleagues. Mansfield found it difficult to return to London. Murry wrote that she 'could settle to nothing. All that she wrote she tore up immediately.' She told him that she longed 'to write and write, and the words simply won't come'.[21] Mansfield was also beginning to be disillusioned with Murry's passivity. He was embarrassed by any physical demonstrations of affection, and was financially and emotionally unreliable,[22] not someone she could lean on. He was often too depressed to be of any help. Dark Bogey, as she called this 'other', was 'a little inclined to jump into the milk jug to rescue the fly'.[23]

The cottage at Runcton, near Chichester, which they rented in 1912, was the place where their first small tragedy played out. They moved from Mansfield's London flat, with her grand piano and furniture bought from Maples on hire purchase. It was their first home together and their dream of a country life – the rural idyll where they would both write great things – with its 'sun-dappled rooms, its walled garden, its medlar trees'.[24] It was the prototype of the fantasy home they would much later name 'The Heron'. At Runcton, Murry wrote that they lived with 'a subtle sense of our own unreality, as though we were only a kind of dream-children, haunting the house'. There, Murry developed what he confessed to be 'a deep desire for a child', shared by Mansfield.[25] She longed for the comfort of a child in her arms and wrote in her notebooks:

> if I had a child I would play with it now, and lose myself in it and kiss it and make it laugh. I'd use a child as my guard against my deepest feeling. When I felt – no I'll think no more of this, its intolerable and unbearable – I'd dance the baby.[26]

For a while they believed that she was pregnant. Murry felt that having a child would make them real, 'We should *be,* in a way in which we were not.' They fantasised about having a little boy and were going to call him Richard, shortened to Dicky, but their hopes evaporated. As they sat in the summer dusk, Murry wrote, 'I could see Katherine's eyes brimming with tears.'[27]

He could not know just how much Mansfield wanted a child, since she had not told him about the baby she had given birth to in Germany, which had not survived. The burden of memory was heavy. Mansfield wrote, 'How I long to talk about IT,' but that was impossible. 'It is ridiculous in me to expect Jack to understand.'[28] The knowledge came as a great shock to Murry after her death. As her health declined, her childlessness haunted her. The idea that she might 'peg out' without having had 'a heron or a heronette' horrified her.[29] Murry firmly believed that if they had had a child together, 'much of the subsequent bitterness of life would have been spared us'.[30]

The publication of *Rhythm* and the *Blue Review* ended in financial ruin for both of them. Mansfield pledged her allowance to pay off a debt that should have been borne by the publisher. They were very young and inexperienced, and, in the end, Murry had to file for bankruptcy. The bailiffs arrived at Runcton. In the space of two years they moved house thirteen times,[31] and this had a detrimental effect on Mansfield's health, her ability to write and their relationship. After they moved from Runcton back to London, both Murry and Mansfield had pleurisy. This was Mansfield's third serious lung infection and she suffered from recurrent coughs and colds throughout the winter. For a time, they moved into cheap rooms with a mattress on the floor and no furniture, before friends lent them a succession of cold, inconvenient, country cottages.

But, after three years together, Mansfield had had enough of poverty, the country and Murry's emotional blindness. She became attracted by the handsome, 'rich and so careless'[32] French author, Francis Carco, and made up her mind to leave Murry. 'We talked of London,' she wrote in her notebook on 31 January 1915. 'Jack understands that I want to live there and apart from him.'[33] Murry, although protesting that he had no sexual feelings for men, had fallen in love with their friend, Gordon Campbell, a barrister and a married man, whose wife, Beatrice, was a friend of Mansfield's. Murry was aware that 'as the bond between Katherine and myself wore thinner, I was turning more and more of my affection towards him'.[34] Murry wrote Campbell an anguished letter, confessing his love for him, but said that he had never had the courage to post it. Campbell, perhaps sensing Murry's growing dependence, failed to arrive for an expected visit on the very day that Mansfield left, and Murry, feeling ill and desperate, went to the Lawrences, where

Lawrence told him that his obsession with Campbell was the reason for Mansfield leaving.[35] Lawrence wanted Murry to subject himself to Freudian analysis, with regard to his relationship with Mansfield, particularly the subject of sex. Murry wrote that Lawrence regarded 'Katherine as a butterfly, and I as a child'.[36] Throughout this period, Mansfield and Lawrence waged a constant battle for the soul of Murry.[37]

'Pas de nougat pour le noël'

Mansfield's return to London, with the aim of leaving Murry and pursuing her relationship with Carco, coincided with the arrival of her brother, Leslie, from New Zealand, eager to play his part in the war in Europe. He was special to Mansfield, being her only brother: younger than herself and someone she felt she had more in common with than her sisters. He was also the only one of her family who remained close to her after she was ostracised over the Garnet Trowell episode. Murry was furious when Leslie gave Mansfield the money to go to Paris to join Carco.

But, in a very short time, she was back in London, disillusioned with her lover and reunited with Murry, although she was adamant about returning to Paris. She had an idea for a new story and wrote to her friend, Koteliansky, that 'I *cannot* write my book living in these two rooms [. . .] and if I do not write this book, I shall die.'[38] She left for Paris to live in Carco's empty flat. Her letters and notebook entries reveal that, even though she was only twenty-six, Mansfield was already unwell. She was suffering chronic joint pain from what she thought was arthritis, and recurrent bouts of pleurisy and a persistent cough. The cold, damp weather in England depressed her spirits and made her body ache, though she does not appear to have consulted a doctor about her symptoms. She complained that she felt old: 'I don't feel like a girl any more, or even like a young woman. I feel really quite past my prime.' She was worried that this premature ageing would affect her relationship with Murry; 'he often talks like a young man to an older woman'.[39] Murry sometimes felt that she treated him as a child by not being frank with him about her feelings. 'Wig,' he wrote in 1915, 'was all our secret life together just a game you played to amuse me as a child?'[40]

The inequality of their financial circumstances was also beginning to undermine their relationship. Murry was earning at least £12 a week from reviewing and journalism, while Mansfield received only £100 a year from her father. Yet Murry expected her to pay all her own expenses. When they set up home together again in London, in a house on Acacia Road, she was expected to pay 50 per cent of the costs. Murry's journals are full of complaints about his own poverty, and laments that he could have treated Mansfield better, if he had only had more money. Mansfield found his lack of generosity repulsive. Even after her father raised her allowance, Murry still earned considerably more than she did.

There was also an element of jealousy in Murry's attitude towards her. It was a paradox that Murry, although he had a poor self-image, suffered from vanity, a curious blind spot, believing himself to be cleverer and more gifted than he actually was and also that he was continually, and unfairly, overlooked. He was obsessed by 'the idea that [. . .] I am not valued'.[41] Murry kept a journal intermittently that records the extent of his self-absorption, where he envisages becoming 'a second Stendhal'. There are pages of self-analysis, written with a conscious eye on the future reader.[42] In it, he sometimes alludes to his admiration (even envy) of Mansfield's gifts, her 'conversation, her power of seizing the essence of persons and books and expressing it with just that touch of caricature which seems to put the thing in its right place'.[43] He admitted later that 'I felt myself to be Katherine's inferior.'[44]

In November 1915, Mansfield's brother, Leslie, was blown up demonstrating a hand grenade at a training camp in Belgium. She was utterly devastated, frozen with grief, writing in her journal that: 'I am just as much dead as he is.' She could not bear to live in the house on Acacia Road any more, because of her memories. Everywhere she heard his voice saying, 'Do you remember, Katie?'[45] She went, accompanied initially by Murry, to stay in France, at Bandol on the Mediterranean coast, where they were both going to write. Mansfield was more convinced than ever that she could not work in England. Murry recalled that France 'gave her back (she said) her power of detailed vision'.[46] But, when they arrived in Bandol, Murry retracted his promise to stay with her, though he found it difficult to explain why. He talked evasively of setting up his own printing press and reviving the magazine he had started with Lawrence. But he confessed later that it was simply a way of covering up his own emptiness, and that his real reason was because 'the death of Katherine's brother had cast a shadow between us'. He could not cope with her grief. 'Sheer cowardice', he admitted. He believed that Leslie had taken up the place in Mansfield's heart that had been his. He had become so self-involved that he could not see that she needed support. Once, when Mansfield was sitting crying on the rocks beside the sea, he burst into a 'fury of anger against her'.[47]After Murry abandoned her and went back to England, Mansfield suffered 'an agony of loneliness' and wrote heart-rending letters which Murry ignored. He later wrote that 'The childishness of some of the beliefs revealed in my letters at this time is astonishing.'[48]

But it was in Bandol, alone, grieving for her brother, revisiting early memories, that Mansfield 'found' her subject-matter, which was to be their shared childhood in 'our undiscovered country'.[49] The only way she could retrieve her brother was to step back into her childhood and fix her memories in prose. She and Leslie had shared secrets: 'We were almost like one child.'[50] This was an additional source of conflict for Murry, as she went back into a childhood experience he could not share. Murry was jealous of Mansfield's close bond with her sibling. He felt that her memories of their 'three year idyll' were being blotted out by a past 'in which I had, nor could have neither part nor lot'.[51] There had always been an element in their emotional interaction that reflected how Mansfield related to her younger brother, her childhood 'playfellow'. This became problematic after Leslie was killed. On one occasion, in bed, feeling 'suddenly passionate', she turned to Murry 'to speak to him or to kiss him' but, in his place, saw 'my brother lying fast asleep – and I got cold. That happens nearly always.'[52]

Eventually, in response to Mansfield's anguished letters as she lay, ill and alone, in a hotel in Bandol, Murry sent a letter agreeing to borrow money from Lawrence and come out to live with her 'immediately'. She wrote back, saying how much happier and better she was, and he wrote retracting his decision, causing her even more distress. Finally, after some procrastination, Murry went to Bandol, where Mansfield had rented the Villa Pauline. Murry described their time there as 'the golden moment of our life together'.[53] They were happy and creative in each other's company.

So much of Mansfield and Murry's intimate life was conducted by letter: letters that crossed in the post with different messages; letters that arrived when a particular mood had changed; letters that arrived late. 'We seem to be fated to suffer because of letters when we are away from each other,' Mansfield wrote.[54] Letters create misunderstandings. There is no body language, no vocal tone to qualify the words, no immediate response to stem a quarrel. Mansfield wrote from France in 1918:

> I am simply *desperate*. I had your two wires today [. . .] but you can never have got a wire I sent immediately after my Friday letter [. . .] No you can't have got it. And there is a letter from you today referring to things I know nothing of – that you have already written about.[55]

Murry's moods swung, according to the content of Mansfield's correspondence. 'My reaction [. . .] was always childishly simple. Was it happy or was it sad? And I was happy or sad accordingly.'[56] When they were together, the misunderstandings ceased.

But the idyll could not last. As Murry put it, their 'stupid sufferings' were fated to go on.[57] Lawrence wrote, inviting them to join him in Cornwall, where he had found two cottages at a very cheap rent. One of them he had already christened 'Katherine's Tower'. Mansfield was against it. She distrusted Lawrence: 'he wants us to join him, but you know we are not made to do that sort of thing, ever'.[58] She had also disliked Cornwall on a previous visit. But Murry wanted to go, and felt under an obligation to join Lawrence, who had written a letter accusing him of being a Judas.[59] This created a problem for Mansfield, who had just promised Murry that their relationship was for 'toujours'.[60] If he was determined to go to England, then she would have to go too. Their lives were full of 'might haves' and 'should haves'. Mansfield should have stayed in Bandol, in a warm climate, for her health and for her work, and things might have been very different if she had been able to, but she had no settled home, an unstable relationship and a restless disposition.

Mansfield was very distressed to leave Villa Pauline, where she and Murry had been 'children of the sun' together.[61] The almond tree in the garden she had loved so much became a symbol of loss and disillusion – 'pas de nougat pour le noël' – but Murry was determined to be loyal.[62] He felt a strong bond with Lawrence which he did not understand. As soon as they arrived in Cornwall, Mansfield hated it and began making plans to leave.

Lawrence proceeded to use their relationship with each other and theirs with him as raw material for his novel *Women in Love.* Lawrence was Rupert, Murry Gerald, and Mansfield Gudrun. Murry was shocked when he finally realised the kind of relationship that Lawrence wanted from him.

> What he really wanted of me he never put into words [. . .] But what he imagined he wanted is stated clearly enough in the novel. There Gerald puts away Rupert's offer of union between the two men, and chooses marriage with Gudrun instead.'

This was exactly what happened with Murry.[63]

A Romantic Disease

By 1917, they were once more living apart in London. Murry was working at the War Office and reviewing French books, earning a very respectable living. Mansfield was renting a studio and working furiously on *Prelude,* which she had drafted at the Villa Pauline. Murry commented in his journal that 'Katherine, when she is Katherine, writes like the

South West wind.'[64] Murry was deeply depressed and feeling isolated by his own inability to sustain relationships. His heart, he wrote in a verse parable, was a child that 'longed to love and to be loved, and in this alone could find happiness and peace'.[65] Mansfield was going through her own trials, with diminishing health and no one to lean on but her schoolfriend, Ida Baker, whom she called 'Lesley' after her brother. It is possible that she already, subconsciously, knew that she had a serious condition. In 1919, she wrote that 'All these 2 years I've been obsessed by the fear of death.'[66]

Murry wrote at length about his relationship with Mansfield in his autobiography, *Between Two Worlds*, which became a kind of justification of his behaviour towards her, as well as a response to Lawrence's accusations. It is a story told slant, with many omissions and some falsehoods, but with childlike transparency. Looking back from the perspective of his third marriage, Murry admits that there was a fundamental difference between himself and Mansfield. She 'lived in the moment, and responded entirely to experience', while he lived in the mind: 'nothing was real to me until my mind had grasped it'. There is a suggestion of envy: 'she had an immediate contact with life, which was completely denied to me'. [67] He writes of his 'devouring love' for her, but states that he had been a little afraid of Mansfield's powerful personality and the demands she might make of him. 'I felt the need of building up some citadel of the soul in which to withdraw.'[68] He describes his own intellectualism and lack of empathy as 'the natural bent of my own mind, which was always poorly furnished with sensuous perception'. He confessed that he often felt an 'instinct for seclusion and separateness', which he felt was 'primitive' and part of his masculinity, generating a need for male company and male conversation. Mansfield, he commented, was 'never very sympathetic to it'.[69]

Both Mansfield and Murry clung to the myth of The Heron – named for Leslie Heron Beauchamp – a settled rural idyll where they would write and have a printing press to print their own work, long after it became obvious that it could never happen. Mansfield had pleurisy once again in London; the doctors were very concerned about her health and advised her to spend the winter abroad. They told Murry the truth they concealed from her – that she had advanced tuberculosis. He confided to his journal that the ground had given way under his soul.[70] Mansfield needed Murry to be upbeat and comforting about her prospects, but he was weighed down with the 'black stone of unbelief' and a morbid conviction that she was going to die, which did nothing for her spirits.[71] Mansfield returned to Bandol, so changed by her illness that no one recognised her. She wrote to Murry that her entire life, her future, their relationship was changed by her illness. 'It's like suddenly mounting a very fresh, very unfamiliar horse – a queer, queer feeling.'[72] While both of them were healthy and able to pursue their careers as authors and editors individually, the relationship had survived. But after Mansfield became terminally ill with tuberculosis, it broke down. Mansfield explained it in her notebook. They had drifted into a relationship where 'we'd been children to each other', carefree and without responsibilities, 'each depending equally upon the other'.[73]

Mansfield's diagnosis came at exactly the moment when they were able to marry, after her divorce from Bowden. But it was not the marriage of two minds and souls they had envisaged. For the first time in their relationship, Mansfield needed someone to look after her, physically and financially. With no welfare state, illness was expensive. Murry was earning very good money at the Foreign Office and for reviewing, earning as much a week as Mansfield received a month from her allowance. Out of the allowance Mansfield received from her father she was paying her own rent and her own medical bills. She economised on food. Money became a point of conflict. She was fiercely independent and would not, on principle, ask for it, but his letters, pleading poverty, made her angry. 'A constant cry about money. He had none; he saw no chance of getting any.'[74] His meanness hurt. At Menton, where she spent months in the Mediterranean sun hoping for a cure, he asked her for half the taxi fare when he took her to the clinic to have a tubercular gland lanced. Mansfield remembered the early years when she had committed all her allowance to pay off Murry's debts for the failure of *Rhythm* and the *Blue Review*.[75] 'I'd been the man and he'd been the woman & he had been called upon to make no real efforts. He'd never really supported me [. . .] it was I who kept him.' But then, she had become ill, the tuberculosis 'getting worse & worse & turning me into a woman and asking him to put himself away and to bear things for me'.[76] What she needed was someone who could look after her needs, leaving her free to write: someone who could support her emotionally through the trauma of terminal illness. Murry was unable to do any of those things. It was Ida Baker who stepped into the role of caregiver. Mansfield claimed that Murry found her illness easier to bear because he thought of it as a 'romantic disease'.[77]

In a moment of great clarity, Mansfield wrote that 'being "children" together gave us a practically unlimited chance to play at life – not to live. It was child love.'[78] It was a love that failed to grow into adulthood. Later, looking back on their relationship, Murry confided to his journal, 'Probably I couldn't love anyone but a girl. I don't know what Woman is and never shall.'[79] What Mansfield was suffering was beyond his capacity to understand. Acknowledging Murry's failure to respond to her anguished letters, Mansfield wrote that 'it hurt him to hear me – I stopped his play.'[80] Yet she still loved him and depended on him, and believed that part of their relationship was still valid; 'we are – apart from everything else – each other's critic'.[81] But her own work had already been elevated to another level. In Bandol for the second time in 1918, writing 'Sun & Moon', she told Murry, 'I am in a way *grown up* as a writer.'[82]

During the final years of Mansfield's life, Murry had two affairs with other women (a pattern he would repeat in subsequent marriages). Princess Elizabeth Bibesco attempted to take Murry away from Mansfield. There were 'poisonous letters'. It was very painful, but Murry denied any physical infidelity. Mansfield wrote: 'I thought a few minutes ago that I could have written a whole novel about a Liar. A man who was devoted to his wife but who lied'.[83] More damaging was Murry's liaison with Mansfield's friend, Dorothy Brett. They played tennis together and went for walks in the country, and there is evidence that they were lovers on at least one occasion – activities Mansfield could no longer take part in. They were, she felt, just waiting for her to die in order to marry. Brett did expect to marry Murry, but was disappointed. It is easy to sympathise with Mansfield on this, but Murry was a young man in his twenties, married to a woman with a terminal illness and no longer able to be a full partner in their relationship. He wrote in his journal on Christmas Day, 1921, that 'Tig's cough in the morning pulls the shutters down on the day for me,' adding, 'I cannot reconcile myself to this utterly frustrated life.'[84]

After a long period at the Isola Bella in Menton, an attempt to live in London and a year in a chalet at Montana in the Swiss Alps, Mansfield returned to Paris with the intention of exploring the 'New Age' beliefs of Pyotr Ouspensky, author of *Tertium Organum*, and the 'Fourth Way' of his mentor, George Gurdjieff. While she was debating whether to leave Murry and follow Gurdjieff, Mansfield wrote a long, painful passage in her notebook, analysing her feelings for Murry and the state of their relationship. 'Face it,' she writes, 'what do you have of him now?' Their life together had become 'simply torture with happy moments'. Because of her illness she had already endured 'five years imprisonment. Someone has got to help me to get out.' It could not be Murry. 'One prisoner cannot help another.'[85] Yet, she preserved the fiction of a perfect relationship, two sides of an organic whole, until the end, writing, in the letter she left for Murry after her death, that 'no other lovers have walked the earth together more joyfully, in spite of all'.[86]

Almost her last wish was to be once again 'a child of the sun'[87] and to live a full personal and creative life to the very end. 'It is hard – it is hard to make a good death!'[88] she wrote, and in the end she had to leave Murry to achieve it. She spent the last months of her life at Gurdjieff's Institute for the Harmonious Development of Man at Le Prieuré des Basses Loges in Avon, near Fontainebleau, where Gurdjieff's philosophical practices, like the activities in a good hospice, helped her to come to terms with the fact that she was dying. It is one of the most curious facts of Mansfield's relationship with Murry that, after months of separation, she sent a letter of reconciliation and asked him to come to Le Prieuré. She died later that day in his presence, as if she had been waiting for their reunion. It was almost as though she had stage-managed her own death.

Murry, devastated, spent the rest of his days making sure that her life and work remained in the public eye. He kept a blotter, bought by Mansfield, on his desk through three further marriages. In the corner she had drawn a heart with an arrow through it, and scribbled in a schoolgirl script, 'KM/JMM – The bes' of all'.[89]

Notes

1. Philip Larkin, *Letters to Monica*, ed. Anthony Thwaite (London: Faber & Faber, 2010), p. 62, (6 October 1951).
2. John Middleton Murry, *Between Two Worlds* (London: Jonathan Cape, 1935), p. 190.
3. Murry, p. 198.
4. Murry, p. 326.
5. Murry, p. 214.
6. Ida Baker, *Katherine Mansfield: The Memories of LM* (London: Virago, 1986), p. 68; Murry, p. 208.
7. Larkin, p. 62 (6 October 1951).
8. Murry, p. 493.
9. Murry, p. 280.
10. Cherry A. Hankin, *Letters Between Katherine Mansfield and John Middleton Murry* (London: Virago Press,1988), pp. 66–7.
11. *Letters* 2, p. 9.
12. Hankin, p. 99.
13. Hankin, p. 100.
14. Murry, p. 414.
15. CW4, p. 275.
16. CW4, p. 275.
17. Middleton Murry family, Private Papers.
18. Murry, p. 216.
19. Murry, p. 278.
20. *Letters* 1, pp. 125–6.
21. Murry, p. 281.
22. Murry, p. 223.
23. CW4, p. 269.
24. Murry, p. 232.
25. Murry, p. 232.
26. CW4, p. 130.

27. Murry, p. 233.
28. CW4, p. 134.
29. *Letters* 2, p. 27.
30. Murry, p. 327.
31. Murry, p. 244.
32. CW4, p. 158.
33. CW4, p. 156; Murry, p. 323.
34. Murry, p. 323.
35. Murry, p. 288.
36. Murry, p. 288.
37. Murry, p. 280.
38. *Letters* 1, p. 175.
39. CW4, p. 148.
40. Hankin, p. 71.
41. Murry, p. 324.
42. Murry, p. 255.
43. Murry, p. 255.
44. Murry, p. 267.
45. CW4, p. 171.
46. Murry, p. 373.
47. Murry, p. 374.
48. Murry, p. 384.
49. CW4, p. 191.
50. CW4, p. 170.
51. Murry, p. 324.
52. CW4, p. 203.
53. Murry, p. 250.
54. Hankin, p. 81.
55. *Letters* 2, p. 159.
56. Murry, p. 389.
57. Murry, pp. 346–7.
58. *Letters* 1, p. 233.
59. DHL to JMM, 18 March 1916, Private Collection.
60. *Letters* 1, p. 219.
61. Murry, p. 393.
62. *Letters* 2, p. 54.
63. Murry, p. 412.
64. Murry, p. 434.
65. Murry, p. 441.
66. CW4, p. 288.
67. Murry, p. 268.
68. Murry, p. 268.
69. Murry, p. 268.
70. Murry, p. 450.
71. Murry, p. 450.
72. *Letters* 1, p. 557; Murry, p. 451.
73. CW4, p. 288.
74. CW4, p. 288.
75. CW4, p. 288.

76. CW4, p. 288.
77. CW4, p. 288.
78. CW4, p. 288.
79. John Middleton Murry, Journal, 30 October 1930, quoted by Katherine Middleton Murry, in *Beloved Quixote* (London: Souvenir Press, 1986), p. 46.
80. CW4, p. 289.
81. CW4, p. 337.
82. *Letters* 2, p. 66.
83. CW4, p. 341.
84. Murry, Journal, 25 December 1921, quoted by Katherine Middleton Murry, p. 32.
85. CW4, p. 433.
86. *Letters* 5, p. 235.
87. CW4, p. 434.
88. CW4, p. 336.
89. Katherine Middleton Murry, p. 173.

The Thoughtful Child: The Sentimental Origins of Katherine Mansfield's Children

Todd Martin

Some people seem to like those 'baby' stories, and I love writing them.[1]
(Katherine Mansfield to Sylvia Payne, 26 December 1904)

Except for *Juliet* and *Maata*, Katherine Mansfield's early – and incomplete – attempts at novel-writing, together with some of her 'vignettes', critics have tended to ignore much of Mansfield's early fiction.[2] Made up predominantly of stories of children speaking in baby talk, the fiction Mansfield was writing prior to the stories that would make up *In a German Pension* (1911) – with a few exceptions, such as 'The Tiredness of Rosabel' – are dismissed as sentimental, which they are. However, that Mansfield takes children as key figures in some of her most memorable, mature fiction suggests that these early child portraits served as studies for such characters as Kezia and Lottie, Sun and Moon. To the extent that Mansfield purposefully designed these stories to evoke emotions – and succeeds in doing so – one should consider these early stories not simply as mere precursors to her later fiction, but more as a means for honing her craft, and thus a key to understanding (at least in part) the mechanics of her later stories.

At the end of 'In a Café' (1907) – published in the *Native Companion* the same year that Mansfield was collaborating with Edith Bendall on a collection of poems and stories for children – one finds this epigram: 'Thus is the High Torch of Tragedy kindled at the little spark of Sentiment, and the good God pity the bearer.'[3] The story itself is self-consciously *un*sentimental. Mansfield draws the reader into the heart of the female protagonist, who – in raising the topic of marriage with her male companion – knows 'the danger of the conversation'.[4] Then Mansfield sets the bait: the man, who in a moment of romantic weakness requested a small bouquet of violets from the woman as a token, casually discards them in the street when he leaves the café. The reader anticipates the crushing effect this will have on the love-struck woman, and Mansfield even teases the reader with the woman's initial response – '[s]he felt herself grow white to the lips'[5] – only to have her kick the flowers into the gutter and laugh it off.

Mansfield's epigrammatic ending to 'In a Café' appears to serve as a commentary on the events portrayed in the story, working as metanarrative to draw attention to the mechanism she uses to manipulate the reader, only then to turn it against itself.[6] Beyond the context of the story, though, I would like to suggest that the epigram provides a clue as to *how* many of Mansfield's later stories work. Mansfield is a master at eliciting emotion in her stories, which often explore the psychological – frequently tragic – impact that certain events or circumstances have on her characters. Yet, the spark of many of her stories – especially those that feature children – is sentiment. Drawing on her ability to create effective (and affective) child characters, a skill honed in her juvenilia, Mansfield draws on the sentiment they help to create to elicit an emotional response from her readers; however, instead of resigning them to the nursery or insulating them from adult concerns, as she does in her 'baby stories', in her mature fiction she has the adult world encroach into their child context. If her early work depends on sentimentality for its effect, in her later stories Mansfield fans that spark into the flame of tragedy.

In a recent article, Marlene Andreson describes a similar dynamic at work in Mansfield's child-centred fiction. While she does not couch her discussion in terms of the tragic, Andreson draws on the sentimentalised portrayal of children in 'Prelude' (1917) and 'Sun and Moon' (1920) to argue that Mansfield uses focalisation to scrutinise the adult world through the eyes of a child.[7] According to Andreson:

> Kezia and Sun's worldview is blissfully ignorant and trans-historical, subscribing to a romantic ideology which favours the individual's autonomy, connection with nature, and imagination. Mansfield, however, does not simply create an escapist retreat into an elusive state of childhood innocence. What makes her stories so profound are the ways in which she employs idealising discourses about childhood, only to dismantle them brutally.[8]

The incursion of the adult world into that of the child – disrupting the child-view of the world – is where the element of tragedy lies.[9] However, as Andreson suggests, the profundity of this effect is dependent upon a sentimentalised portrayal of the child, a device whose rhetorical power Mansfield began developing before she was publishing professionally.

What Mansfield calls her 'baby stories' were written between 1903 and 1904, when she was only fourteen or fifteen, and several of these were published in the *Queen's College Magazine* during this period;[10] they clearly capture her early infatuation with children, a fascination evident in the letters she was writing during this time as well. On 26 December 1904, Mansfield wrote to her friend, Sylvia Payne. After fawning over the photo she received of her cousin, Elizabeth von Arnim's, daughter, Felicitas (evidently the inspiration of some of her 'baby stories'), Mansfield writes:

> There is another baby here. She is four and a half. Her name is Estherelle. She is beautiful with long gold hair far past her waist, and great blue wonderful eyes. When she kneels in front of the fire with the light on her hair, & the heat flushing her dear little face, she is like a fairy or a little picture child. She sings in a little shaky voice about a black-bird, and says the drollest things. She has been telling me about an ''a'gusting mis'able mouse' all the morning, and is so affectionate. Are you very fond of small children? They always will captivate me –[11]

Even as she works to capture the innocence of Estherelle here, her 'baby stories' allowed her to show how clever she was in portraying children and encouraging her audience to delight in the sentimentalised view of childhood.

Then, between 1907 and 1908 – during the time Mansfield was working on a children's book, for which she wrote some child-verses in the vein of Stevenson's *A Child's Garden of Verse* and for which Edith Bendall was to provide the illustrations – she was also writing her Thoughtful Child stories.[12] The discovery of three previously unknown Thoughtful Child stories by Chris Mourant, combined with the three culled from Mansfield's notebooks – all written around the same time – suggests that these were to be a part of the children's book on which Mansfield was collaborating with Bendall.[13] Confirming such a supposition is the fact that a drawing of two small children by Bendall (see cover image; see also Figure 1), housed at the Newberry Library in Chicago, includes a hand-written caption by Bendall taken directly from Mansfield's story, 'The Thoughtful Child'.[14] Thus, while they, like the 'baby stories', are 'sickly-sweet meditations on the innocence of childhood and nature', as Mourant describes them,[15] they had a much clearer target audience – children – suggesting that Mansfield was purposeful in her development of the stories. In fact, rather than 'the literary value of these stories [being] negligible',[16] I would like to suggest that understanding Mansfield's early perspective on and portrayal of children in both her 'baby stories' and Thoughtful Child stories can enrich our readings of

Figure 1. Edith Kathleen Robison (*née* Bendall), pencil drawing of a little girl with a fringe, MS-Papers-11923-19, Brownlee Jean Kirkpatrick Papers, Alexander Turnbull Library, Wellington, New Zealand.

Mansfield's later child-focused fiction and enhance critical approaches such as that put forth by Andreson.

The late Victorian and Edwardian periods, during which Mansfield spent her formative years, had a romanticised view of childhood, an idealisation that, according to Cherry Hankin, 'persisted until well after [Mansfield's] death, even among educated people'.[17] This Romantic view derived from the combined influence of John Locke and Jean-Jacques Rousseau. Locke, of course, contributed the notion of the *tabula rasa,* or 'blank page', which suggests that children need to be nurtured and protected from corruption, that they need guidance to develop into socially adjusted adults. Thus, many Victorian texts – especially those written for children – emphasised the instruction of the child. Rousseau, on the other hand, emphasised children's 'natural wisdom', which provided them with greater insight into humanity and the natural world. Particularly during the Edwardian era, the notion that 'the innocent play and pleasure of childhood had value in their own right' became much more prominent; 'the "child" became a model of a certain life-style: lighthearted and playful, robust and authentic'.[18] Once this became a more entrenched view of the child, according to Perry Nodelman, writers could 'find charm in poems pretending to be spoken in the voices of children [. . .]. Other writers could then invest voices and attitudes of children with great power and use them to attack the supposed rationality and wisdom of adults [. . .].'[19] Among the books that signalled this transition were Edward Lear's *Laughable Lyrics* (1877), Robert Louis Stevenson's *A Child's Garden of Verse* (1885) and Gelett Burgess's *Book of Goops and How to be Them* (1900), works that most middle-class, late Victorian children would have known, and to which Mansfield specifically alludes in some of her early stories.[20]

That Mansfield was influenced by such views of children is evident in her story, 'I am afraid I must be very old-fashioned', written in late 1903 when she was fifteen. The narrator is a woman who initially prides herself on being quite 'Modern'. However, when she and her husband attend a lecture on 'Physical Culture' – a fad not unlike recent trends in exercise and nutrition – she begins to question the views of the speaker, Miss Mickle, who suggests, 'Why teach an infant the entirely foolish and senseless rhyme of Jack Horner for instance. How much better it would be for him to learn the position of his heart and the Circulation of the Blood.' The mother, however, views this as undermining the child's imagination. She reflects: '[Miss Mickle] pulled down, and cast into the fire, all the little things that seem to be part of our childhood. And where the little rose-covered summer houses had stood for so long, she erected great dull stone buildings and parallel bars.'[21] At the end of the story, she and her husband call their children to them during tea, and the father recites 'Little Jack Horner' to them.[22]

Likewise, in a story from 1907, 'She and the Boy', Mansfield introduces her Thoughtful Child character, and she and her brother visit the 'Funny-Old-Thing', an imaginary character who lives in a little house called 'Step-Inside-and-Find-Out', which leads to the 'Heart of the World' where the Funny-Old-Thing appears to be keeping the world running. With a significant nod to the Romantic notion of childhood, the narrator recounts an exchange in which the Funny-Old-Thing scolds the Thoughtful Child for whispering – a carryover from the didacticism of early children's literature. However, in the vein of Rousseau, she exclaims, '"Never whisper in public [. . .] if you have anything sensible to say, you may depend upon it everybody wants to hear you. And if you haven't there's no sense in whispering. You look far too young to talk nonsense."'[23] This statement that the child is too young to speak nonsense implies that nonsense and a lack of wisdom are left to the adults.

Mansfield suggests that children (and, in some instances, their parents, by virtue of association) have a knowledge beyond that of adults, a notion she carries over into 'The Thoughtful Child, Her Literary Aspirations' (1908). In this Thoughtful Child story, a young girl is learning her letters so that she can (with her father) write a book

> for all those Poor Things who have no babies of their own to look after but other people's children [. . .] that they may therein read about the private and particular language of the Secret Society – to which every respectable child belongs – their customs and demands.[24]

But even adults who have children of their own lack, by degrees, a depth of imagination. In one of the stories that Chris Mourant discovered in the archives at King's College London, entitled 'Hand-in-Hand with the Thoughtful Child' (1908), a father reads nursery rhymes to his daughter, who exclaims after hearing one, '"Oh, such a beautiful hymn, Father,"' raising it to the level of the sacred. The father in turn reflects, 'and to me, too, it seemed fraught with most delicate suggestion'.[25] But when the father and daughter fall asleep together, 'one of [his] hands clasped firmly in hers', it is the Thoughtful Child who leads the father through the streets of dreamland, where they see Curly Locks, Jack and Jill, Little Bo-Peep and The Old Woman who Lived in a Shoe. When the father asks, '"Are you never lost, Daughter mine?"' she responds, '"Oh, no, Father dear, this is *our* town . . . ."'[26] The Thoughtful Child knows the layout of the town and is greeted by name; the father, on the other hand, is the interloper and must be guided along, having things explained to him.

Of course, the children in Mansfield's later fiction are not any less imaginative. One need merely recall the animal game the children play in the washhouse in 'At the Bay' (1921). However, what Mansfield does in these later stories is to expose the children more directly to the adult world. In 'At the Bay', Linda Burnell is cold and aloof, while Stanley Burnell bullies his wife and thinks only of himself. In the story, 'One Day' (1904), by contrast, one finds a very different family dynamic. The mother is sweet and patient with the children as they wash up and get ready for the day, and the father takes time to play 'engines' before breakfast. Then, when the father must go off to work after breakfast,

> They all stood on the front steps. Handkerchiefs and 'good-byes' were as fervent and numerous as though he was leaving home for a year.
> 'Bring me back a pony, daddy' Jinks cried.
> 'Me too' from Beggles.
> 'An' me barley sugar' piped Luls, hopping on one leg.
> 'Bring back yourself, dear' mother said smiling.[27]

This is a far cry from the relief that the women of the Burnell family feel once Stanley has left for work in 'At the Bay'.

Such differing family dynamics help establish the dividing line between Mansfield's children's stories and her more mature work about children. In her early stories, home is a safe place. In fact, the story titled simply 'The Thoughtful Child' (1908) begins:

> They had lived together for a very long time – Father, Mother and she, in the white house on the Hill. Other people lived a great way off, and seemed a little unreal to the thoughtful child. She had no time for them, and so many 'really truly' friends with her always.[28]

According to Adrienne Gavin, 'The construct that predominates in Edwardian fiction is of childhood as a world (or worlds) apart from that of adults, both in time and imaginative possibility.'[29] So, while in these earlier stories the children interact with their fathers and mothers, these parents (just like the children) are idealised: they protect their innocent children from the adult world, and for the most part, the children are insulated from the world outside of the family. In the later stories, though, the children are in danger of losing their innocence as the adult world encroaches on the world of childhood.

However, more than just the prominence of the adult world separates Mansfield's early stories about children from those she wrote as a mature author. Before Mansfield produced her more renowned stories *about* children, she was writing specifically *for* children. The Thoughtful Child stories, as suggested above, were similarly geared towards a child audience, for Mansfield was drawing on a genre that had gained prominence: children's books were aggressively merchandised during the late Victorian period and it was taken seriously as an art form. According to Rebecca Knuth, new children's picture books 'were reviewed in art journals, and the genre was discussed at length in literary magazines'.[30] Thus, some of Mansfield's early works emulate the characteristics of children's literature of the time, which included a strong dose of sentimentality.

The Thoughtful Child stories demonstrate a greater awareness of audience and utilise a tone reminiscent of the children's literature of the day. Much Victorian and Edwardian children's fiction is filtered through an adult narrator who, while he or she may provide the perspective of the child, often comments on the events from an adult point of view. Because adults would typically read the stories to children, the adult narrators (and the authors creating them) are often self-conscious of the fact that they are speaking to children in the presence of other adults.[31] As a result,

> their narrators will address child narratees overtly and self-consciously, and will also address adults, either overtly, as the implied author's attention shifts away from the implied child reader to a different older audience, or covertly, as the narrator deliberately exploits the ignorance of the implied child reader and attempts to entertain an implied adult reader by making jokes which are funny primarily because children will not understand them.[32]

This phenomenon is called either 'double address' or 'double audience'.

Mansfield employs 'double address' in several of her early stories about children, but especially in her Thoughtful Child stories in which the father–narrator seems to nod to the adult audience as if they were in on a joke at the child–narratee's expense, incorporating comments and information that an adult audience would appreciate, but not necessarily a child. The father–narrator often incorporates narrative intrusions which appear, at first, to acknowledge the narratee's understanding but which actually work as a sort of a wink to the adult audience, showing how gullible the child is. The story, 'She and the Boy', for instance, begins:

> Well. The Thoughtful Child and The Boy ('Yes, silly names, I quite agree with you' . . . 'No, I can't possibly change them') had been a little crabby together. And you know that really means 'pinching', which is an awful terrible thing that even well brought up crabs don't think of doing.[33]

Here, the narrator is clearly addressing children within the story, and the implied author is setting this up to create a friendly relationship between the narrator and the narratees, showing a degree of intimacy that a strictly third-person limited narration would not provide. But even as the narrator engages the questions of the children – implied by the responses given in parentheses – there is a degree of mockery in the way the narrator responds, a sideways glace at the adult reader, suggesting how clever these children are for asking such questions. Likewise, the narrator talks down to the children by instructing them about pinching and how 'well brought up crabs' should act. This, too, could be construed as a nod to the listening adults, who would approve of this correction of behaviour and who might even smile at these mischievous, spirited children. Later in the story, when the narrator introduces the Funny-Old-Thing, he again intrudes: '("You know what that means, don't you? Yes – I beg your pardon for being so insulting").'[34] Again, the aside is supposed to take the children into his confidence, acknowledging their cleverness, but the message to the adult reader is a nudge at how precocious these children are, evoking sentimentality.[35]

Interestingly, the Thoughtful Child stories discovered in the King's College London archives have a different feel to them, suggesting Mansfield may have been transitioning from their imagined child audience toward an adult one, thus anticipating the later fiction, which reflects a more nuanced view of reality. Two of the stories in particular, 'The Thoughtful Child and the Lilac Tree' and 'The Thoughtful Child. In Autumn', appear to be companion pieces. Both remain sentimental, developing the traditional theme of childhood innocence, but the adult narrator is much more reflective. Rather than portraying the antics of the child–subject in order to entertain, the narrator meditates: 'She [Thoughtful Child] is transfigured this Spring and I look at her radiant little face with awe. The world is a bran tub of perpetual "dips" and her astonishment at each fresh sweetness is so infectious that Mother and I feel it too [. . .]', and then, 'Just now, for the Thoughtful Child, all life is centred in the blossoming lilac tree . . . her little child soul seems to have found its mate in the song of the brown bird.'[36] Similarly, in the latter story, the narrator contrasts the Thoughtful Child's spring-like attitude with the onset of autumn, concluding the story: 'My little Thoughtful Child – you are still looking out upon the world with the blue eyes of Spring, with the pink cheeks of Morning,'[37] which both recognises the child's innocence (the 'pink cheeks of Morning') even as it anticipates the loss of innocence with the coming of autumn (and evening). These two stories, when contrasted with the Thoughtful Child stories gleaned from Mansfield's notebooks, demonstrate either a shift in the focal audience from children to adults or else a failure to engage the younger target audience effectively. The prominence of the parental perspective feels much more intrusive than in some of the other stories of the same ilk, and without a focus on the words and acts of the child to capture the essence of innocence, the sentimentality becomes too introspective and falls flat. In her more mature work, like those stories centred around the Burnells, she would more effectively 'show' the contrast between the child and adult worlds without relying on such overt introspection.

Mansfield's more successful Thoughtful Child stories, however, remain much more aware of their 'double audience', with an emphasis on entertaining the child while evoking an emotional response from the adults. Accomplishing this effect, though, necessitates idealising the child, which results in a caricature – really the root of sentimentality, which tends to sacrifice complexity for the sake of the emotional effect.[38] This caricature, stemming as it does from a Romantic view of children, also finds a source in earlier, religious portrayals of children. Instead of the 'saintly hero of evangelistic fiction', however, late Victorian and Edwardian authors of children's literature tend to focus on 'the secular innocent child'. Gillian Avery notes that, after this shift toward the secular, the child's

> little naughtinesses are not sin, but delicious childish mischief. The authors take great pains to include nothing which might frighten child readers. However, one can be certain that the creators of both sacred and secular innocents derived the same shivers of delight from contemplating the sweetness they had portrayed.[39]

To create this 'sweetness', writers of the time often incorporated baby talk into their stories; it elicits a sentimental response to the children that the audience find so puerile yet nonetheless entertaining. Mary Louisa Molesworth, whom Mansfield read and emulated in her early work, according to Kimber,[40] was the most prolific and successful purveyor of baby talk and one of the writers most imitated in this vein.[41] Evidence of this influence can be found in Mansfield's early letters, which are sprinkled with descriptions of small children in which she often incorporates baby talk. Likewise, Mansfield finds ways of incorporating baby talk into her stories to draw readers into the innocent, safe world of her children. For example, in her 'baby story', 'One Day', the mother is taking the children for a walk and the youngest child begs her sister not to take the dolly's pram: 'Not the pwam. . . . Please not the pwam. You always wheels it over me feets.'[42] After a bit of thought, the older child finally relents. This reveals that Mansfield's use of baby talk was not merely a personal fetish, but rather a key element for much of the children's literature that would have influenced Mansfield as she was developing her own book for children. Mansfield was following suit with the numerous other authors of children's literature who drew from the qualities and tone of Molesworth, and who aimed 'to please and amuse, but [who were] earnestly careful to exclude non-nursery matter and anything that could destroy a child's faith in its parents, and its sense of security'.[43] And Mansfield occasionally draws on this technique even in her later work to evoke similar sentiment, such as Pip's green 'nemeral' (an emerald) and Kezia's 'ninseck' (an insect) in 'At the Bay';[44] however, Kezia's sobbing 'Head back! Head back!' in 'Prelude'[45] – given the context of having just witnessed handyman Pat chop the head off a duck – best demonstrates the emotional potential of contrasting the innocence of the child's world with the realities of death, a motif Mansfield would revisit in the touching scene between Kezia and her grandmother when they discuss mortality in 'At the Bay'.

Death's intrusion, interestingly, is one exception to the otherwise insulated child-worlds of Mansfield's early stories, even those geared towards a child audience. Portraying the death of a child in order to elicit an emotional response from readers, however, was a device used even in the children's literature of the time. Few things evoke sentiment more than the death of an innocent, especially a child. Adult audiences would obviously be affected by the death of a young, angelic child, and the figure of a child entering into her heavenly reward contributed to the didactic effect, motivating good behaviour in children.[46] According to Joanna Smith, 'The queen of the deathbed scene was Charlotte Yonge,' whom Antony Alpers claims was a staple read for Mansfield and the other boarders at Queen's College by Clara Finetta Wood (known as 'Woodie'), who ran the hostel which served the school and where the Beauchamp girls were housed.[47] But one need look no further than Charles Dickens to find an influence for Mansfield's portrayal of child deaths. In 'Mansfield and Dickens: "I am not Reading Dickens *Idly*"', Angela Smith references a passage in Mansfield's notebooks in which she indicates, '"I could make the girls [at Miss Swainson's private school] cry when I read Dickens in the sewing class,"' which, Smith suggests, must have been the passage in *Dombey and Son* that depicts the death of Paul.[48] Certainly, Mansfield would have sought the same emotional effect in her own early stories.

Mansfield's story entitled simply 'The Thoughtful Child', written in 1908, fully combines the sentimentality of the death of a child with the innate and innocent wisdom of a child; it may also be an allusion to the death of Gwendoline, Mansfield's sister, who died in 1891 at the age of three months.[49] The story begins (as noted earlier) with the narrator explaining that the child character feels that other people seem unreal; she is insulated from the world around her, beyond her own home and garden. The Thoughtful Child is at home in nature, and she particularly enjoys playing in the small woods near her house. The narrator explains, 'When she went into the wood, somehow she never felt "jokey", but almost like Church time.'[50] Likewise, she seems to have a greater sense of communion with the natural world as she interacts with the fairy-like creatures she calls the 'Shadow Children', beings that adults, of course, cannot see. These Shadow Children appear in several of the other Thoughtful Child stories, and here they serve as the playmates who, unlike other people, are more real to her and are her 'really truly' friends. While she does not speak aloud to the Shadow Children – 'she answers them inside her' – she understands all that they tell her, 'but she could not "say it back" to anyone, not even to Father and Mother, because they would not understand now. They had stopped being Fairies for so long,'[51] reaffirming the Romantic notion that the child is closer to nature, and to the ephemeral.

When the Thoughtful Child discovers that she is going to have a 'real' brother, she becomes jealous of the time her parents spend with him and not with her. But when her brother becomes ill and dies, 'She did not see her Brother again, though Mother and Father were always with her now. They were sad, and never played, but just sat and looked at her, and did not even smile.'[52] It is in the midst of this grieving, as the winter passes into spring, that the Thoughtful Child goes into the woods, where 'someone caught hold of her hand. She looked down and saw it was her brother smiling at her';[53] he has become one of the Shadow Children. She spends the day with him, swallowing sunbeams, a trick the Shadow Children had taught her, and then she brings the glad tiding to her parents:

> 'Don't be sad dears' she said, 'Brother's here. I've been playing with him in the garden. He lives in the wood and he sends his love.'
>
> And the sunbeams that she had swallowed grew so big that when she started laughing they flew out – all except one, and filled the whole house.[54]

Thus the story ends with this child of nature, and her own innocent perspective on death lightens the hearts of her parents even amidst their sadness. The ending is simplistic, certainly. But the death of one child and the insight offered by another encapsulate the essence of sentimentality that many writers of children's fiction were trying to achieve in their work.

Desiring to 'restore the sentimental *within* modernism', Suzanne Clark argues that the predominance of male modernists resulted in the use of 'aesthetic antisentimentalism to make distinctions, to establish a position of authority against mass culture', which was 'a feminized enemy'.[55] According to Clark,

> The sentimental is at issue because no discourse can escape appealing to the emotions of its audience, and yet modernist criticism pretended to do so. No discourse can escape some relationship with its readers' narcissism or its readers' nostalgia; no criticism can be so objective that it avoids calling up the issues of ideology and subjectivity in its appeal to its audience. No text can escape issues of transference. Yet modernist criticism attempted to export all this out of its domain, to maintain the poem as an aesthetic object.[56]

For Clark, the modernist tenet of 'art for art's sake', which emphasises the art-object itself, attempts to eliminate emotion and ideology by removing the work from its authorial context and – more importantly – is critical of any work that fails to achieve such disinterestedness. Arguing that this put women writers at a disadvantage, Clark asserts that such critiques are disingenuous because they ignore the fact that any discourse is necessarily tied to sentiment. Concurring with such an argument, Michael Bell agrees that 'feeling' is certainly a part of modernism; however, he stops short of identifying it with sentimentalism. Instead, seeking greater nuance, he traces the evolution of the nature of sentimentalism, distinguishing between true and false feeling. In general, Bell suggests that appeals to emotion in modernist writings are hidden rather than overt, and what makes sentimental appeals so evident is that they depend upon an 'ideal object' to evoke their effect; in other words, the false feeling of sentimentalism elides realism to evoke emotion.[57]

Otherwise, what distinguishes Bell's discussion from Clark's is that Clark emphasises the importance of how a text *works*, arguing against 'the practice of separating literature from rhetoric'.[58] Thus, while Bell's distinction between true and false feeling is convincing – for readers certainly recognise when they are being manipulated towards an emotional end – the feelings that modernist texts arouse still often depend upon similar rhetorical devices to those found in sentimental literature for their effect, albeit within the context of realism. This is what I want to suggest about Mansfield's more mature work: she draws on rhetorical practices – such as baby talk – that she honed in her early writing, writing that was influenced by a romanticised view of children and the sentimental appeals of the children's literature that she was emulating.[59]

Even in her own criticism, Mansfield – who was critical of works that lapsed into unadulterated sentimentality – acknowledged sentimentalism's affective role when used appropriately. On the one hand, Mansfield takes Patience Worth to task in 'Three Women Novelists', a review published in the *Athenaeum* in April 1919. Mansfield categorises Worth's *Hope Trueblood* (1918) as a 'pastime novel', which 'never for one moment touches the real world or the realm of faery [. . . and] where Melodrama has his castle and Sentimentality is the weeping lady of the tower'.[60] On the other hand, in 'Mr. De Morgan's Last Book', published only a few months later, Mansfield claims that William de Morgan, author of *The Old Madhouse* (1919), 'knows just how large a pinch of sentimentality will stimulate our jaded sympathies'; Mansfield even notes that 'he has a taking way with the lower orders, with small children and pet animals'.[61] Likewise, Mansfield's own later stories retain a 'pinch' of sentimentality from her earlier stories, but she uses this for a tragic end. After all, as James Chandler contends in *An Archaeology of Sympathy*, the goal of sentimentality is empathy, to 'imagine ourselves in the place of the other', to experience their emotion or passion vicariously,[62] and such is at least one understanding of the Aristotelian notion of catharsis.[63]

Many of Mansfield's professionally published writings that are centred on children generally emphasise the tragic loss of innocence through the incursion of the adult world upon that of the uninitiated child: Laura comes face to face with death in the figure of the carter in 'The Garden Party' (1921), as do Kezia and the other children who witness the beheading of the duck in 'Prelude'; Leila glimpses her fate, dancing with a fat, older gentleman in 'Her First Ball' (1921); and Isabel models her socialisation, imposing her adult-like authority upon the other children in 'Prelude' and 'The Doll's House' (1921), even as Kezia undermines that worldview by inviting the downtrodden Kelveys to see the doll's house. As Andreson notes, 'these brutal [. . .] transitions from childhood to adulthood highlight in Mansfield's stories the child protagonist's complexity and stylistic richness – a potential of which the writer knew how to take full advantage'.[64] To enhance further our understanding of the complexity that Andreson identifies, it is valuable to recognise the sentimental origins of Mansfield's later child characters, for it is from these emotive sparks that she is able to kindle her tragic effects.

Notes

1. *Letters* 1, p. 15.
2. A notable exception is Gerri Kimber's *Katherine Mansfield: The Early Years*, in which she provides one of the only extended discussions of Mansfield's 'baby stories' (Edinburgh: Edinburgh University Press, 2016). See also Kimber's 'Katherine Mansfield, Fairy Tales and Fir Trees: "the story is past too: past! past! – that's the

way with all stories"', in Gerri Kimber and Janet Wilson, eds, *Re-forming World Literature: Katherine Mansfield and the Modernist Short Story* (Stuttgart: ibidem, 2018), pp. 231–50.

3. CW1, p. 88.
4. CW1, p. 87.
5. CW1, p. 88.
6. The enigmatic last phrase, 'and the good God pity the bearer', may allude to the modernist disdain for anything hinting at sentiment, thus sounding a warning to anyone using it as a device.
7. Marlene Andreson, 'Seeking Blissful Ignorance: Katherine Mansfield's Child Protagonists in "Prelude" and "Sun and Moon"', in Enda Duffy, Gerri Kimber and Todd Martin, eds, *Katherine Mansfield and* Bliss and Other Stories (Edinburgh: Edinburgh University Press, 2020), pp. 91–104 (p. 91).
8. Andreson, p. 97.
9. For a similar argument, see Delphine Soulhat, 'Kezia in Wonderland', in Janet Wilson, Gerri Kimber and Susan Reid, eds, *Katherine Mansfield and Literary Modernism* (London: Continuum, 2011), pp. 101–11. According to Soulhat, the children in stories like 'Prelude' and 'At the Bay' occupy a liminal space: 'the imaginary realm where light and darkness compete, and where dream and nightmare merge. The passage from childhood to adult reality crosses a form of limbo' that signals a loss of innocence (pp. 104, 109). Janet Wilson, however, argues that stories like 'Something Childish But Very Natural' reveal Mansfield's understanding that such a transition into adulthood is necessary for autonomy. See Wilson, 'Katherine Mansfield's Stories 1909–1914: The Child and the "Childish"', in Janka Kascakova and Gerri Kimber, eds, *Katherine Mansfield and Continental Europe: Connections and Influences* (Houndmills, Basingstoke: Palgrave, 2015), pp. 221–35.
10. For an extended discussion of stories Mansfield published in *Queen's College Magazine* and the influence of children's literature and fairy tales on her early work, see Kimber, 'Katherine Mansfield, Fairy Tales and Fir Trees'.
11. *Letters* 1, p. 15.
12. In *The Early Years*, Kimber suggests that Mansfield was also likely to be 'emulating her cousin, Elizabeth von Arnim, who in 1900 had written a little book called *The April Baby's Book of Tunes*, with delightful colour illustrations by the well-known Victorian illustrator Kate Greenaway' (p. 195).
13. See Chris Mourant, '"A Little Episode": The Forgotten Typescripts of Katherine Mansfield, 1908-1911', in Janet Wilson, Gerri Kimber and Delia da Sousa Correa, eds, *Katherine Mansfield and the (Post)colonial* (Edinburgh: Edinburgh University Press, 2013), pp. 154–66 (p. 161). The stories found by Mourant include: 'The Thoughtful Child and the Lilac Tree', 'The Thoughtful Child. In Autumn' and 'Hand-in-Hand with the Thoughtful Child'. Those from Mansfield's notebooks are: 'The Thoughtful Child. Her Literary Aspirations', 'The Thoughtful Child' and 'She and the Boy; or, the Story of the Funny-Old-Thing'.
14. The caption on the front of the image, written in Bendall's hand, reads, 'She saw his eyes looking that way – and she wondered about it –.' The passage from 'The Thoughtful Child' that this alludes to occurs just after the Thoughtful Child's baby brother is born: 'Brother used to be carried on to the lawn, never into the wood – it was too shady, but often when the Thoughtful Child looked at him, she saw his eyes looking that way, looking, looking, and she wondered about it' (CW1, p. 126). Her

brother's looking toward the woods, where the Shadow Children live, suggests a possible connection with his sister, for whom the Shadow Children are her 'really truly' friends; it may also foreshadow his death and joining of the Shadow Children at the end of the story.

15. Mourant, p. 161.
16. Mourant, p. 161.
17. Cherry Hankin, 'Katherine Mansfield and the Cult of Childhood', in Roger Robinson, ed. *Katherine Mansfield: In from the Margin* (Baton Rouge: Louisiana State University Press, 1994), pp. 25–35 (p. 27).
18. Rebecca Knuth, *Children's Literature and British Identity: Imagining a People and a Nation* (Lanham, MD, Toronto and Plymouth, UK: Scarecrow Press, 2012), p. 96.
19. Perry Nodelman, *The Pleasures of Children's Literature* (White Plains, NY: Longman Publishing Group, 1992), p. 26.
20. Gerri Kimber and Vincent O'Sullivan note several of these connections in CW1. For example, 'The Thoughtful Child' includes an allusion to Lear's *Laughable Lyrics* (p. 127, n. 1); 'The Thoughtful Child. Her Literary Aspirations' evokes Stevenson's *A Child's Garden of Verse* directly (p. 120); and 'One Day' references Burgess's *Book of Goops* (p. 28, n. 6).
21. CW1, pp. 17, 18.
22. In *The Early Years*, Gerri Kimber equates Miss Mickle to Charles Dickens's Thomas Gradgrind (pp. 145–6).
23. CW1, pp. 74–5.
24. CW1, p. 119.
25. CW1, p. 535.
26. CW1, pp. 536–7.
27. CW1, p. 26.
28. CW1, p. 124.
29. Adrienne E. Gavin and Andrew F. Humphries, 'Worlds Enough and Time: The Cult of Childhood in Edwardian Fiction', in Gavin and Humphries, eds, *Childhood in Edwardian Fiction: Worlds Enough and Time* (Houndmills, Basingstoke: Palgrave Macmillan, 2009), pp. 1–20 (p. 4).
30. Knuth, p. 89.
31. Barbara Wall, *The Narrator's Voice: The Dilemma of Children's Fiction* (New York: St Martin's Press, 1991), pp. 9, 13.
32. Wall, p. 35.
33. CW1, p. 73.
34. CW1, p. 74.
35. This seems to be a reversal of what Andreson suggests occurs in 'Prelude' and 'Sun and Moon', where it is the perspective of the child that reflects on the adult world.
36. CW1, pp. 529, 530.
37. CW1, p. 533.
38. According to James Chandler, sentimental literature often ignores 'probability' – 'codes of expectation and understandings of chance, design, and casality' – in order to create a particular effect on the audience (p. 203); however, it is precisely because of this obvious manipulation of such codes for an affective end that Michael Bell suggests modernists reject the sentimental mode (pp. 5, 64). See James Chandler's *An Archaeology of Sympathy: The Sentimental Mode in Literature and Cinema* (Chicago: University of Chicago Press, 2013), and Michael Bell's *Sentimentalism, Ethics and the Culture of Feeling* (Houndmills, Basingstoke: Palgrave 2000).

39. Gillian Avery, *Nineteenth Century Children: Heroes and Heroines in English Children's Stories 1780–1900* (London: Hodder and Stoughton, 1965), p. 174.
40. Kimber, *The Early Years*, pp. 71, 144.
41. Joanna Smith, *Edwardian Children* (London: Hutchinson, 1983), p. 90.
42. CW1, p. 27.
43. Avery, pp. 173–4.
44. CW2, pp. 350, 361.
45. CW2, p. 82.
46. Mansfield's 'Two Ideas with One Moral' (1903) follows in this vein, showing two different children, one apparently well-behaved and the other not, and the undertaker's final assessment of their lives after their deaths. Interestingly, Mansfield appears to be parodying the genre, for the 'sweet' girl 'had never heard of the verb "to think" and as to "reason" why it was Greek to her', whereas the 'nasty' girl 'always worried other people with wishing for unnecessary knowledge, she babbled solely of the verb "to think" and as to "reason", why it was life to her!' (CW1, pp. 18–19). This reveals her developing rebelliousness, rejecting the traditional middle-class expectations for girls/women.
47. Joanna Smith, p. 91; Antony Alpers, *The Life of Katherine Mansfield* (New York: Viking Press, 1980), p. 26. See also Kimber, *The Early Years*, p. 120.
48. Angela Smith, 'Mansfield and Dickens: "I am not reading Dickens *Idly*"', in Gerri Kimber and Janet Wilson, eds, *Celebrating Katherine Mansfield: A Centenary Volume of Essays* (Houndmills, Basingstoke: Palgrave Macmillan, 2011), pp. 189–201 (pp. 189–90).
49. Mary Burgan suggests that 'Mansfield's fascination with infant death was the symptom of anxiety brought about by the *real* witnessing of the *real* death of her sister at close range' (p. 11), which is certainly valid; however, while Burgan focuses on the clinical implications of Gwen's death, she overlooks the literary tradition from which Mansfield would likewise have been drawing. See Mary Burgan, *Illness, Gender Writing: The Case of Katherine Mansfield* (Baltimore: Johns Hopkins University Press, 1994).
50. CW1, p. 125.
51. CW1, p. 125.
52. CW1, p. 126.
53. CW1, p. 127.
54. CW1, p. 127.
55. Suzanne Clark, *Sentimental Modernism: Women Writers and the Revolution of the Word* (Bloomington: Indiana University Press, 1991), pp. 4, 5. Although Clark's study on sentimentality focuses on American literature, this does not preclude its relevance and application to Katherine Mansfield or British literature more widely.
56. Clark, p. 6.
57. Bell, pp. 66, 123.
58. Clark, p. 25.
59. Cherry Hankin, however, suggests that, in order to become more modern, Mansfield turned away from 'the facile Edwardian idealization of children in fiction toward a far more profound and "modern" psychological investigation of the workings of a child's mind' (p. 30). While I would agree with the tenor of Hankin's statement, I am not so sure that Mansfield completely abandoned her view of the child, and certainly not her means of evoking in the reader an affective response to her children. In fact, as I have suggested, it is precisely the contrast between a sentimentalised portrayal of

children and the reality of the adult world that results in the complexity of her more mature work.

60. CW3, p. 445.
61. CW3, p. 503.
62. Chandler, p. 150.
63. See Bence Nanay, 'Catharsis and Vicarious Fear', *European Journal of Philosophy*, 26 (2018), pp. 1371–80.
64. Andreson, p. 103.

Katherine Mansfield's Play Aesthetics

Imola Nagy-Seres

> As I came into the town all the babies were flocking in the streets looking at the Xmas toys. Heaven knows they are a sorry little show, but you should have heard the screams of joy. [. . .] I began to look too & I nearly bought an elephant or a dog with one ear standing up, or a *lovely* tea set with roses painted on it & a sugar basin with a tiny strawberry for the handle on the lid.[1]

Toys occupied an important role in Katherine Mansfield's life, both as a child and as an adult. She loved to play with miniatures – traditional toys and everyday/natural objects alike – as a child in New Zealand, and her enthusiasm for play did not diminish as she grew up. Some of her most vivid memories of places she visited are coloured by her engagement with toys. When, in 1915, due to her fragile health, she had to spend Christmas on her own in a hotel in Bandol, she found solace in browsing the toys displayed in the Christmas market, a magical sight that filled her with delight and a childish desire to buy a tiny animal or a '*lovely* tea set with roses painted on it', and mingle among the screaming children. Toys also feature frequently in her correspondence with her husband, John Middleton Murry, especially the two Japanese dolls, Ribni and O Hara San, which Mansfield treasured greatly, not least because they represented an affective bond between her and Murry when they were separated by geographical distance.[2]

Play, with traditional toys and miniature everyday objects, as well as role-play, represents an important topic in Mansfield's œuvre. In her short fiction she created unforgettable child characters with unique thoughts and feelings, and not invisible members of a larger family network. As George Shelton Hubbell, a reviewer for *The Sewanee Review* wrote in 1927:

> Time was when 'John Smith and family' would satisfactorily designate a whole household. Nowadays 'Mr and Mrs John Smith and family' will generally do. But in the Mansfield stories each child must be treated separately, and the parents are lucky if they get as much attention as their offspring, or as much respect.[3]

Through her detailed and nuanced descriptions of children's play, Mansfield allowed a glimpse into her young characters' thoughts and their unique perspective on the world. In recent years, critics have shown a vivid interest in Mansfield's treatment of children. Tracy Miao has argued that the children's way of looking at the world reveals Mansfield's 'serious thought process on art and the artist', while Meghan Marie Hammond has examined child characters' embodied feelings, reading Mansfield's stories in tandem with William James's and Carl Lange's theories on emotions.[4] Janka Kascakova has recently written on the playing child figure in Mansfield's works, arguing that Mansfield '[brought] children into adult literature in order to somehow complete it', and show the potential of 'childlike qualities [. . .] to enrich lives'.[5] This chapter offers a new perspective on Mansfield and childhood by reading her portrayal of playing children in parallel with early twentieth-century pedagogical trends, with special emphasis on the work of Maria Montessori, whose theories Mansfield must have been familiar with, as I will discuss later.

This essay will focus on the aesthetic and political role of play in 'Prelude' (1918), 'At the Bay' (1921) and 'Marriage à la Mode' (1921), stories in which Mansfield critiqued didactic definitions of play as activities with predetermined learning outcomes. In Mansfield's view, play mostly represented a free act of imagination, unstructured by adult guidance but not completely divorced from the external world, including other people and non-human species. As Marina Warner has put it: play 'weave[s] the fabric of subjectivity, fastening the ties between self and other and patterning relations within the immediate group of kin and the more distant but no less demanding groups of society, tribe, nation, and even species'.[6] For Mansfield, creating a fantasy world was not synonymous with the negation of reality, as Montessori thought, but imaginative play honed the child's aesthetic, social and ecological sensibility, representing a form of reaching out to and forging intimate bonds with others.

'Play Learning' and 'Toy Teaching'

From the late seventeenth century, many philosophers and educators, including John Locke, Jean-Jacques Rousseau and Richard and Maria

Edgeworth, had written on the significance of play in the context of children's early education. However, the theorisation of playful learning started to become widespread in Europe in the nineteenth and early twentieth centuries. In the first half of the nineteenth century, the German educator Friedrich Froebel founded the first kindergartens and became a passionate advocate of play in early education. Froebel saw play as infants' most authentic mode of existence, which determined their physical and spiritual development. He created a wide range of educational toys, called 'gifts', including soft, colourful balls, cubes and cylinders, and encouraged children to use their hands in exploring and understanding the world.[7] Froebel's kindergartens were introduced to England in the mid-nineteenth century, and educational toys became widespread during this period.[8] By the end of the nineteenth century, concepts such as 'play learning' and 'toy teaching', had been widely used in the British media: in the section for newly published books, the *Athenaeum* advertised an instruction book entitled *The Child's Instructor; or, Learning Made Easy by Toys* (1883), which served as guiding material for teachers and parents who wanted to sharpen children's cognitive skills through play.[9]

Similar to Froebel, Montessori also placed great emphasis on the role of the senses in children's cognitive development. Her theories were based on her observations of children in the *Casa dei Bambini* (Children's House) in Rome. Montessori claimed that young children could easily learn the three Rs (reading, writing and arithmetic) by using their senses instead of rote memorisation. In *The Montessori Method* (1912), she explained how children in the Children's House learnt to read:

> I prepare a number of little cards made from ordinary writing-paper. On each of these I write in large clear script some well-known word, one [. . .] which represents an object actually present or well known to them. If the word refers to an object which is before them, I place this object under the eyes of the child, in order to facilitate his interpretation of the word. I will say, in this connection, the objects used in these writing games are for the most part toys of which we have a great many in the 'Children's Houses.' Among these toys, are the furnishings of a doll's house, balls, dolls, [. . .] various animals, tin soldiers, railways, and an infinite variety of simple figures.[10]

What is interesting, however, is not the method Montessori used, but the conclusions she drew from this experiment:

> But what was my amazement, when the children, having learned to understand the written cards, *refused* to take the toys! They explained that they did not wish to waste time in playing, and [. . .] preferred to draw out and read the cards one after another![11]

This and similar learning experiments corroborated Montessori's hypothesis that children possess an inner desire to learn and understand the world by actively and purposefully engaging with objects and not passively listening to a teacher. At the same time, her dismissal of toys and free play in favour of cognitive development is already present in her early work and represents one of the main reasons why her theories became criticised. Although there were traditional toys in the Montessori classroom, they were used for specific didactic purposes, and children were not supposed to play with them freely. Montessori designed special educational toys, including colourful wooden objects of different geometrical forms, reading cards, and balls to sharpen children's ability to process sensory impressions.

One of the most enthusiastic supporters of Montessori in England was school inspector Edmond Holmes, who published *The Montessori System of Education* in 1912. When Montessori visited London in September 1919, she received a royal welcome. Her lectures and training courses were very popular among teachers and intellectuals, and she quickly became widely known in Britain.[12] *The Times* advertised her two-month training course in London, which was highly overbooked: over two thousand teachers had applied but only a quarter could enrol.[13] Though many British educators were fascinated by her theories, others criticised her approach as rigid and unwilling to accommodate changes. Education reformer Charlotte Mason wrote that the Montessori method is too restrictive, fails to encourage free play, and places too much emphasis on small children's cognitive skills, such as writing and reading.[14] Even Holmes, though continuing to support Montessori, showed concern that her teaching might be too dogmatic and inflexible for English schools, and the absence of free play and fairy tales in her approach might become problematic for British educators and parents.[15]

Mansfield must have been familiar with Montessori's theories: she explicitly mentions Montessori's name at least once in her personal writings. In a letter addressed to her friend, Violet Schiff, in July 1920, Mansfield writes about her encounter with Bessie Moult, the wife of journalist Thomas Moult:

> Bessie is a smaller quieter creature who is everything that is good and kind but will talk to me about Madame Montessori and persist in telling me it's not so important to attract the child's attention as to guide it. This, because I am bad and wicked, bores me. I do not see why you should have to endure such people.[16]

Mansfield's impatient and ironic tone makes it clear that she does not share Bessie's and Montessori's views on child education. Mansfield's last sentence remains ambiguous: it is not entirely clear whether the dismissive phrase 'such people' refers to Bessie or Montessori (or both). Mansfield must have noticed what critics of Montessori, including Mason and Holmes, had also drawn attention to: the rigidity of the Montessori method, its interpretation of play as having the sole role of enhancing children's cognitive skills, and its failure to embrace imaginative play and creative storytelling. Montessori dismissed creativity for its own sake because she considered it an abstract indulgence and a rejection of reality rooted in bodily–sensuous perception:

> Man [*sic*] is guilty of a like sin against the intelligence when he employs his creative activity of thought for its own sake, without basing it upon truth; by so doing he creates an unreal world, full of error, and destroys the possibility of creating in reality, like a god, producing external works.[17]

According to Montessori, the child's cognitive development takes place through empirical learning, and not through the construction of fantasy worlds completely divorced from reality.

Education 'à la Mode'

Mansfield was intuitive about childhood and sympathetic to the child's point of view from a very young age; this intimacy with children is the key to her depictions of family love in her earliest writings. The importance of being childlike, allowing children free play and intimate adult engagement in children's play, is evident in her juvenilia, especially in the stories she wrote during her studies at Queen's College, London. In 'One Day' (1905), 'Daddy' plays 'a game of engines [with the children] before breakfast', and towards the end of the story, the children give a 'concert' using the edge of the table as a piano and a 'headless wooden horse' as a violin.[18] The parents participate in the game, singing along with the children instructive verses and rhymes, 'strong moral lesson[s]', the aim of which is to teach infants polite manners and middle-class etiquette.[19] In an earlier story, 'I am afraid I must be very old-fashioned' (1903), Mansfield explicitly rejects a didactic approach to play by ridiculing the figure of Miss Mickle, the 'Physical Cultured' woman, who gives a lecture on children's education, claiming that young infants should not be taught the 'foolish and senseless rhyme of Jack Horner' but they should rather learn 'the position of [their] heart and the Circulation of the Blood'.[20] The narrator, a young mother, strongly disagrees with such theories, and observes with relief that her 'beloved' shares her views: after dinner, when the 'babies' ask for a story, the father tells them 'Little Jack Horner', an English nursery rhyme with 'a high Moral value'.[21] While, in Mansfield's early writings, parents recognise the emotional benefits of play and they fully participate in their children's games, these stories are imbued with a strong sense of Edwardian morality, which is absent from her later work.

In her mature writings, children's relationship to play and their engagement with the world through play becomes more complex. Her mature stories are not so much interested in the moral consequences of play but rather in its psychological–emotional, aesthetic and social benefits. In 'Marriage à la Mode' (1921), Mansfield portrays the protagonist, Isabel, as a mother who embraces modern pedagogical trends, including the use of educational toys. Her husband, William, resents the fact that she has discarded their children's old toys because she considers them too sentimental:

> But nowadays they had Russian toys, French toys, Serbian toys – toys from God knows where. It was over a year that Isabel had scrapped the old donkeys and engines and so on because they were so 'dreadfully sentimental' and so 'appallingly bad for the babies' sense of form'.[22]

If the time setting of the story is contemporaneous with its writing, and Isabel got rid of the old toys 'over a year [ago]', then she must have adapted her new pedagogical principles towards the end of 1919 – the period when Montessori held training events in London, and the theories of various education reformers were hugely popularised in the media. Isabel rejects a purely emotional attachment to toys, which does not facilitate the cognitive development of children. In her view, if children fail to engage with educational toys from a young age, they risk growing up with a distorted 'sense of form':

> 'It's so important,' the new Isabel had explained, 'that they should like the right things from the very beginning. It saves so much time later on. Really, if the poor pets have to spend their infant years staring at these horrors [old toys], one can imagine them growing up and asking to be taken to the Royal Academy.'
>
> And she spoke as though a visit to the Royal Academy was certain immediate death to any one. . . . (p. 271)

While Isabel dismisses 'dreadful sentimentality' in her children's education, her sentences abound in exaggerations and hyperbolic language: 'poor pets', 'these horrors', 'asking to be taken to the Royal Academy'. Isabel's worry about her sons' wish to be taken to an art gallery seems not only ridiculous, but also illogical, taking into account that she threw away the old 'sentimental' toys precisely because she thought that they would interfere with the children's ability to appreciate art. Through Isabel's character, Mansfield mocks an uncritical subscription to theories and trends 'à la mode', educational and artistic alike. Isabel's ideas about education and the role of 'right' toys for children's mental development reveal her own distorted views on what constitutes great art and intimate familial relationships.

After surrounding herself with her bohemian and superficial friends, Isabel's aesthetic taste and affective attachments change significantly. William remembers how the 'old' Isabel used to play with the children in the 'old' house, which, after meeting her new friends, suddenly became small and claustrophobic for her:

> They were having rides on the leopard skin thrown over the sofa back, or they were playing shops with Isabel's desk for a counter, or Pad was sitting on the hearthrug rowing away for dear life with a little brass fire shovel, while Johnny shot at pirates with the tongs. Every evening they each had a pick-a-back up the narrow stairs. (pp. 273–4)

Before moving to a bigger house and dedicating her attention to 'new people and new music and pictures' (and fancy foreign toys), Isabel did not guide her sons' imagination from an exterior (and superior) perspective, but participated in their play. The mother's presence and willingness to enter the fantasy world created by the boys transformed the drawing-room into an intimate and magical space. The affective bonds between family members suffer significant changes in the new house, where characters, especially the children, can be defined by their constant absence. The reader never encounters Paddy and Johnny in the present time of the narrative: they appear only in William's memories, or in the brief dialogues between the parents. When William wants to spend time with them, the boys either are asleep or are taken out by the nurse for the whole day. They become gaps in both the architectural space of the new home and the narrative structure of the short story.

The children's absence can be partly explained by their rigid daily routine, planned and imposed by the nurse, who seems to have more authority than Isabel herself. When William prepares to go back to London on Sunday afternoon, Isabel becomes apologetic: '"I'm so sorry the babies have been out all day, but Miss Nail had arranged it"' (p. 278). Both parents seem pathetically helpless and unable to take their children's care into their hands. William might be 'dreadfully sentimental' when reminiscing about their life in the old little house, but in contrast with Isabel, at least he notices that his sons' strict routine of eating, sleeping and playing might lead to psychological damage. As such, 'Marriage à la Mode' might be read as Mansfield's implicit critique of early twentieth-century infant care theories which advocated a rigorous, at times cruel, daily routine that often ignored children's individual differences, and their need for unstructured play time and intimacy. As Trudi Tate has argued, Mansfield might have heard about the New Zealand-born child health reformer Truby King, whose baby care theories became popular in Britain after the First World War. King advised mothers to feed their babies in determined time intervals, regardless of whether they were hungry or not, and the infants were supposed to be left on their own to sleep, preferably in the fresh air, far from their carers.[23] Tate reads Mansfield's 'Bliss' (1918) as a critique of King's principles, suggesting that 'the *emotional* centre of the story is [. . .] the lost potential of the relationship between mother and baby'.[24] Following Tate's argument, 'Marriage à la Mode' can be read as a story centred around the lost potential of the relationship not only between mother and children, but also between father and children, and wife and husband.

One of the most ironic (and sad) moments in the story is when Isabel addresses her friends as 'my children', trying to dissuade them from buying a gramophone that would disturb William's peace of mind. While, for Isabel, caring for her children means buying them sophisticated toys, she fails to notice that, under the influence of her new pseudo-artistic friends, her own aesthetic and emotional sense have been severely distorted.[25] When William finds himself alone in the house, while the children are sleeping and Isabel is out with her friends, he observes sadly the lurid and tawdry design of the sitting-room:

> On the wall opposite William some one had painted a young man, over life-size, with very wobbly legs, offering a wide-eyed daisy to a young woman who had one very short arm and one very long, thin one. Over the chairs and sofa there hung strips of black material, covered with big splashes like broken eggs, and everywhere one looked there seemed to be an ash-tray full of cigarette ends. (p. 276)

Mansfield's satirical wit culminates in this scene, when she portrays Isabel not only as a superficial mother and spouse but also as a person lacking artistic sensibility. While she talks about her sons' potential visit to the Royal Academy with horror, and thinks about herself as someone who knows how to shape the children's 'sense of form', her own aesthetic sense, influenced by her friends, is 'wobbly' and 'broken'. William's discomfort in the garish room is further enhanced by his nostalgic memories of the old family house, where one could see toys scattered on the floor:

> Nowadays, when one felt with one hand down the sides, it wasn't to come upon a sheep with three legs or a cow that had lost one horn, or a very fat

> dove out of the Noah's Ark. One fished up yet another little paper-covered book of smudged-looking poems. . . .' (p. 276).

The presence and arrangement of objects in the house corroborate William's feelings of despair and helplessness, also suggested by the ellipsis at the end of the sentence, which translates into a typographic sigh. Mansfield describes Isabel's and her friends' artistic taste with words related to filth and fragmentariness: 'strips of black material', 'splashes like broken eggs' and a smudgy poetry book. William feels unable to deal with the aesthetic and affective disarray of his home, which he contrasts to his family's life in the old house, where broken toys lay on the drawing-room floor, suggesting the imperfect yet intimate ties between family members. William's familiarity with the minute details of the wooden animals from Noah's Ark show his care for his children and his willingness to participate in their play, a form of pleasure he has been denied in the new home.

Creative Play and Empathy

While Isabel and William's sons are subordinated to a strict educational routine that discourages free play, the Burnell sisters in 'Prelude' (1917) and 'At the Bay' (1921) engage in various imaginative play activities that foster their creative and caring attitude towards the surrounding world. Play represents a central theme in 'Prelude', in which entire sections are dedicated to children: section VIII, for example, focuses on the sisters' imaginary dinner party. At first, the reader feels disorientated as new character names are suddenly introduced into the narrative: Mrs Smith and her twin children pay a visit to Mrs Jones. However, we soon realise that the Burnell sisters are role-playing, and although the narrator does not tell us which girl is Mrs Jones, Mrs Smith and the former's maid, there are subtle hints that help to solve the puzzle. The guest Mrs Smith is probably Isabel, the eldest sister, who pays special attention to social conventions. She thinks that she should not be introduced to the servant: 'I don't think you ought to introduce me to the servant. I think I ought to just begin talking to her' (p. 104). Isabel makes great efforts to imitate adult behaviour, and she is more aware of the concept of social status than her younger sisters. Regarding the identity of the other two characters, one would assume that Kezia is Mrs Jones and Lottie the maid, since the latter is the youngest and the one who is usually given the most menial roles. However, it is most likely that Kezia plays the role of the maid and Lottie is Mrs Jones, a gesture that shows Kezia's dismissal of hierarchy and her unselfish love for her little sister. Kezia often protects Lottie when others try to hurt her, but in the dinner party game, Lottie is the one who defends Kezia when Isabel talks derogatively about the maid: 'Well, she's more of a lady-help than a servant and you do introduce lady-helps, I know, because Mrs Samuel Josephs had one' (p. 104). Kezia prevents any possible quarrels by nonchalantly saying: 'Oh, well, it doesn't matter' (p. 104). While all of the sisters are familiar with social hierarchy, it is Kezia who dismisses it the most firmly.

Besides Kezia's social sensibility, the dinner party play also draws attention to her highly sophisticated aesthetic affinity. The way she prepares the dinner and sets the table acquires artistic qualities:

> [She was] beating up a chocolate custard with half a broken clothes peg. The dinner was baking beautifully on a concrete step. She began to lay the cloth on a pink garden seat. In front of each person she put two geranium leaf plates, a pine needle fork and a twig knife. There were three daisy heads on a laurel leaf for poached eggs, some slices of fuchsia petal cold beef, some lovely little rissoles made of earth and water and dandelion seeds, and the chocolate custard which she had decided to serve in the pawa shell she had cooked it in. (p. 104)

Kezia's dinner table becomes an ephemeral art object in which shapes and colours create a perfect aesthetic harmony, and which shows, to borrow Rishona Zimring's words, Mansfield's celebration of 'the transformative creativity of the small, intimate, and unassuming'.[26] Kezia's delicate arrangement of the plant crockery and cutlery on the pink cloth, and the poise of her movements when setting the table, create a sense of harmony evident in the narrative pace: the staccato rhythm of the shorter sentences culminates in the final meandering sentence that contains the entire menu – in the form of a list – served by the child. Kezia's play unites the aesthetic and the ecological, two categories that have not been often discussed together. Yet, as Hannah Freed-Thall notes, 'these modalities of thought share a concern with strategies of non-domination, techniques of freeing objects or life forms from the hubristic concepts and categories we habitually impose on them'.[27] At the same time, the little girl's aesthetic and ecological sensibility is coupled with a subtle affective awareness. When Isabel asks Kezia to fill in the bottle of the twins (probably Isabel's dolls) 'at the dairy', Kezia thinks of fetching real milk from the kitchen, instead of water: '"Oh, all right," said Gwen, and she whispered to Mrs Jones: "Shall I go and ask Alice for a little bit of real milk?"' (104). While fully absorbed in the fictional universe of the dinner party, Kezia nevertheless remains in contact with reality; she can easily transcend the boundaries between the two realms. During play time, the volume of the real world is slightly turned down to a whispering level, but its murmurs are nevertheless audible.

However, before Kezia has the chance to fetch real milk, the dinner party is suddenly disrupted by the arrival of the girls' cousins, Pip and Rags Trout. The sisters run to the front door, and the table is left almost entirely forlorn:

> But someone called from the front door and the luncheon party melted away, leaving the charming table, leaving the rissoles and the poached eggs to the ants and to an old snail who pushed his quivering horns over the edge of the garden seat and began to nibble a geranium plate. (p. 104)

After the children abandon the dinner table, the narrator continues the play with her own (uninvited) guests: the ants and the snail. The narrator shares Kezia's delicate attention to detail and the little girl's love for the natural world, which unite in the intimate depiction of the snail.

Child-sized dish sets represented popular toys in the nineteenth and twentieth centuries, and they were often used in nurseries and schools. Montessori used miniature cooking accessories in the Children's House:

> The *rectangle* of which I make use is the plane of one of the children's tables, and the game consists in laying the table for a meal. I have in each of the 'Children's Houses' a collection of toy table-furnishings [. . .]. Among these are dinner-plates, soup-plates, soup-tureen, saltcellars [. . .], etc. I have them lay the table for six, putting *two places* on each of the longer sides, and one place on each of the shorter sides. One of the children takes the objects and places them as I indicate. I tell him [*sic*] to place the soup tureen in the *centre* of the table; this napkin in a *corner*.[28]

Montessori children's play with 'table-furnishings' differs strikingly from the Burnell sisters' imaginary dinner party. While the Burnell children embody different roles, and Kezia arranges the table freely listening to her aesthetic instincts (though partly imitating adult social conventions), Montessori pupils lay the table by following rules and the teacher's directions, which have specific didactic purposes: to teach numbers, geometric forms and spatial relations, as the italicised words show. Children in Montessori schools were not encouraged to make up imaginary dinner parties but were taught (mainly) mathematical concepts through the playful activity of table setting. The slightly commanding tone of the passage, suggested by the verbs 'indicate' and 'tell', corroborates Montessori's aim of achieving specific cognitive outcomes through play. At the same time, this extract might help us better understand Mansfield's rejection of Montessori's principle of subordinating play to learning.

Mansfield did not dismiss 'play learning' and 'toy teaching', but she thought that free play was crucial for the development of children's aesthetic, affective and ecological sensibility. In 'At the Bay', Mansfield satirises extreme educational reforms through the portrayal of the Samuel Josephs, the Burnells' former neighbours:

> The whole family of Samuel Josephs was [on the beach] already with their lady-help, who sat on a camp-stool and kept order with a whistle that she wore tied round her neck, and a small cane with which she directed operations. The Samuel Josephs never played by themselves or managed their own game. If they did, it ended in the boys pouring water down the girls' necks or the girls trying to put little black crabs into the boys' pockets. So Mrs S. J. and the poor lady-help drew up what she called a 'brogramme' every morning to keep them 'abused and out of bischief.' It was all competitions or races or round games. Everything began with a piercing blast of the lady-help's whistle and ended with another. There were even prizes [. . .]. The Samuel Josephs fought fearfully for the prizes and cheated and pinched one another's arms –they were all expert pinchers. (p. 289)

One can notice a sharp contrast between the Burnell sisters' and the Samuel Josephs' mode of playing. The latter are not allowed to engage in free play but are under the constant surveillance of their 'lady-help', who makes up rigorous 'brogrammes' for them. Mansfield portrays the maid in militaristic terms: she wears a whistle around her neck and 'directs operations' with a cane. Mansfield not only rejects this form of prescribed play, but also suggests its inherently violent nature through the use of military vocabulary and the (perhaps not) accidental slip of tongue 'abused'. At the same time, violence operates in two directions: while the Samuel Josephs children are subordinated to violence, they also become perpetrators, hurting each other and other children through play. Subordinated to a strict play regime, the Samuel Josephs incorporate the language and behaviour of military routine into their interactions with others, both in and outside of the realm of play. The nurse's educational regime is doomed to failure: instead of honing the children's affective and cognitive skills, it transforms them into 'awful' 'savages', leaping on the lawn (p. 289) and 'beating the table with their tea-spoons' ('Prelude' p. 81).

Comparing the workings of a child's mind to that of 'savages' represented a common trend in the early twentieth century. Montessori described children's mentality as differing from adults' thinking, in that the child 'loves to wander in the fascinating worlds of unreality, a tendency which is also characteristic of savage peoples'.[29] She identified education as the most effective antidote for infants to surpass the 'savage state': 'education *should help the child* to overcome it; it should not *develop the savage state*, nor *keep* the child therein'.[30] Mansfield's depictions of play question Montessori's definition of 'savage state': Mansfield critiques rigid, didactic 'brogrammes' and the meticulous guidance of children's play, which, as her portrayal of young characters suggests, can backfire: instead of becoming more 'civilised', the Samuel Josephs engage in an abusive and domineering form of play. While Kezia becomes more empathetic through free-imaginative play, her mind being 'a place of profusion, making [her] share [her] human space with the vegetable, mineral, and animal', the Samuel Josephs fail to show any compassion for their environment.[31]

However, though Kezia seems to possess an innate affective and ecological sensibility, Mansfield's stories also suggest that careful attention to the natural world is something that children have to learn, often through unpleasant experiences. At the end of 'Prelude', Kezia goes into her aunt's room to tell her that she is expected downstairs. After Beryl leaves the room, Kezia puts her calico cat on her aunt's dressing-table and attaches the lid of a cream jar to its ear, making fun of the animal:

> The calico cat was so overcome by the sight [in the mirror] that it toppled over backwards and bumped and bumped onto the floor. And the top of the cream jar flew through the air and rolled like a penny in a round on the linoleum – and did not break.
>
> But for Kezia it had broken the moment it flew through the air, and she picked it up, hot all over, and put it back on the dressing-table. Then she tiptoed away, far too quickly and airily. . . . (p. 120)

Kezia's feelings might be explained by her fear of being scolded by her aunt, an act not without precedence. But her complex and contradictory bodily reaction of feeling at once hot and weightless can also be read as a sensation of shame, caused by her realisation of her careless treatment of the cat. The animal's 'disobedience' reminds Kezia that the cat is a living creature with individual needs, not a toy to be carried 'under [the] arm' and used for playful experiments (p. 120). Through her interactions with animals in 'Prelude', Kezia learns that an animal is not a toy that can be mended once broken. When the handyman decapitates the duck, she suffers a shock not only due to her witnessing of the bloody action but also because of the painful lesson she learns: once killed, the head of the duck cannot be 'put back' like that of a broken doll (p. 109).[32]

In 'At the Bay', written a few years after 'Prelude', Kezia seems to have learned her lessons about animals. In 'the later story, the three sisters and their cousins play a card game that presupposes their imaginary transformation into animals. While the Trout boys and Isabel can easily choose an animal identity, Kezia and Lottie encounter some difficulties. Lottie is too young to comprehend the rules of the game fully, or to decide which animal she wants to be, and Kezia's choice to identify with the bee leads to some controversy among the children:

> 'You can't be a bee, Kezia. A bee's not an animal. It's a ninseck'.
>
> 'Oh, but I do want to be a bee frightfully', wailed Kezia. . . . A tiny bee, all yellow-furry, with striped legs. She drew her legs up under her and leaned over the table. She felt she was a bee.
>
> 'A ninseck must be an animal', she said stoutly. 'It makes a noise. It's not like a fish.' (p. 303)

The children's dialogue and Kezia's definition of the category of 'ninseck' reveal their lack of zoological knowledge and 'the superficiality of their method', which is perfectly understandable, taking into account their age.[33] The lack of theoretical facts, however, does not hinder Kezia in acquiring an intimate knowledge about the bee, most probably based on her previous observations of the insect. In contrast with the other children, Kezia's familiarity with her chosen animal is not limited to onomatopoeic words: she describes the bee with delicacy, while experiencing a whole-body metamorphosis, which demonstrates, as Melinda Harvey has put it, Mansfield's 'critique of anthropocentrism and [her] pursuit of an animal-centred discourse'.[34] Kezia might not know whether a 'ninseck' classifies as an animal, but she is intimately familiar with the shape, colour and texture of the bee, as well as its posture, which she imitates with her own body, proving her playmates wrong and showing them that, within the boundaries of the game, she can indeed be a bee (pun intended).

In contrast with some early twentieth-century education reformers, Mansfield advocates the importance of free-imaginative play instead of pedagogical play with educational toys, which has predetermined learning outcomes. Throughout her career, she remained deeply engaged with the psychology of childhood and, in her mature fiction and letters, was highly critical of the disruptive effects on childhood creativity, and on family relationships, of new educational methods that sought to transform children's play into learning activities. For Mansfield, free and unstructured play represents a form of creative liberty, a way of acquiring knowledge about the world and forging intimate ties with others. Through the character of Kezia, Mansfield creates the figure of the child artist, showing how creative play can hone the child's aesthetic affinity and empathy for the immediate group of family circle and for the more distant but equally important others, including the socially disadvantaged and the non-human. By linking the aesthetic and the ecological through the image of play, Mansfield encourages her readers to create an empathetic mode of reading the (story)world – a realm in which humans, plants, animals and other natural elements can co-exist as playmates.

Notes

1. *Letters* 1, p. 231.
2. Mansfield often sent her regards to the dolls in her letters to Murry. In a letter from January 1918, she wrote: 'Kiss [Ribni] for me –.' *Letters* 2, p. 5.
3. George Shelton Hubbell, 'Katherine Mansfield and Kezia', *Sewanee Review*, 35: 3 (1927), pp. 325–35 (p. 326).
4. Tracy Miao, 'Katherine Mansfield's "Innocent Eye"', *Journal of New Zealand Literature*, 32 (part 2, 2014), pp. 143–66 (p. 144); Meghan Marie Hammond, 'Mansfield's Psychology of the Emotions', in Claire Hanson, Gerri Kimber and Todd Martin, eds, *Katherine Mansfield and Psychology* (Edinburgh: Edinburgh University Press, 2016), pp. 56–67.
5. Janka Kascakova, 'Katherine Mansfield's Children at Play', in Joyce E. Kelley, ed., *Children's Play in Literature: Investigating the Strengths and the Subversions of the Playing Child* (New York: Routledge, 2018), pp. 124–42 (p. 139).
6. Marina Warner, 'Out of an Old Toy Chest', *Journal of Aesthetic Education*, 43: 2 (2009), pp. 3–18 (p. 10).
7. Mary Ruth Moore and Susan Hall Rodney, 'Friedrich Froebel', in Rodney P. Carlisle, ed., *Encyclopedia of Play in Today's Society* (Thousand Oaks, California: 2009), p. 247.
8. Some of these toys were on display at the South Kensington Museum (later Victoria & Albert Museum) in the Education Collection. See James Macauley, 'The South Kensington Museum', *The Leisure Hour*, 14 April 1859, p. 234.
9. Published by Ward, Lock & Co., advertised in the *Athenaeum*, 3 November 1883, p. 579.
10. Maria Montessori, *The Montessori Method*, trans. by Anne E. George (New York: Frederick A. Stokes, 1912), p. 298.
11. Montessori, p. 300.
12. Sol Cohen, 'The Montessori Movement in England, 1911–1952', *History of Education*, 3: 1 (1974), pp. 51–67 (p. 56).
13. *The Times*, 1 September 1919, p. 13.
14. *The Times*, 3 December 1912, p. 4.
15. Cohen, p. 54.
16. *Letters* 4, p. 20.
17. Maria Montessori, *The Advanced Montessori Method*, trans. by Florence Simmonds (New York: Frederick A. Stokes, 1917), p. 243.
18. CW1, p. 25; p. 27.
19. CW1, p. 27.
20. CW1, p. 17.
21. CW1, p. 18.
22. Katherine Mansfield, *Selected Stories*, ed. by Angela Smith (Oxford: Oxford University Press, 2002), p. 271. Further references to Mansfield's stories are placed in the text.
23. Trudi Tate, 'King Baby: Infant Care into the Peace', in Trudi Tate and Kate Kennedy, eds, *The Silent Morning: Culture and Memory After the Armistice* (Manchester: Manchester University Press, 2013), pp. 104–30 (p. 117).

24. Tate, p. 119.
25. Isabel's attraction to foreign toys might have been influenced by her visit to Paris with her friend Moira. In the first decades of the twentieth century, artistic toys were popular in France. Many French intellectuals believed that children should be taught, from a young age, to 'hate ugliness' and 'to love that which is pretty, elegant, harmonious'. See the French review *L'Art et l'enfant*, 4: 21 (1908), p. 63. Since children's aesthetic taste could be shaped most effectively by the toys with which they played, artists (including painters, illustrators and architects) were encouraged to design artistic toys that would hone children's ability to appreciate beauty.
26. Rishona Zimring, 'Mansfield's Charm: The Enchantment of Domestic "Bliss"', in Delia da Sousa Correa, Gerri Kimber, Susan Reid and Gina Wisker, eds, *Katherine Mansfield and the Fantastic* (Edinburgh: Edinburgh University Press, 2012), pp. 33–50 (p. 39).
27. Hannah Freed-Thall, 'Thinking Small: Ecologies of Close Reading', in David James, ed., *Modernism & Close Reading* (Oxford: Oxford University Press, 2020), pp. 228–41 (p. 229).
28. Montessori, *The Montessori Method*, p. 243.
29. Montessori, *The Advanced Montessori Method*, p. 255.
30. Ibid.
31. Delphine Soulhat, 'Kezia in Wonderland', in Janet Wilson, Gerri Kimber and Susan Reid, eds, *Katherine Mansfield and Literary Modernism* (London: Continuum, 2011), pp. 101–11 (p. 103).
32. In the years when she was working on 'Prelude' and 'At the Bay', Mansfield showed a vivid interest in broken toys. In a letter written to Murry in 1915 from France, she playfully scolded him for 'decapitating' O Hara San: 'Darling, what a frightful adventure with O Hara San. What a Minx to take off her head like that – but you ought to have known, Bogey.' See *Letters* 1, p. 205. In October 1920, she wrote an enthusiastic letter to Murry, urging him to bring along her other doll, Ribni, when he visits her in Menton: 'Can you bring Ribni at Xmas? There is a shop in Nice which cures poupées cassées. When I read of it I almost telegraphed for Ribni. I want him to be made good as new again. He haunts me. Ah, I can see a story in this idea.' *Letters* 4, p. 76.
33. Derek Ryan, 'Katherine Mansfield's Animal Aesthetics', *Modern Fiction Studies*, 64: 1 (2018), pp. 27–52 (p. 38).
34. Melinda Harvey, 'Katherine Mansfield's Menagerie', in Wilson, Kimber and Reid, pp. 202–10 (p. 202).

Katherine Mansfield's Sleeping Boys

Erika Baldt

The first story that Katherine Mansfield ever published, aged eleven, was about the death of a child. The recently discovered[1] 'His Little Friend' is a brief account of the friendship that develops between the 'aged', childless Mr Long and 'little Bobbie', a boy who lives in the village.[2] The story bears the hallmarks of Mansfield's mature work: an ear for dialect and children's speech ('I fought you was never comin'. I'se been waiting for you every day'), class issues as seen through innocent eyes ('mother's ill, and we hasent got nofing to eat')[3] and, perhaps surprisingly, a young life cut short. For although Mansfield is arguably best known for breathing life into the 'firm compact little girls' and 'tender, delicate-looking little boys'[4] of her mature stories like 'Prelude'[5] and 'At the Bay', she also invests the dead with similar qualities. Regardless of age, the deceased are almost uniformly described like the 'little lad' of her first story, whose innocent, smiling face beaming from his pillow suggests untroubled sleep, rather than death.[6]

Such a representation was not new, however. According to Emily Vermeule, the ancient Greeks imagined sleep as 'death's twin or little brother'.[7] While the eleven-year-old Mansfield was surely unaware of such a connection, I would argue that the more mature writer saw a deeper potential in the imagery. I have written elsewhere about Mansfield's tendency to employ classical motifs in her work, despite not being considered to have the same interest or education in the subject as many of her contemporaries.[8] At the very least, however, she was extremely widely read, and her letters and notebooks[9] indicate not only a familiarity with classical sources, but 'a really vivid memory' of them,[10] which would suggest that she was making a conscious effort to situate her work within a tradition that stretches back to the origins of literature. Presenting the deceased as a sleeping boy in her later stories,

Mansfield echoes depictions of 'the youth and gentleness of the dead' that go back to the Bronze Age[11] in order to reflect the tragic losses of her own day.

In the wake of the Great War, death was, unfortunately, for the young; the aged, like 'the Boss' in 'The Fly', were left to mourn, imagining their sons 'lying unchanged, unblemished [. . .] asleep for ever'.[12] Youth was, in a way, immortalised in death, 'unchanged', a 'paradox' that Jean-Pierre Vernant identifies in Homeric epics 'of the values of life, youth, and beauty, which one can ensure for oneself only by losing them, which become eternal possessions only when one ceases to be'.[13] Losing his life in the bloom of youth, a hero was, at the same time, fixed forever in that state, and Mansfield sought to capture the same 'paradox' in her work. Writing to her husband, John Middleton Murry, in 1919, she claimed, 'We see death in life as we see death in a flower that is fresh unfolded. Our hymn is to the flower's beauty – we would make that beauty immortal because we *know*.'[14] Even before 'The Fly', Mansfield personified this fresh, unfolded flower as a sleeping boy in stories like 'The Garden Party', 'Psychology' and 'Six Years After', preserving, in the manner of the ancient Greeks and Romans, the beauty of those young men who perished in the prime of their lives.

Welcoming Death in 'The Garden Party'

Early on, however, Mansfield's stories owed more to fairy tales and popular culture than the classics. As 'His Little Friend' demonstrates, she was fixated on the death of children, but her models were rather more contemporary. The 'shadow children', whose ranks the narrator's brother joins upon death in Mansfield's 1908 story 'The Thoughtful Child',[15] for example, could have any number of sources, from Hans Christian Andersen,[16] to Louisa May Alcott,[17] to Robert Louis Stevenson.[18] It is in 'A Fairy Story' of 1910, however, that the direction begins to change, in spite of the piece's title. The story follows 'the Girl', who wanted to 'find [her]self', and her companion 'the Boy', who wanted to find 'the world'.[19] He describes to her his fantasy, in which

> people will point at me crying, 'See, there he goes, the boy who has found the world; the boy who has conquered the world.' And I shall sit in a bower made out of my laurel wreaths, and you shall be the queen and hold my hand. And I shall never be old, and always be beautiful.[20]

Though he talks of castles and dragons, the Boy's image of himself as eternally young and crowned with laurels is closer to the Greek or Roman ideal of the conquering hero, while his death echoes that of the mythical Narcissus, in that his obsession with this vision of himself ultimately kills him.[21] His corpse is placed on a bed with 'his flaxen hair [. . .] spread upon the pillow,' and a smile on his face,[22] thus fulfilling his prophecy that he will 'never be old'.

Though satirical, the Boy's preoccupation with perfection seems to prefigure the idealisation of young men that flooded the media with the arrival of the First World War. Propaganda posters sought the enlistment of 'boys'[23] and 'lad[s]'[24] who would be led by the armed, Athena-like figure of Britannia[25] as, according to Theodore Koulouris,

> the presence of the heroic ideal inherited from the iron grip of Hellenism over the cultural and political context of early twentieth-century Britain was, indeed, pervasive. The Homeric heroes constituted an inspiration for the young officers who left their universities and swapped their books for arms.[26]

Mansfield, however, was against making such connections explicit, arguing instead, in the same letter to Murry in which she presents her views on 'death in life', that she could never mention the war 'bang out' but instead 'might write about a boy eating strawberries or a woman combing her hair on a windy morning'.[27] A good example of this technique is explained by Christine Darrohn in her essay, '"Blown to Bits!": Katherine Mansfield's "The Garden Party" and the Great War', in which she argues that 'The Garden Party' is actually a story about the losses of and anxieties created by the Great War, specifically the loss of Mansfield's own brother, Leslie Beauchamp, who was killed in a grenade accident. Darrohn explains how Mansfield rewrote her brother's death:

> In 'The Garden Party' that terrifying image [of Leslie] is transformed into a picture of beautiful, peaceful, still wholeness, an image to assuage anxieties that the war raises – not merely for Mansfield, but for an entire society – about the vulnerability of the male body to violence.[28]

The story contains no references to war, but the figure of the deceased, fixed 'into a picture' of youth and beauty, recalls those of the Greek heroes who died in battle.

The character in question is a working-class man called Scott, whose skull is crushed when he is thrown from his horse. Like that of the Boy in 'A Fairy Story', however, the corpse that the protagonist Laura encounters is without blemish. Taking her first glimpse of death, Laura sees

> a young man, fast asleep – sleeping so soundly, so deeply, that he was far, far away from them both. Oh, so remote, so peaceful. [. . .] His head was

> sunk in the pillow, his eyes were closed [. . .] He was wonderful, beautiful. While they were laughing and while the band was playing, this marvel had come to the lane. Happy . . . happy . . . All is well, said that sleeping face. This is just as it should be. I am content.[29]

With his head 'sunk in the pillow' and no sign of age on his 'happy' face, Scott's depiction not only echoes those of the boys in Mansfield's earlier stories, but also follows the tradition of ancient Greek funeral rites. For although Darrohn suggests that 'the metaphor of sleep' is 'perhaps the most radical revision of the corpse',[30] it was actually the preferred representation, according to Vermeule, as the corpse was

> laid on a bed or bier, usually with the feet toward the door, facing the journey. The house was hung with wreaths and sprays of leaves, and these were also offered to the dead man. There was special use of marjoram and celery, myrtle and laurel leaves. [. . .] The bier was usually dressed like a bed with mattress, blanket and pillows, part of the old association between sleep and death which is still natural for us.[31]

Scott's appearance and placement match the ancient model, as does the mourning that occurs around him. 'The Scotts' house is distinctly gendered female',[32] as Darrohn puts it, because in ancient Greece, the funeral rites 'are family responsibilities of the women in the household who loved the dead dearest and miss him most. The dead are helpless, and need comfort or mothering like infants.'[33] Even, or especially, adult men were both perceived and presented like children in death, which is evident in the story, as well, for though considerably more mature than Laura in age and experience, the first adjective used to describe Scott from her perspective is 'young', his 'peaceful' sleep lending his figure an innocence it no longer possessed in life.

But what of Laura herself? She is not bound by any 'family responsibilities' to the deceased, but her connection with death is signalled throughout the story by her fascination with particular trees and flowers. Emmanouil Aretoulakis explores the symbolism of the vegetation with which Laura seems to have a special affinity:

> on the one hand, the karaka-tree seems to be a celebration of life, while on the other, it is inextricable from death. By associating emotionally with the karaka-tree, Laura acts out that 'in-betweenness' which keeps life and death – or beauty and ugliness – separate but also symbiotic. Similarly, the lilies 'growing in her breast' may be symbolic of her closeness to death as well as life.[34]

Though not the marjoram or celery of the Greek rites, the connotations of the karaka and lily are appropriate to the story's New Zealand setting.

However, what Aretoulakis does not take into account is Laura's own name, which is notable for breaking the pattern of *Little Women* allusions established with the names of her other siblings, Meg, Jose and Laurie.[35] Certainly, her name is meant to connect her with her beloved brother Laurie, suggesting a kind of twinning like that of sleep and death. The name Laura itself, though, is derived from that of the laurel tree,[36] which not only gave the karaka its common name of New Zealand laurel,[37] but was, from ancient times, used in funeral rites, as Vermeule notes.[38] With her basket of food and her wonderment at the figure before her, Laura herself becomes an offering to the dead man, enacting the ritual that will give his short life meaning. As Vernant explains, 'Death is overcome when it is made welcome instead of merely being experienced, and when it makes life a perpetual gamble and endows it with exemplary value.'[39] It is only by allowing Laura to perceive the corpse as a beautiful, sleeping youth that Scott's death is 'made welcome'. In this way, 'death is overcome' not just for Scott, or, by extension, Leslie Beauchamp, but for all those boys and men that lost their lives and for all the families that mourned them.

'Psychology': The First 'Marvel'

Yet 'The Garden Party' is not the first time that Mansfield invoked the classical imagery of death. Following Darrohn's lead to a story that 'perhaps seems worlds away from the Great War',[40] I would argue that Mansfield's 'Psychology'[41] of 1920 precedes 'The Garden Party' in its use of the figure of a sleeping boy as a symbol for those who have died. For though 'Psychology' seems, on the surface, to be about a failure of communication between two writers over tea and cake, the story is another example of 'the ways survivors of war employ imagination and language to represent and recuperate from the costs of war'.[42] The story describes a brief encounter between two unnamed characters, one male and one female, as they attempt to navigate a social situation without giving in to their desire for one another. However, while critics often focus on the characters' discussion of psychological symptoms, as the story's title asks us to do,[43] I would argue that it is not the desire for each other that threatens to disrupt their pleasantly superficial evening, but their feelings for what appears to be a small sculpture in the woman's studio.

The objects with which the woman surrounds herself almost become characters in their own right, as 'all these gay things round her were part of her – her offspring – and they knew it and made the largest, most vehement claims'.[44] She is, however, more accepting of 'claims' of affection from inanimate objects than from humans, and the story turns when the male character admits to deeper feelings:

> 'Often when I am away from here I revisit it in spirit – wander about among your red chairs, stare at the bowl of fruit on the black table – and just touch, very lightly, that marvel of a sleeping boy's head'.
>
> He looked at it as he spoke. It stood on the corner of the mantelpiece; the head to one side down-drooping, the lips parted, as though in his sleep the little boy listened to some sweet sound. . . .
>
> 'I love that little boy', he murmured. And then they both were silent.[45]

The silence that follows his admission is in stark contrast to the banter that they seem to cultivate as a sign of their unproblematic friendship. But what is it about the sculpture of a child that could open such an 'unfamiliar pool' between them?

That the figure is sleeping suggests, of course, what Vermeule calls the 'old association' with death, and the term that the man bestows upon it, 'marvel', prefigures Laura's interpretation of Scott's corpse in 'The Garden Party'. Moreover, the head is described with a very particular phrase: 'down-drooping'. Though it indicates the angle of repose, it also echoes a passage in Alexander Pope's 1899 translation of *The Iliad.* In the short scene, the Greek warrior Teucer has taken aim at the Trojans' greatest hero, Hector, but hits Hector's kinsman instead:

> He miss'd the mark; but pierced Gorgythio's heart,
> And drench'd in royal blood the thirsty dart.
> [. . .]
> As full-blown poppies, overcharged with rain,
> Decline the head, and drooping kiss the plain;
> So sinks the youth: his beauteous head, depress'd
> Beneath his helmet, drops upon his breast.[46]

The simile of the dying hero's head 'drooping' like a poppy is translated on to the sculpture, whose lips are parted so that it too seems to 'kiss the plain'. Meanwhile, the rest of the room's furnishings, the red chairs and the black table, recall the flower's well-known colours. Yet another layer of meaning is added when we consider that the poppy became a symbol of remembrance for the Great War, most notably in John McCrae's 1915 poem 'In Flanders Fields', which ends

> If ye break faith with us who die
> We shall not sleep, though poppies grow
>   In Flanders fields.[47]

Taking these allusions into account, it is no wonder that 'silence' suddenly overwhelms the characters.

As McCrae's poem suggests, the sleep of the dead is fitful, and it is important to note another, possibly troubling, aspect of the sleeping boy: the piece is never described as a sculpture or referred to as a representation of a full-length figure. When mentioned in the text, it is referred to only as a head without a body. This fragmentation recalls Mansfield's description of a vision of her brother that, Darrohn suggests, was the impetus for 'The Garden Party':[48]

> when I leaned out of the window I seemed to see my brother dotted all over the field – now on his back, now on his face, now huddled up, now half pressed into the earth. Wherever I looked there he lay I felt that God showed me to him like that for some express purpose.[49]

While she makes no mention of severed limbs, it is certainly implied, revealing that, for Mansfield, just as for the ancient Greeks, one of the greatest fears was the dismemberment of a corpse. The idea that 'in losing its formal unity the human body is reduced to the condition of a thing along with its disfigurement'[50] is made manifest in 'Psychology', as the sleeping boy is counted as only one of the female character's many 'gay things'. However, the related concern with dismemberment for the Greeks was its potential to sever the ties between the deceased and the loved ones left behind. If the hero's remains were scattered and left to the elements, there would be

> no place of burial [. . .] no location for his body that would mark for his society the site where he is to be found; there he would continue his relations with his country, his lineage, his descendants, or even simply with the chance passers-by. Excluded from death, he is equally banished from human memory.[51]

Here, being 'excluded from death' does not mean that the hero would become immortal, but that he would be forgotten, and Mansfield could not accept such a fate for Leslie. In the same notebook entry, she notes that 'When I am not writing I feel my brother calling me & he is not happy. Only when I write or am in a state of writing – a state of "inspiration" do I feel that he is calm.'[52] It is as if Leslie is enacting the final lines of 'In Flanders Fields', threatening that he will not 'sleep' if Mansfield 'break[s] faith' with his memory.

In Homeric epics, the dismembered corpse could be made whole only through divine intervention. According to Vernant,

> the gods perform the human rituals of cleansing and beautification but use divine unguents: these elixirs of immortality preserve 'intact', despite all the abuse, that youth and beauty, which can only fade on the body of a living man, but which death in battle fixes forever on the hero's form.[53]

The goal was not to undo the hero's death, but to ensure that his 'youth and beauty' could live on. While there are no magic 'elixirs' in Mansfield's 'Psychology', the story is not completely free of references to divine authority, and, though satirical, the invocation of the Book of Genesis early on in the story[54] nonetheless draws attention to divine intervention in human life, as well as providing a link back to Mansfield's diary entry of seeing Leslie's body in the field. There, she uses an unexpected syntax, 'God showed *me* to *him*,' in a way that suggests that she is the instrument by which the hero, whether Leslie or any casualty of the Great War, will be once again made 'intact', though not through 'divine unguents' but 'inspiration'. The boy in the story sleeps peacefully, despite his fragmentation, because he has been turned into art.

The Spirits of 'Six Years After'

Josiane Paccaud-Huguet also sees a connection with Leslie Beauchamp in 'Psychology', suggesting that the 'pool of silence [that] falls between the two friends' is 'a poetic evocation of the dark side of the world where Mansfield's little sun/son has dropped'.[55] In one of her final stories, 'Six Years After', Mansfield returns to 'the dark side of the world', New Zealand, and expands the pool into an ocean. The unfinished piece is often read as Mansfield's exploration of her mother's grief after Leslie's death, but, like 'Psychology', it is also a pastiche of classical references that expands the personal to the universal. The story begins with a married couple settling in on a steamer voyage. Left to her own thoughts, the woman falls into a waking dream in which she is importuned by 'a presence', who 'cried to her alone'.[56] The vision crystallises into the figure of her son, 'a little slender boy – so pale – who had just waked out of a dreadful dream'.[57] Though the text does not suggest it for several more paragraphs, Mansfield's use of the image of a sleeping boy should alert the reader to the fact that the woman's son has died.

An earlier fragment of the story indicates that the son was actually a young man and a soldier, as the mother 'press[es] her head against the cold buttons of his British warm'.[58] As the Greeks did, however, Mansfield exaggerates the boy's youth, and the dream he describes also follows a classical precedent. After asserting that his mother is 'forgetting'[59] him, the boy recalls that

> I dreamed I was in a wood – somewhere far away from everybody, – and I was lying down and a great blackberry vine grew over me. And I called and called to you – and you wouldn't come – you wouldn't come – so I had to lie there for ever.[60]

This dream of a blackberry vine echoes Mansfield's earlier poem on Leslie's death, 'To L.H.B.', in which the speaker dreams of encountering her brother in a similar setting: 'By the remembered stream my brother stands / Waiting for me with berries in his hands. . . .'[61] As with the sleeping boy's head in 'Psychology', however, there is an even earlier precedent for this image in epic poetry.

The idea of a son killed and his corpse subsumed by foreign soil 'far away from everybody' can be traced back to another Trojan, Polydorus, the youngest son of King Priam and Queen Hecuba, who is sent to neighbouring Thrace that he might survive the war with the Greeks. Unbeknownst to his parents, however, he is murdered by his host, and his body is left unburied. Like Gorgythion, Polydorus is mentioned only briefly in *The Iliad*,[62] but his fate was described with lasting effect by Virgil in *The Aeneid*. Recounting his journey from Troy, the hero Aeneas describes his arrival at Thrace, and his attempt to remove a myrtle tree in order to build an altar. In doing so, he

> had sight of a gruesome prodigy
> Beyond description: when the first stalk came torn
> Out of the earth, and the root network burst,
> Dark blood dripped down to soak and foul the soil

and 'a groan came from the mound'.[63] The spirit of the dead Polydorus identifies himself from beneath the roots, and, to ensure that Aeneas does not mistake what he sees for the dark juices of the myrtle berries, states that 'this blood drips from no tree'.[64] Dante then took up this image in the seventh circle of hell. There, the souls of those who died by their own hand are imprisoned within trees that bleed when their branches are torn. Such injury is the only way that the spirits are allowed to speak, so that 'there came words and blood together'.[65] With these allusions in mind, it is easy to see why Janet Wilson refers to 'Six Years After' as 'Mansfield's most overtly haunted story'.[66] Here, the concern for the integrity of the corpse, only hinted at in 'Psychology', is amplified to become a source of torture not just for the spirits, whose cause of death prevented their burial,[67] but for the living, as well. Just as Aeneas's discovery throws him into 'a maze of dread',[68] and Dante 'stood transfixed by fear',[69] Mansfield's text assigns similar feelings to the mother in 'Six Years After': 'This is anguish! How is it to be borne? Still, it is not the idea of her suffering is unbearable – it is his. Can one do nothing for the dead? And for a long time the answer had been – Nothing!'[70]

The question 'Can one do nothing for the dead?' is one with which, as 'Psychology' and 'The Garden Party' suggest, Mansfield continuously wrestled. It is also one that can help the reader make sense of the story's next paragraph. Following that exclamation, which the reader assumes to have been the mother's, there is a pause in the text: '. . . But softly without a sound the dark curtain has rolled down. There is no more to come. That is the end of the play.'[71] While some have interpreted it allegorically, as Katherine Dickson Murphy does, suggesting that 'The Mother's anguish over death is not defeat but persistence in the belief that one can go on although life may be only an illusion, a drama at the end of which there is nothing,'[72] no critic has yet provided an explanation for the sudden interjection of these lines, which interrupt and redirect both the woman's thoughts and the reader's attention. Yet if Mansfield was truly looking to the model of Polydorus, it is very possible that these lines refer to an actual stage production that dramatised his story.

Long before Virgil, Euripides wrote two plays that focus on Hecuba, Polydorus's mother. While it is certain that Mansfield and most of her readers would have been familiar with the character from the player king's speech in *Hamlet* and the eponymous prince's famous line, 'what's Hecuba to him or he to Hecuba [. . .]?',[73] it is also likely that they would have had some knowledge of the source material as well, since the plays of Euripides were undergoing a resurgence in London during the turn of the twentieth century, due in large part to Gilbert Murray's translations and productions.[74] While Murray himself noted the prevalence of the plays in popular culture at the time,[75] William L. Chenery further explained why Euripides himself was the model needed for the current times:

> It is Euripides [. . .] who concerns the great awakening world of 1914. The intellectual battles which Euripides fought on behalf of Athens have been waged again and often for the millions who slumber and are content. They are being fought now with an intensity unprecedented. So it brings courage and it brings calm to realize the continuity of the conflict, and to recall the signal victories of the olden days.[76]

Published four months before the Great War, Chenery's words take on a prophetic cast and provide a compelling rationale for why Mansfield might have turned to Euripides in the war's aftermath.

Both of Euripides' plays featuring the Queen of Troy deal with a mother's grief over the fate of her children. The first, simply titled *Hecuba*, opens with the ghost of Polydorus, whose corpse in this version is not overgrown by vines but left at the edge of the sea, recalling the setting of 'Six Years After', as does his goal 'to win a grave [. . .] to find a tomb and fall into my mother's hands'.[77] Yet while the second and better-known play, *The Trojan Women*, does not mention Polydorus, focusing instead on the tragedies that befall Hecuba's other children, it is possible that

Mansfield conflated the two texts, as Virgil did in *The Aeneid*,[78] in order to heighten the pathos of the boy's death. The question 'Can one do nothing for the dead?' is one that Hecuba asks almost verbatim over the body of her grandson Astyanax after he, too, has been killed by the Greeks.[79] Astyanax is only a small child, closer in age to the boy in 'Six Years After' than Polydorus would be, and in both texts, it is the youth of the victim that compounds the tragedy, as the lost future is mourned as much as the child himself. That Astyanax has been robbed of 'the sweets of manhood, of marriage, and of godlike power'[80] compounds Hecuba's grief, just as the mother's projection of her son's future 'wedding and [her] first grandchild' is the cause of renewed sorrow, not only to her but to her son as well: 'Oh, Mother, it's not fair to me to put these ideas into my head! Stop, Mother, stop! When I think of all I have missed, I can't bear it.'[81] Just as Mansfield doubles Polydorus and Astyanax in the figure of the son, she doubles the son and the mother, as his final words – 'I can't bear it!' – become hers. In making the child much younger than the figures mentioned by Virgil or Dante, Mansfield both corresponds to the earlier Homeric model that focuses on the youth of the deceased and heightens the perception of his suffering.

Yet there is another double for Polydorus in *Hecuba*. His sister Polyxena is sacrificed by the Greeks on the tomb of Achilles, just as his own body is being recovered from the shore.[82] Immediately, the matching names for brother and sister, Polydorus and Polyxena, recall the brother and sister pairing of Laurie and Laura in 'The Garden Party' and provide a clue as to why Mansfield may have been captivated by this source material in the first place: in the wake of the news of Leslie's accident, Mansfield wrote often of her wish to join him in death.[83] Though removed from that period by the same length of time as the story's title, Mansfield was again facing her own mortality when she wrote 'Six Years After', albeit far less willingly.[84] By indirectly projecting herself into the story, she ensures that, in fiction at least, 'brother and sister may be laid on the same pyre and buried side by side'.[85]

Conclusion

Only a few months before she began sketching out ideas for 'Six Years After', Mansfield composed a brief fragment in her journal that begins, 'Little children run in and out of my world, never knowing the danger.'[86] From her very first story to one of her last, Mansfield was compelled to portray children in a way that acknowledged the perils that surrounded them. Some of her young characters thrived but many also died, reflecting not only Mansfield's own personal 'world', but the wider one, in which young sons and brothers departed for foreign shores and never returned. In fact, Mansfield makes it clear that the beauty of youth exists not in spite but because of this 'danger', and it is this juxtaposition of 'death in life', as she calls it, with which she imbues the figure of the sleeping boy in her stories. By wrapping his memory in references to the epics and tragedies in which young men made the ultimate sacrifice, Mansfield turns the personal loss of one particular boy into a universal symbol in a way that itself hearkens back to ancient times: 'This easy sliding from present to past to present is a characteristic of the way myth functioned in Greek society, where conjunction with the figures of old poetry could confer heroic stature on present mortals.'[87] While it may not 'confer heroic stature', Mansfield's placement of her sleeping boys within this classical tradition ensures that, though they will never wake, they will not be forgotten.

Notes

1. See Matt Stewart, 'Eleven-year-old Mansfield's first published work unearthed by Wellington author', *stuff*, 3 August 2017, available at <https://www.stuff.co.nz/entertainment/books/95433477/elevenyearold-mansfields-first-published-work-unearthed-by-wellington-author> (last accessed 15 July 2020).
2. Katherine Mansfield, 'His Little Friend', *The New Zealand Graphic and Ladies' Journal*, 13 October 1900, pp. 710–11, available at <https://wellington.recollect.co.nz/nodes/view/2515#idx3023> (last accessed 15 July 2020).
3. Mansfield, 'His Little Friend', p. 711.
4. CW2, p. 351.
5. CW2, pp. 56–93.
6. Mansfield, 'His Little Friend', p. 711.
7. Emily Vermeule, *Aspects of Death in Early Greek Art and Poetry* (Berkeley: University of California Press, 1979), p. 145.
8. See for example, Erika Baldt, '"A god instead of a mortal": Katherine Mansfield and the Orphic Mysteries', in Aimée Gasston, Gerri Kimber and Janet Wilson, eds, *Katherine Mansfield: New Directions* (London: Bloomsbury Academic, 2020), pp. 110–24.
9. Mansfield made notes on Shakespeare's *Troilus and Cressida*, which focuses on the Trojan War, in a notebook entry for 1916, and describes Chekhov's 'The Steppe' as 'a kind of Iliad or Odyssey' in a letter to S. S. Koteliansky in 1919. See CW4, p. 201, and *Letters* 2, p. 353.
10. See Mansfield's letter of 1922 to Dorothy Brett (*Letters* 5, p. 156), about James Joyce's *Ulysses*, in which she tells Brett not to read the novel unless she can 'really worry about it' because 'one needs to have a really vivid memory of The Odyssey and of English literature to make it out at all'. Such advice suggests that Mansfield herself had the requisite background to read and 'worry about' the text.
11. Vermeule, p. 21.
12. CW2, p. 478.
13. Jean-Pierre Vernant, 'A "Beautiful Death" and the Disfigured Corpse in Homeric Epic', in Douglas L. Cairns, ed., *Oxford Readings in Homer's Iliad* (Oxford: Oxford University Press, 2001), p. 334.

14. Cherry A. Hankin, ed., *Letters Between Katherine Mansfield and John Middleton Murry* (London: Virago Press, 1988), pp. 211–12. Italics original.
15. CW1, pp. 124–7.
16. Andersen's 'The Shadow' was first published in 1847 and describes a shadow that detaches from its human owner and continues to exist after the human dies. See Hans Christian Andersen, 'The Shadow', in *Hans Andersen Forty-Two Stories*, trans. by M. R. James (1930), available at <https://gutenberg.ca/ebooks/andersen-shadow/andersen-shadow-00-h.html> (last accessed 15 July 2020).
17. See Louisa May Alcott, 'Shadow-Children', in *Aunt Jo's Scrap-Bag* (Boston: Roberts Brothers, 1882), pp. 104–23, available at <http://www.gutenberg.org/files/27567/27567-h/27567-h.htm#Page_104> (last accessed 15 July 2020).
18. Robert Louis Stevenson, 'My Shadow', in *A Child's Garden of Verses* (New York: Charles Scribner's Sons, 1905), available at <http://www.gutenberg.org/files/25609/25609-h/25609-h.htm#MY_SHADOW> (last accessed 15 July 2020).
19. CW1, p. 202.
20. CW1, p. 202.
21. See Ovid, 'Narcissus and Echo', *Metamorphoses*, trans. by David Raeburn (London: Penguin, 2004), pp. 109–16. Narcissus dies as a result of becoming obsessed with his own reflection. His body is then transformed into the flower of the same name. In Mansfield's 'A Fairy Story', the Boy is crushed by the books that he believed would allow him to find the world (p. 203) and buttercups grow on his burial place (p. 204).
22. Mansfield, 'A Fairy Story', p. 204.
23. W. H. Caffyn, 'Come along, boys! Enlist to-day' (London: The Haycock-Cadle Co., 1915), available at <https://www.loc.gov/item/2003662913/> (last accessed 11 July 2020).
24. 'Come lad slip across and help' (Harrow: David Allen & Sons Ld., 1915), available at <https://www.loc.gov/item/2003675293/> (last accessed 11 July 2020).
25. E. Kemp-Welch, 'Remember Scarborough! Enlist now' (Harrow: David Allen & Sons Ld., 1914), available at <https://www.loc.gov/resource/cph.3g11361/> (last accessed 11 July 2020).
26. Theodore Koulouris, *Hellenism and Loss in the Work of Virginia Woolf* (Farnham: Ashgate, 2011), p. 123.
27. Hankin, p. 212.
28. Christine Darrohn, '"Blown to Bits!": Katherine Mansfield's "The Garden-Party" and the Great War', *Modern Fiction Studies*, 44: 3 (Fall 1998), pp. 513–39 (p. 520).
29. CW2, p. 413.
30. Darrohn, p. 521.
31. Vermeule, p. 13.
32. Darrohn, p. 526.
33. Vermeule, p. 14.
34. Emmanouil Aretoulakis, 'Colonialism and the Need for Impurity: Katherine Mansfield, "The Garden Party" and Postcolonial Feeling', in Gerri Kimber, Delia da Sousa Correa and Janet Wilson, eds, *Katherine Mansfield and the (Post)colonial* (Edinburgh: Edinburgh University Press, 2013), pp. 45–62 (p. 56).
35. Louisa M. Alcott, *Little Women, Or Meg, Jo, Beth, and Amy* (Boston: Little, Brown, and Company, 1880), available at <https://www.gutenberg.org/files/37106/37106-h/37106-h.htm> (last accessed 15 July 2020). Two of the sisters in the novel are named Meg and Josephine, while their male neighbour and friend goes by the nickname Laurie.

36. Iseabail C. MacLeod, *The Wordsworth Dictionary of First Names* (Ware: Wordsworth Editions, 1995), p. 130, available at <https://archive.org/details/wordsworthdictio0000macl> (last accessed 15 July 2020).
37. 'Corynocarpus laevigatus Tree Record', *SelecTree*, 1995-2020, available at <https://selectree.calpoly.edu/tree-detail/corynocarpus-laevigatus> (last accessed 15 July 2020).
38. Vermeule, p. 13.
39. Vernant, p. 320.
40. Darrohn, p. 514.
41. CW2, pp. 193–8.
42. Darrohn, p. 517.
43. See Allan Pero, '"Jigging away into nothingness": Knowledge, Language, and Feminine Jouissance in "Bliss" and "Psychology"', in Claire Hanson, Gerri Kimber and Todd Martin, eds, *Katherine Mansfield and Psychology* (Edinburgh: Edinburgh University Press, 2016), pp. 100–12, and Josiane Paccaud-Huguet, 'A Trickle of Voice: Katherine Mansfield and the Modernist Moment of Being', in Gerri Kimber and Janet Wilson, eds, *Celebrating Katherine Mansfield: A Centenary Volume of Essays* (Basingstoke: Palgrave Macmillan, 2011), pp. 131–43.
44. CW2, p. 194.
45. CW2, p. 195.
46. Homer, *The Iliad of Homer*, trans. by Alexander Pope (1899), p. 247, available at <https://www.gutenberg.org/files/6130/old/6130-pdf.pdf> (last accessed 16 July 2020).
47. John McCrae, 'In Flanders Fields', *Poetry Foundation* (2020), available at <https://www.poetryfoundation.org/poems/47380/in-flanders-fields> (last accessed 16 July 2020).
48. Darrohn, p. 518.
49. CW4, p. 203.
50. Vernant, p. 337.
51. Vernant, p. 337.
52. CW4, p. 202.
53. Vernant, p. 340.
54. See CW2, p. 194: 'it's the kind of cake that might have been mentioned in the Book of Genesis. . . . And God said: "Let there be cake. And there was cake. And God saw that it was good."'
55. Paccaud-Huguet, p. 137.
56. CW2, p. 423.
57. CW2, p. 424.
58. CW2, p. 425.
59. CW2, p. 423.
60. CW2, p. 424.
61. CW3, p. 96.
62. Homer, p. 610.
63. Virgil, *The Aeneid*, trans. by Robert Fitzgerald (New York: Vintage, 1990), p. 66.
64. Virgil, p. 66.
65. Dante, *The Inferno*, trans. by John Ciardi (New York: Signet, 1954), p. 120. In the poem, the character of Virgil states that Dante had seen these images 'in my verses'.
66. Janet Wilson, 'Mansfield as (Post)colonial-Modernist: Rewriting the Contract with Death', in Kimber, Da Sousa Correa and Wilson, pp. 29–44 (p. 38).

67. Historically, individuals who died by suicide were often denied Christian burial. See Robert Barry, 'The Development of the Roman Catholic Teachings on Suicide', *Notre Dame Journal of Law, Ethics & Public Policy*, 9: 2 (1995), pp. 449–501, available at <http://scholarship.law.nd.edu/ndjlepp/vol9/iss2/4> (last accessed 17 July 2020). During Dante's time, there was also a 'custom of humiliating the corpse to deter future possible suicides' (Barry, p. 475). It is possible that Mansfield could be equating Leslie's accidental death with suicide, since the grenade exploded in and by his own hand.
68. Virgil, p. 67.
69. Dante, p. 120.
70. CW2, p. 424.
71. CW2, p. 424.
72. Katherine Dickson Murphy, *Katherine Mansfield's New Zealand Stories* (Lanham, MD: University Press of America, 1998), p. 62.
73. *Hamlet*, II, ii, 569.
74. See Edith Hall, Introduction, *Euripides Hecuba, Trojan Women, Andromache* (Oxford: Oxford University Press, 2000), p. xiv.
75. Gilbert Murray, *Euripides and His Age* (London: Williams and Norgate, 1913), available at <https://www.gutenberg.ca/ebooks/murraygga-euripidesandhisage/murraygga-euripidesandhisage-00-e.html> (last accessed 13 July 2020).
76. William L. Chenery, 'An Ancient Radical', in *The Little Review*, 1: 2 (April 1914), p. 29, available at <https://repository.library.brown.edu/studio/item/bdr:509350/PDF/> (last accessed 13 July 2020).
77. Euripides, *Hecuba*, trans. by E. P. Coleridge, in Whitney J. Oates and Eugene O'Neill, Jr, eds, *The Complete Greek Drama*, vol. 1 (New York: Random House, 1938), available at <http://www.perseus.tufts.edu/hopper/text?doc=Perseus%3Atext%3A1999.01.0098%3Acard%3D1> (last accessed 16 July 2020).
78. See H. May Johnson, 'Virgil's Debt to the Hecuba and Troades of Euripides', in *The Classical Weekly*, 3: 7 (20 November 1909), p. 50: 'The second and third books of the Aeneid are written in the spirit and contain many of the incidents of the Trojan Women and the Hecuba.' Murray also seems to have combined elements of *Hecuba* and *The Trojan Women* into a single adaptation called 'Hecuba's Lament', set to music and performed at the British Museum in 1911. See 'Hecuba's Lament' (1911), *Archive of Performances of Greek & Roman Drama*, available at <http://www.apgrd.ox.ac.uk/productions/production/11969> (last accessed 18 June 2020).
79. Hecuba's line is, 'What can I do for you, luckless one?' Euripides, *The Trojan Women*, trans. by E. P. Coleridge, in *The Plays of Euripides*, vol. I (London: George Bell and Sons, 1891), available at <http://www.perseus.tufts.edu/hopper/text?doc=Perseus:text:1999.01.0124:card=782> (last accessed 16 July 2020).
80. Euripides, *The Trojan Women*, n.p.
81. CW2, p. 424.
82. Euripides, *The Trojan Women*, n.p.
83. See CW4, pp. 171–2.
84. CW4, pp. 372, 385.
85. Euripides, *The Trojan Women*, n.p.
86. CW4, p. 380.
87. Vermeule, p. 22.

Kezia a 'ninseck', Kezia the Bee

Janka Kascakova

> 'You can't be a bee, Kezia. A bee's not an animal. It's a ninseck.'
>
> 'Oh, but I do want to be a bee frightfully', wailed Kezia. . . . A tiny bee, all yellow-furry, with striped legs. She drew her legs up under her and leaned over the table. She felt she was a bee.
>
> 'A ninseck must be an animal', she said stoutly. 'It makes a noise. It's not like a fish.' (CW2, p. 361)

It would be hard to discuss Katherine Mansfield's depiction of children without at least a brief mention of her most memorable creation, the imaginative and original Kezia of some of the New Zealand stories. And although she has often been discussed by critics in passing and in detail, her allure and depth are such that she keeps enticing scholars to look into her world and its workings time and time again. The focus of this chapter is the very entertaining and seemingly random moment in part IX of 'At the Bay' (1921), when Kezia decides, against the implied rules of the game, to be a bee. More specifically, this essay will concentrate on and examine two significant elements of the short passage included above: one is Kezia's, but more importantly Mansfield's, choice of the bee 'animal' as a play persona; the other, equally vital and no less intriguing, is the inclusion of the insects versus animals taxonomic controversy. It will explore the implications of both, arguing that closer scrutiny of the symbolical connotations of bees adds further layers to the reading of the story, and that Kezia's defence of insects communicates and supports Mansfield's belief in alternative approaches to the treatment and perception of children, women or animals, expressed in other parts of this particular story as well as in some of her other New Zealand stories.

When discussing this passage of 'At the Bay', most scholars offer only brief comments and do not venture into deeper analysis. Cherry Hankin, for example, claims that 'Kezia, who is sensitive but able to hit back, is given the role of a bee with power to sting,'[1] thus suggesting that every child's choice of animal is simply a reflection of his or her character and position within the group. Saralyn Daly observes that '[o]nly Kezia runs counter to the conventions. Despite protests, she is a bee, an insect (like Jonathan) rather than an animal.'[2] Unlike Hankin, Daly puts emphasis on Kezia's rebellion and makes an interesting, yet unexplored, connection between Kezia and her uncle, Jonathan Trout, but does not attempt an interpretation of the symbolism of the scene. Similarly, Peter Mathews links Kezia with Jonathan, maintaining that his 'comparison of himself to a desperately trapped insect is also, however, an ironic echo of Kezia's choice of animal in the previous section. Kezia's ninseck is affirmed because of the noise it makes.'[3] Neither Daly nor Mathews, however, seeks to explain the discrepancy between the obviously unhappy and 'trapped' insect of Jonathan Trout, and Kezia's struggling but clearly free bee. Delphine Soulhat maintains that the children's impersonation of animals in this scene 'is no mere disguise – it is role play, the closest stage to transformation',[4] but does not comment any further on the particularities.

In his discussion of the role of animals and animality in Mansfield's writing, Derek Ryan offers a much more detailed interpretation of the passage. He proposes to read 'the tension between classification and transformation [. . .] in zoological terms: that is, between the taxonomic study of animals, which deals in lifeless specimens, and the theory of evolution, which brings to life the biological and ethological history of species'. He maintains that 'the scene's focus on the children's trying out of various actions and behaviors in order to imitate certain animals reflects some of biologists' early attempts to understand evolutionary processes'.[5] Elsewhere, I have examined this part of the story, discussing the symbolism of the respective children's choice of animal, and reading 'Kezia's emphasis of a bee's ability to produce sound' as a sign of 'her desire to be accepted, to be allowed to express herself freely and be heard despite her unorthodox views that distance her from the rest of the family'.[6] Further, I have discussed Kezia's bee with a focus on Stephen Nachmanovitch's belief in the inevitable presence of an awareness of death in the most successful works of art.[7] Here, I will expand on the symbolical usage of bees and its possible implications for my reading of the story.

Throughout history and across different cultures and mythologies, bees have occupied a significant place, and their appearance in literature carries many symbolic connotations, one such being their connection to death, resurrection and immortality. In the folklore of many European nations, bees served as messengers between the world of the living and the world of the dead: hence the tradition of 'telling the bees' when somebody in the family passed away.[8] In ancient Greece they were also linked to seers and soothsaying; the buzzing noise the seers were producing indicated that they were in the middle of making a prophecy.[9] Bees were also associated with poets who were seen as prophets, the 'privileged guild of mortals who were divinely inspired to reveal the past, present, or future to their less perceptive brethren'.[10] The divine inspiration was administered by spreading honey on their lips. A similar notion reappeared in the Christian tradition in the person of St Ambrose, the patron saint of beekeepers. He was said to have been visited by a swarm of bees and left with a drop of honey on his lips while still in his cradle, a sign of his future greatness and eloquence.[11] Finally, many philosophers and political theorists throughout history have regarded bees and the organisation of beehives as a metaphor for human society.[12]

It is hard to gauge the extent to which these connotations would have been known to Mansfield; her concerns regarding the gaps in her education contradict the scope of her knowledge evident in her personal writings. She read extensively and her letters show that, like other modernists, she was knowledgeable about classical cultures and mythologies, and could hold her own in debates about them.[13] Given the context of the story, the inclusion of a bee character in 'At the Bay' seems to indicate that Mansfield would have been aware of most, if not all, of the above. The bee as an intermediary between the living and the dead is especially relevant in the case of 'At the Bay'. Although it was originally 'Prelude' that sprang from Mansfield's need to process the death of her younger brother Leslie and to pay him tribute, the four years between its publication and that of 'At the Bay', as well as several deaths among Mansfield's close relatives in the meantime, meant that the latter became a memorial to other members of her family, especially her beloved grandmother. What is more, Mansfield was already dying too, literally standing at the threshold between the two worlds, telling the stories of 'the past, present and future' through Kezia, the idealised version of her young self, immortalising her dead family members, as well as herself, in the process.[14] This reading is supported by one of the most memorable scenes in Mansfield's stories, the discussion between Kezia and her grandmother about dying in part VII of 'At the Bay'. Kezia's reluctance to die or to let the most beloved member of her family die is both a moving glimpse into the psychology of a child and a statement of intent; although unable to avoid physical death, she can at least make sure that those who are dear to her will live on in her art.

The prophetic dimension of the bee symbolism is also apparent in this and other stories featuring Kezia. She often acts/is treated like a prophet by the other, more conventional, children, as well as by adults, in the sense of the biblical notion that 'a prophet is not without honour, but in his own country, and among his own kin, and in his own house'.[15] Kezia is regarded as 'different', spoken to with disdain and suspicion, or even scolded and punished, but despite all opposition, she keeps doing what she believes is right. Her actions, often incomprehensible to others, constantly suggest fresh ideas and alternatives for a better, more meaningful life. Several times in the New Zealand stories in which she appears, she goes against rules and traditions, and sees what others overlook: for example, the importance of the little lamp and the rightness of defying orders by bringing the Kelveys to see the doll's house in the eponymous story; the value and meaning of treating real and imaginary food as art in 'Prelude'; and the necessity to speak up against rules that restrict freedom and creativity in children's games in 'At the Bay'. By all these actions she demonstrates that, although fraught with difficulties and not guaranteed, there is the possibility of an alternative to the existence that swallowed her mother, Aunt Beryl and Uncle Jonathan Trout.

Mansfield approaches the organisation of bees as a metaphor for human society in a very different way to her predecessors, mostly male and philosophers. Their main interest was always humanity, and while the animal kingdom might have provided some interesting insights, their approach was decidedly anthropocentric and patronising. They would observe them from their hierarchical position on high, using only what they perceived to be useful, and discarding or disregarding everything else. In contrast, Melinda Harvey reads Mansfield's interest in the animal as 'a corollary of her identification with the underdog',[16] and interprets her depiction of animals as anti-anthropocentric, arguing that, for her, 'animals are seldom merely emblems of human meaning, but rather co-actors, moving and doing in their world, of which humans are a part'.[17] Similarly, Ryan makes the connection between Mansfield's interest in the treatment of animals and women in patriarchal societies, but he is less categorical when dealing with her attitude to anthropocentrism. Instead of 'rushing to claim her as part of an antianthropocentric group of contemporaneous writers', he argues that her animal aesthetics are not straightforward and unified: '[r]ather than altogether disposing of hierarchical oppositions between human and animal [. . .] she often probes and plays on species boundaries, occasionally reinscribes and sometimes redraws them, and yet rarely moves entirely beyond them'.[18] As will be argued later, Mansfield, while still using fauna for symbolical purposes, is at least trying to approach them from the position of equality, not concentrating on their placement with respect to other species but rather on their otherness, seen as a welcome variety and possible inspiration for humans. She thus suggests a more open-minded and non-judgemental observation of nature.

The combination of Kezia's play-acting as a bee and her fervent defence of insects, her advocating for them to be included among animals, further underpins this reading. While, according to both Isabel and the conventions of biology, Kezia is wrong, she is, as usual, also very right in her own, unique way. She is simply applying a different set of rules from the rest of her family, or even society in general. This conflict between what society understands as correct and Kezia's repeated unorthodox approaches is most obvious in the interactions between her and Aunt Beryl, who sometimes seems positively allergic to the child. Kezia does not understand Aunt Beryl's excessive animosity and interprets it as a sign of chaos that is impossible to comprehend. When scolded for creating a river in her porridge and 'eating the banks away', she expresses her confusion by first wondering what she had done and then mentally commenting on 'How unfair grown-ups are!'[19] Aunt Beryl, in her turn, sees the child as 'messy',[20] which, too, means disorderly or chaotic. Their discord seems to match and possibly even represent the conflict between the Edwardians and the modernist artists, especially in the belief of the former that modernist art was random and chaotic, and that it was an attack on 'normality' that needed to be lambasted and fought against.[21] For the modernists, just as for Kezia, however, there was a rhyme and reason to their work, even if it was not immediately apparent: what Vincent O'Sullivan defines as the 'sense of order through the apparently random'.[22]

This sense of order, which might seem counterintuitive or completely incorrect with respect to Kezia's placement of insects among animals, can be found when following the direction of Ryan's reading of the children's play in light of the developments in embryology, and Daniel Aureliano Newman's discussion of the connection between biology and modernist literature, especially the experimental *Bildungsroman*. Newman demonstrates and persuasively argues that the modernists' fascination with the new developments in sciences included biology, and that the emerging or reclaimed biological theories influenced the way that the modernists narrated development in a more profound way than was previously acknowledged.[23]

Newman's central claim is that the traditional *Bildungsroman* of the Victorian era mostly reflected the way society understood development: that is, as linear, correlating with the perceived linearity of time. This belief was based on the so-called biogenetic law, also known as the theory of recapitulation. The biogenetic law holds that the development of every individual (ontogeny) copies the stages in the development of its whole kind (phylogeny). The consequences of this seemingly innocuous claim are, however, far-reaching. As Newman points out, '[b]ecause recapitulation assumes perfectibility, groups deemed imperfect were thus primitive, immature or degenerate, and the standard of perfection was unsurprisingly white, male, heterosexual and upper class'.[24] The theory thus endorses – if not directly engenders – such ideologies as colonialism, imperialism, sexism and racism, as well as speciesism. Women, children, animals or members of 'primitive' nations were seen as lower on the developmental ladder and that justified their treatment as lesser creatures, dominated by those who were perceived as more developed and higher.

This view of development was, however, challenged by many other theories already arising in the nineteenth century. Newman refers to them as either 'modernist biologies' or theories of reversion, and they include, for example, atavism, interrupted development, Mendelism, heterochrony or neoteny. Discussing them in detail by using examples from some of the most famous modernist novels, Newman not only contests the idea of modernism as presenting 'a bleak picture of wasted potential, stunted growth, perpetual adolescence, or premature senescence', but also claims that 'modernism's apparently unnatural ways of narrating development might be to some extent mimetic – not in a naïve or literal sense, but in the sense that they resemble or even borrow from the natural world revealed by modernist biology'.[25] In other words, what seemed like an introduction of randomness or deliberate disruption into literature, might be, in fact, just a different way of narration, based on a revised understanding of development.

Mansfield's 'strange company assembled in the Burnells' washhouse after tea' indeed seems to be an illustration of the tension between recapitulation and the theories of reversion.[26] Just as the children in 'Prelude' mimic the actions of the adults in their play, here, too, they retain the power structures and the hierarchy of adult society and emulate the ways it perceives animals. The two elder children are the leaders, although Pip, the patriarch in training, is at the top: the bull, but also the bully. Isabel, the rooster, compensates for her apparent weaknesses by supporting the bull against the 'lesser animals' and acting like a herald of his ideas. It is no accident that, in 'Prelude', Isabel claims to be the goddaughter of Queen Victoria.[27] Although not her real godmother, Queen Victoria is indeed Isabel's *ideological* godmother: a strong and capable woman at the helm of an empire, nevertheless refusing female emancipation, trumpeting patriarchal theories, allying herself with men and their agenda. What seems like a random non sequitur in the middle of the children's play in 'Prelude' gains its full meaning in 'At the Bay'. What Mansfield thinks of such alliances is subtly expressed by the pairing of the two animals. A bull and a rooster, or, in other words, the 'cock and bull', are complicit in 'spinning corresponding stories for their younger siblings'.[28] Furthermore, this female disloyalty was what Mansfield had in mind when she claimed that women were 'held with the self-fashioned chains of slavery',[29] and its representation also finds its expression in 'At the Bay'. Although it is not stated explicitly who utters the categorical 'you can't be a bee, Kezia', it can be no one else but Isabel. Pip is busy with his own importance, bellowing 'I'm a bull. I'm a bull.'[30] For Rags and Lottie, it would be completely out of character to say something like that, while it perfectly fits Isabel's personality and the history of her interactions with Kezia and the other children, to whom she likes to preach. It is Isabel, a grown-up in miniature, who makes sure the rules are enforced, even when the 'man' forgets about them, paying attention to his own greatness and importance.

Rags and Lottie either choose or have chosen for them animals that are considered meek, obedient, stupid or, in the case of the dog, possibly uncritically loyal to its master. The irony of these choices is that all of these animals, including the bull and the rooster, are, in fact, domestic animals, serving somebody else whose aims and intentions can be in direct conflict with their own interests and well-being, as exemplified by the poor dog Snooker or the headless walking duck in 'Prelude'. Kezia was probably expected to choose some equally low animal, but she disrupts the status quo by her daring deviation from what is expected of her, and the intensity and manner of her disruption are significant. She does not just fight the supremacy of the two elder children by choosing a tiger or an elephant, both animals that are bigger, stronger and louder than the bull and the rooster. Although that would enable her to play within the rules, it would also mean endorsement of their validity. Rather than breaking rules she does not believe in, she suggests a new set of rules in which, seemingly against logic, an insect is suddenly included among animals. Kezia's clumsy biological classification translates Mansfield's suggestion that other models of development should be taken into consideration, in which a bee will not be on the lower scale of the ladder but equal in importance to other creatures. Kezia, the modernist, rejects the simplistic hierarchy of recapitulation and intimates that there are different possibilities of understanding the world that, despite sounding impossible or outrageous, can make more sense than longstanding theories that are taken for granted.

The reasons why Mansfield chose insects to represent the new biological theories are manifold and complex. She was obsessed with them, possibly because, as Harvey claims, they are 'the last animals on earth who remain uncoopted, who observe unobserved, who can live life without dependency or fear of human beings'.[31] She was also a member of the generation for which insects, as Rachel Murray explains, became closely associated with the First World War, both as constant unwelcome companions of the soldiers in the trenches and the metaphorical representation of how they felt and perceived themselves. On the one hand, 'troops were regularly disinfected with chemicals designed to halt the spread of lice'; on the other, 'soldiers were also being subjected to poisonous gases from the enemy, some of which had previously been used as insecticides'.[32] Most importantly, many of the alternative biological theories were derived from the observation and study of insects, which was widespread in the first decades of the twentieth century. The general public's knowledge of insectology must have been wide, as Mansfield herself casually refers to the French entomologist Jean-Henri Fabre on at least two occasions.[33] However, it is important to realise that this moment in 'At the Bay' is possibly the only one when the insect she chooses is not obnoxious and its connotations are not negative.

By the slight shift from the usual fly to a useful, although still potentially harming, bee, Mansfield further emphasises the need for a new approach to one's existence, free from detrimental patterns based on no longer valid theories. That is why there is, indeed, an important difference between Kezia and her uncle, Jonathan Trout, although both see themselves as insects. While Jonathan feels trapped in his social role, acknowledging only a theoretical possibility of freedom, Kezia pictures herself as a part of a community and working with others, yet still free. As a matter of fact, she openly distances herself from Jonathan when she states a bee 'is not like a fish'.[34] Her distinction between them, the ability to make noise, might seem confusing at first; Jonathan is complaining about his fate after all. However, empty whining does not qualify as 'noise'; it is not meaningful and, as such, it is not likely to lead to change or to any kind of result. What is more, unlike a fly, a bee is not seemingly useless, unimportant, easily killed and forgotten. It has its place and function in its society and the legacy of the work it helps to create will continue, even when it is gone.

One more interesting aspect of the biological reading of Kezia's bee is how it can alter the perception of other well-known parts of Mansfield's stories. Although Newman's analysis concerns primarily modernist novels, many of his claims can be easily applied to Mansfield's short stories as well. What is more, within some of his theories, one could potentially justify classifying her very loosely linked New Zealand stories as a *Bildungsroman* of sorts, where development is not narrated in a linear way, but in a series of fits and starts. Additionally, while space limits the opportunity to discuss particular biological theories of reversion in detail, it is useful to give at least a taste of some of them to illustrate either how they informed Mansfield's writing or, more probably, how, within her own belief of not 'turning life into a case',[35] they prove yet again her impressive powers of observation and the ability to translate them into her art. Particularly relevant, for example, is Newman's discussion of new developments in such fields as ethology and ecology with respect to the portrayal of children. According to him, childhood is no longer seen as a stage in development; a young person is considered to be a being in its own right, having its own needs in the same way as an adult. This notion is also reflected in modernist writing which, according to Newman, strives

> to render the experience of childhood rather than its recollection from a position of wise and ironic adulthood. If maturity is no longer idealised as the only significant part of life, its deferral may not be as problematic as some critics imply when they cite the modernist trope of delayed or arrested development.[36]

On the one hand, his claim illustrates perfectly the way Mansfield approaches children; on the other, it offers a more positive view of her alleged childishness and inability to grow up, which were mostly commented on in negative terms. Against the seemingly obvious belief in the necessity of maturity to reach one's full potential, Newman puts Gerald Heard's assertion that the survival of humanity depends on the 'sporadic outcrop of men who manage to retain, with full mental stature, the radical originality and freshness of a vigorous child'.[37]

The close relationship between Kezia and her grandmother can also be viewed through the lens of biological theories of reversion. If the biogenetic law held true, then every new generation would be an improvement on the previous one, which is obviously not the case in the Fairfield family. The two (possibly even three) daughters of Mrs Fairfield are what Edward Carpenter calls 'an *impasse* and a point of arrest', and the remedy, according to him, is 'a return to an earlier and more primitive stage in social development, as to a point from which to branch out afresh'.[38] While Isabel, emulating her mother's behaviour, is well on the way to growing up into this point of arrest, Kezia, although in many respects like her mother too, by force of returning to the starting point that is her grandmother, has a chance of branching out afresh in a different, possibly better and healthier, direction.

Kezia's 'ninseck' of a bee in 'At the Bay', while easily overlooked and seemingly inconsequential, proves yet again how complex and multi-layered Mansfield's writing is and how she manages to communicate complex agendas through simple means. What is more, having a child impersonate an insect expresses the deepest truths about what she referred to as 'Life'; she places both on the same level as adults and humans, until then seen as superior, envisioning the change from a world based on hierarchical structures to an existence in which different kinds of people and different species live in mutual respect, for the benefit of all.

Notes

1. Cherry A. Hankin, *Katherine Mansfield and her Confessional Stories* (London: Macmillan, 1983), p. 230.
2. Saralyn R. Daly, *Katherine Mansfield* (New York: Twayne, 1965), in *Twayne's English Authors Series on CD-ROM*. Twayne, 1997, n.p.
3. Peter Mathews, 'Myth and Unity in Mansfield's "At the Bay"', *Journal of New Zealand Literature*, 23: 2 (2005), pp. 47–61 (pp. 55–6).
4. Delphine Soulhat, 'Kezia in Wonderland', in Janet Wilson, Gerri Kimber and Susan Reid, eds, *Katherine Mansfield and Literary Modernism* (London: Continuum, 2011), pp. 101–11 (p. 106).
5. Derek Ryan, 'Katherine Mansfield's Animal Aesthetics', *Modern Fiction Studies*, 61: 1 (2018), pp. 27–51 (p. 38).
6. Janka Kascakova, 'Katherine Mansfield's Children At Play', in Joyce E. Kelley, ed., *Children's Play in Literature: Investigating the Strengths and the Subversions of the Playing Child* (New York: Routledge, 2019), pp. 124–42 (p. 138).
7. Stephen Nachmanovitch, *Free Play: Improvisation in Life and Art* (New York: Tarcher/Putnam, 1990), p. 23.
8. See, for example, Colleen English, 'Telling the Bees', *JSTOR Daily*, 5 September 2018, available at <https://daily.jstor.org/telling-the-bees/> (last accessed 2 September 2020).
9. Susan Scheinberg, 'The Bee Maidens of the Homeric Hymn to Hermes', *Harvard Studies in Classical Philology*, 83 (1979), pp. 1–28 (p. 25).
10. Scheinberg, p. 25.
11. Richard Stracke, 'Saint Ambrose of Milan: The Iconography', available at <https://www.christianiconography.info/ambrose.html> (last accessed 20 October 2020).
12. Scheinberg, p. 25.
13. Even her stories demonstrate her familiarity with ancient literature; Mathews, for example, identifies many parallels between 'At the Bay' and Homer's *Odyssey* (p. 57).
14. Kascakova, p. 139.
15. Mark 6: 4.
16. Melinda Harvey, 'Katherine Mansfield's Menagerie', in Wilson, Kimber and Reid, eds, pp. 202–10 (p. 205).
17. Harvey, p. 206.
18. Ryan, p. 31.
19. CW2, p. 347.
20. CW2, p. 347.

21. For a more detailed discussion of the conflict between Beryl and Kezia, see Janka Kascakova, '"Eating the Banks Away": The Conflict Between the Traditional and the Modernist in Katherine Mansfield's New Zealand Stories', *in esse: English Studies in Albania,* 10: 1 (2019), pp. 18–30.
22. Vincent O'Sullivan, 'Katherine Mansfield, the New Zealand European', in Roger Robinson, ed., *Katherine Mansfield: In from the Margin* (Baton Rouge: Louisiana State University Press, 1994), pp. 9–24 (p. 18).
23. Daniel Aureliano Newman, *Modernist Life Histories: Biological Theory and the Experimental Bildungsroman* (Edinburgh: Edinburgh University Press, 2019).
24. Newman, p. 11.
25. Newman, p. 4.
26. CW2, p. 361.
27. CW2, p. 77.
28. Kascakova, p. 138.
29. CW4, p. 91.
30. CW2, p. 361.
31. Harvey, p. 209.
32. Rachel Murray, 'Why World War I cultivated an obsession with insects', *The Conversation,* 27 July 2017, available at <https://theconversation.com/why-world-war-i-cultivated-an-obsession-with-insects-80355> (last accessed 2 September 2020).
33. One is in a letter to Dorothy Brett, 9 March 1922, *Letters* 1, p. 449; the other to John Middleton Murry, 27 September 1920, *Letters* 4, p. 54.
34. CW2, p. 361.
35. *Letters* 4, p. 69.
36. Newman, p. 43.
37. Gerald Heard, *Man the Master* (New York: Harper, 1941), p. 160; qtd in Newman, p. 159.
38. Edward Carpenter, *Angels' Wings: Essays on Art and its Relation to Life* (London: Swan Sonnenschein, 1898), pp. 246–7; qtd in Newman, p. 22.

'Real Childhood': The Daring of Katherine Mansfield and Alice Meynell

Ann Herndon Marshall

Katherine Mansfield followed in the footsteps of Alice Meynell in boldly portraying 'real children'. In an introduction to Meynell's work, Vita Sackville-West points out that a focus on children need not be compromised by cloying emotion:

> It is something of an achievement to write on dangerously sentimental subjects ('the darling young' sounds full of pitfalls) without provoking even one anticipated quiver of embarrassment in the reader; and this may be especially true of women, whose reader, aware of the sex, is thereby the more inclined for suspicion.[1]

Sackville-West corrects 'misapprehensions' about Meynell as a latter-day Victorian author and frames her focus on children as a daring choice. Meynell had done much to prepare the way for Mansfield's fresh take on childhood. It is a case of like-mindedness, for both writers emphasise the problem of adult condescension and the unnecessary suffering of real children. Like Meynell, Mansfield writes against the grain of her Victorian inheritance. Kezia from 'Prelude' is no clichéd child. Kezia is Mansfield's best-known example, but from the time of the early story 'Mary', she strives to free her literary children. Both writers go beyond simple attacks on Victorian sentimentality; they resist modern trends as well, fashions that underestimate the individuality of children and fail to acknowledge their difference from adults.

Meynell's essays on children appeared each week in the *Pall Mall Gazette* in the 1890s, under the heading *The Wares of Autolycus*, a column which featured unsigned articles by 'one of six distinguished ladies'.[2] Alice Meynell was a poet, essayist, suffragist, and along with her husband, Wilfrid Meynell, a professional editor and critic; she often based her *Autolycus* columns on one or more of their eight children.[3] The poet Katharine Tynan recalls the importance of the *Pall Mall Gazette* at a time when it was led by the writer and politician Harry Cust: 'He himself wrote his leaders, the brilliant audacity of which kept literary London in a delighted exhilaration which could hardly bear the time between one issue and the next.'[4] Meynell later collected and published her *Autolycus* essays along with some new compositions as *The Children* (1897; 1911) and *Childhood* (1913).[5] Their influence was widespread in the first half of the twentieth century, providing 'invaluable insight on the development and care of personalities before [Abraham] Maslow and [Benjamin] Spock'.[6]

Meynell's essays were admired for their 'Athenian ingenuity, their Spartan terseness, their mediaeval clearness and profundity'.[7] Not overburdened by a didactic purpose, her approach is gently satirical and anecdotal. An editor and critic by trade, Meynell also considers closely the successes and failures of literary predecessors who portray children. She fends off conventional assumptions about children in a witty chapter from *Childhood*, which begins: 'It is for fear of the grown-up, or at least out of respect towards them, that a chapter must be given to fairies.'[8] She goes on to point out the 'officiousness' of 'authors, parents, uncles, godmothers, or imaginative adult persons of any kind', who impose on their charges their notions of such 'properly child-like' pleasures as fairies.[9] For example, she calls out her friend, the 'great poet' Francis Thompson, for burdening the child with a cherished notion of the whimsical and credulous.[10] Meynell ironically mimics all such officious grown-ups: 'If the children do not care very much for fairies, they must be made to care. "Who is to care if they do not? Who is to be properly childlike if they are not?"'[11]

Meynell objects when adults expect to find certain endearing qualities in children. If even great writers have misunderstood the nature of children, there is much clarification to be done. Her *sang-froid* in challenging old assumptions offers to Mansfield and her contemporaries a new awareness of children as fascinating, misunderstood subjects worthy of fresh examination. Given her widespread influence in Mansfield's time, it is worth considering how Meynell's insights can illuminate important moments in Mansfield's 'child stories', as she proudly dubbed them, especially 'How Pearl Button Was Kidnapped', 'Sun and Moon', 'Prelude' and 'At the Bay'.[12] Meynell's critical scrutiny of child characters anticipates Mansfield's struggle in her early story, 'Mary', to leave behind old models and treat children as vital, embodied subjects capable of a range of feelings often denied them by Victorian writers.

Mansfield's Knowledge of the Meynell Family

Friendship with the Meynell family would have alerted Mansfield to Alice Meynell's literary reputation and very likely to the well-known essays on children. Mansfield's acquaintance with the family began in London in 1909, when the aspiring writer was still boarding at the Beauchamp Lodge and attending musical evenings at the home of Monica Meynell Saleeby and her husband, a science writer and eugenicist. Mansfield records an upcoming date in her notebook: 'Saturd: Dr [Caleb] Saleeby'.[13] At one of these gatherings, she met her first husband, George Bowden, and their engagement was announced at the Saleebys' home.[14]

Both Mansfield and John Middleton Murry encountered Alice Meynell, along with several of her children, when visiting the family's country estate at Greatham in Sussex in 1915. Through friendship with D. H. Lawrence and through letters from Murry, Mansfield learned more of the Meynells. Murry observes them in February 1915 when staying with the Lawrences, in a cottage borrowed from Meynell's daughter, the novelist and short story writer Viola Meynell.[15] He is disparaging in his comments: 'The lady of high degree left today and left me wondering (as I've done before) how women who have such a lot of knowledge can be so essentially stupid & useless. It was an amazing exhibition of ineffectuality.'[16] A 'lady of high degree' could refer to Viola or her mother; Alice spent much of her time at Humphrey's Homestead in Greatham rather than in London during the war years.[17] It seems an odd way to refer to his contemporary, Viola;[18] in any case, Murry blames his irascible mood on a cold. Mansfield was in France, pursuing her brief affair with Francis Carco, and Murry writes to her, reporting on Viola's cottage, a welcome change from their own leaky Rose Tree Cottage, which had probably hastened Mansfield's escape to France:

> Of course this cottage is a palace. One enormous dining-room with great beams, the size of a good barn, three bedrooms, a bath-room and a wonderful kitchen [. . .] I must confess I envy these people their money. Its the kind of cottage we could live in so much better than they.[19]

Murry then describes the proximity of other Meynells as a burden, even though the family treats him as a celebrity:

> This afternoon we had to go to Monica Saleeby's cottage (she lives next door) for coffee.
>
> What I cannot imagine after seeing her is how she ever managed the aesthetic-sugeric [*sic*] stunt with the bearded doctor. She's fat, quite amiable and kindly, and perfectly stupid, *so stupid* that Frieda L[awrence]

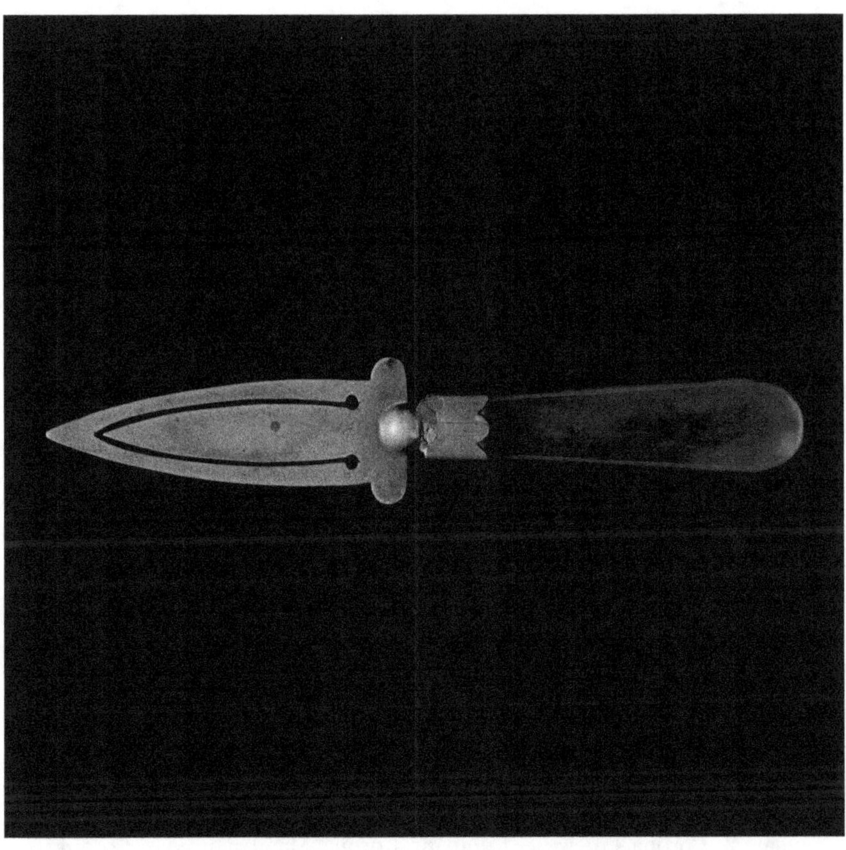

Plate 1. Silver and greenstone combination bookmark and paper knife formerly owned by Katherine Mansfield. Alexander Turnbull Library Ref: Curios-018-005. Photograph courtesy of Alexander Turnbull Library, National Library of New Zealand.

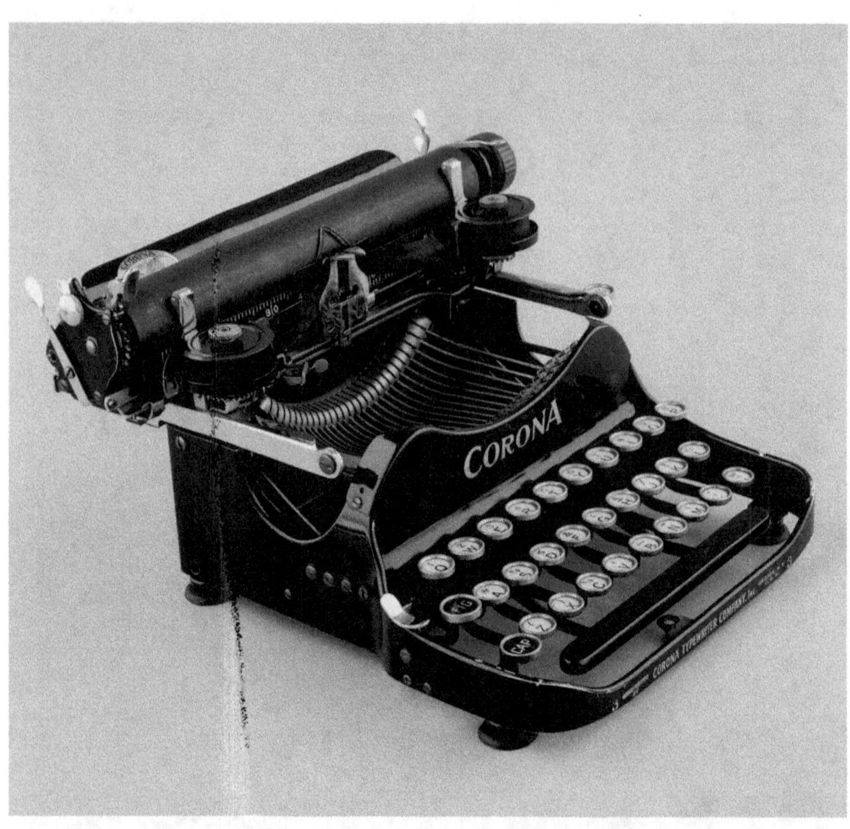

Plate 2. Corona Typewriter Company: Corona. Manufactured by Corona Typewriter Company Inc., Groton, N. Y., U. S. A. [Number] 3, manufactured 1920, formerly owned by Katherine Mansfield. Alexander Turnbull Library Ref: Curios-018-1-010. Photograph courtesy Alexander Turnbull Library, National Library of New Zealand.

> seems a paragon of wit and ingenuity beside her. Then there is the famous Sebastian – again an amiable fellow utterly dull. I am afraid his amiability mainly consists in the pleasant conceit of myself he manages to give me, by hanging onto my words in awestruck reverence.[20]

Self-absorbed, Murry seems unaware of Sebastian Meynell's depression.[21] Unable to continue in publishing, at his parents' urging, 'Bastian' had retired for a time to Greatham. Murry's reference to the Meynells as 'these people' may carry over from conversations with Lawrence, who was ambivalent about their largesse.[22]

While Murry returned to London in search of lodging, Mansfield made her own visit to the Lawrences, who were still at Greatham in March. A second-hand account comes from Virginia Woolf's diary:

> Katherine Mansfield described a visit to the house in Sussex – All the M[eynell]s in barns & cottages; & the daughters singing long monotonous ballads, & then, by way of contrast & to surprise a scallywag I daresay with their liveliness breaking into music hall songs taught them by their brothers in law. Katherine described them like so many B[urne] J[ones] mermaids with long lush hair, plucking at mediaeval instruments & intoning those verses. Mrs. M[eynell] sat by.[23]

One can imagine the pleasure Mansfield took in being among the musical and possibly costumed Meynells, who were, through Madeline's husband, Percival Lucas, also associated with the preservation of Morris dancing.[24] Writing to Murry, Mansfield agrees: '[Viola's] is a very nice cottage & and I feel like you that ours is sordid in comparison';[25] however, she differs with Murry over Monica Saleeby's appeal. She enjoys their intimacy and includes a report on ten-year-old Mary Saleeby who looks forward to Murry's return:

> I have seen Mrs Saleeby – she called me 'Katherine' – I don't know why that touched me. I like her but she seems to me unhappy – she appeals to me – Mary keeps your letters but you said you were coming here soon & Mrs Saleeby says if the promise is not kept 'there will be no holding Mary'.[26]

A teasing humour accompanies the description of Mary's robust attachment.

At the Meynell colony, family is nurtured and children are foregrounded. At the same time, Mansfield recognises that Monica's marriage to Saleeby is unhappy.[27] The sense that Monica needs her sympathy enters into a dream, which she describes to Murry from Paris:

> Just as I was saying I never had and never could love [George Bowden] *etc.* Mrs. Saleeby appeared & seeing us together she came up to me and kissed

> my hands and said 'Oh Katherine I always felt such love for you – & now I know why' – & she pressed me to her and said 'Caleb is at home digging in the garden'[.] This so touched me that I nearly sacrifiged [*sic*] myself on the spot but I knew you were waiting for me in a little house in South Kensington [. . .].[28]

The dream dramatises her sympathy for another's untenable marriage, and it has a convenient ending to reassure Murry. It also conveys Mansfield's continued awareness of the Meynell children and her warm feelings, in contrast to Murry's censure.[29]

The Dombey Factor: Navigating the Legacy of Victorian Child Characters

Alice Meynell is acutely sensitive to inauthentic versions of children. She sniffs out adult condescension in even the most vaunted Victorian child characters, and this awareness makes her essays valuable to a new generation writing about children. Like Mansfield, she is devoted to Dickens. She finds in him 'the most perfect memory of childhood'; at the same time, she calls 'little Nell' 'strangely over-praised' and admires just 'certain brief passages of Paul Dombey'.[30] She objects to adults over-determining children's 'attitudes': Paul Dombey's stoicism is poignant, but portraits of children only earn her full approval when they appear 'from within the boundaries of a child's nature, from a child's stage of progress, and without the preoccupation and attitude of older experience'.[31] She commends Robert Louis Stevenson's verse when he 'looks steadily and intelligibly into the child's eyes'; he is willing to examine children afresh and not just perpetuate clichés.[32]

Mansfield's early story, 'Mary' (1911), shows her struggling to handle a poignant child character; she was not far from her girlhood triumph with *Dombey and Son*: she 'could make the girls cry' in her sewing class when she read them the death of Paul Dombey.[33] Fondness for Dickens's invalid character may have helped inspire the character of Mary, but Mansfield's invalid is a pale shadow against the vividness of Paul Dombey, or, for that matter, against her own later child characters. To borrow Mansfield's terms, Paul Dombey is a little 'pa-man', directing entrances and exits from his deathbed.[34] Despite denials from adults, he is in tune with natural processes: he intuits the passage of his life through awareness of the river's tide. In Mansfield's 'Mary', there are hints of an interesting and active spirit: Mary holds a duck for Pat to slaughter, and she loves games with boys. There is even a Dickensian touch in the father's referring to her tubercular cough as 'Poor old Mary's bark' (p. 168), but finally, the Victorian tradition of the innocent fey invalid overwhelms the portrayal of Mary.[35]

Implausibly, Mary is 'utterly unsuspecting' when her sister Kass arranges with her teacher to have Mary, a poor reciter, win the prize that regularly goes to Kass (p. 170). In the story's most convincing scene, a subdued Kass returns home to grown-ups who assume she is sulking over Mary's rare triumph. They do not suspect the complexity of Kass's emotions. By bedtime, she regrets her charity: 'the Devil entered into my soul. I decided to tell Mary the truth. From that moment I was happy and light again but I felt savage' (p. 171). Stories of selfless siblings, like Florence Dombey, so faithful at little Paul's bedside, set a high bar for Kass, but in the end, her sister Mary's angelic influence saves her: 'The moon shone through the window straight on to Mary's bed. She lay on her side, one hand against her cheek, soundly sleeping. [. . .] one button of her nightdress was undone, showing her flannel chest protector' (p. 171). Mary's innocence and chest protector trump Kass's awakened competitiveness. Her 'savagery' would have gained nuance in Mansfield's later career, and if Mansfield had taken an even greater risk and complicated Mary's interior life, the story might have broken new ground. The story does confront its own sentimentality: Kass is a new sort of child character, struggling to emerge, whilst Mary remains a disappointing stereotype.

In 'Mary', we see Mansfield wrestling with Victorian precedents, but by 1919, she has penned several successful child stories, and she celebrates Dickens's influence in her flattering review of a sequel, *The Gay-Dombeys* (1919) by Sir Harry Johnston. Feigning a hoary old age, she values her reading of the Victorians: 'there are delights reserved for us elderly creatures which are quite out of sight [. . .] of the golden boys and girls'.[36] She compares the staying power of one of Dickens's best characters to 'a meeting with an old play-fellow who is just come from the country of our childhood'.[37] Old fictional 'playfellows', like memories of her own childhood, are grist to her writer's mill, offering opportunities well taken in Johnston's 'fan fiction'. As she celebrates the afterlives of the characters, she identifies with what she imagines as Dickens's nostalgia to hold on to characters like the beloved Paul Dombey: '"Shall I never be that dying boy again, waving my hand at the water on the wall?"'[38] An accomplished writer of children herself, she no longer strives against the interference of Victorian literary children. A store of classics read in childhood, which Meynell also credits, is part of an ongoing source of inspiration. Like Mansfield, Meynell was especially connected to Dickens. In truth, her life was bookended by him and his fictional 'playfellow', Paul

Dombey: Dickens first brought Meynell's mother to her father's attention, and the author remained a family friend; when Meynell, on her deathbed, uttered, 'This is not tragic. I am happy,' she paraphrased Paul Dombey's repeated reassurance: '"Don't be sorry for me, dear Papa. Indeed I am quite happy."'[39]

'Near the Ground': A Call for Real, Embodied Children

Like Meynell, Mansfield highlights the existential integrity of children and shows a striking awareness of children's bodies and movements. In a fantasy of childlike togetherness with Murry, Mansfield emphasises the distinction between their 'Grown-Up Selves' and child selves: 'my G.U.S. looks on through the window. And she sees us stop and touch the gummy bark of the trees, or lean over a flower and try to blow it open by breathing very close.'[40] The child's physical intimacy with the natural world is set apart from the aloof adult. Meynell makes similar observations in 'Near the Ground': '[Adults] lose, by mere growing, something of the good habit of familiarity with the old and fresh earth – the familiarity, especially, of the eyes and hands.'[41] In 'Real Childhood', Meynell again marks off the separation when writing in the second person to herself as a child: 'While your elders passed over some particularly tedious piece of road [. . .] in their usual state of partial absence of mind, you, on the contrary, perceived every inch of it.'[42] In yet another essay, she comments on the obsolete notion that children are simply primitive adults: 'Time was when childhood was but borne with, and that for the sake of its mere promise of manhood.'[43]

Meynell anticipates Mansfield in explaining how children see the world in fundamentally different ways from adults, especially in their perception of time, resistance to empirical facts and closeness to Nature. Of the child's love of Nature, Mansfield might agree with Meynell's conviction, 'Wordsworth cannot say too much.'[44] Children are not aloof but always 'busy at close quarters'.[45] Like Meynell, Mansfield harbours scepticism about the receptivity of the grown-ups who are distant from the earth. However, she does not explicitly, as Meynell frequently does, tie her scepticism to religious faith. Meynell's Catholicism supports her resistance to empirical assumptions about reality that make it so difficult to cross the divide between adult and child, and imagine the world as the child does.[46] To illustrate the child's faith and resistance to empiricism, she tells of her son Francis's belief in a nursery story, despite her efforts to contradict it: 'The man with two heads had become his play, and so was perhaps bringing about his sleep by gentler means than the nurse had intended.'[47]

Child's Time in 'How Pearl Button Was Kidnapped' and 'At the Bay'

Writing about the child's perception of time, Meynell anticipates an important idea for Mansfield. It is difficult for a child to endure the dawdling pace of 'talkative, easy-living, occupied people' and 'the special and singular duration some such space as your elder, perhaps called half-an-hour'.[48] Meynell begins 'Real Childhood' with the child's experience of time while trapped by a distracted adult:

> when your mother's visitor held you at his knee, while he talked to her the excited gibberish of the grown-up, he little thought what he forced upon you; what the things he called minutes really were, measured by a mind unused; what passive and then what desperate weariness he held you to by his slightly gesticulating hands that pressed some absent-minded caress, rated by you at its right value, in the pauses of his anecdotes. You, meanwhile, were infinitely tired of watching the play of his conversing moustache.[49]

A similar ennui begins 'How Pearl Button Was Kidnapped'. Pearl Button is a captive child: her Pākehā mother, ironing in the kitchen, is distracted. The Māori women passing by diagnose her need for something new as they watch her swing on the gate and sing 'a small song'.[50] It is a lovely afternoon of a 'sunshiny day', and it seems only fair to them that she should glimpse 'beautiful things' (pp. 285–6).

Unlike Meynell's child, who suffers the disappointment of a visitor's 'absent-minded caress', Pearl Button experiences the full-on attention, soothing caresses and pleasing scents of the Māori women:

> One of the women [. . .] caught Pearl Button up in her arms and walked with Pearl Button's head against her shoulder and her dusty little legs dangling. She was softer than a bed and she had a nice smell – a smell that made you bury your head and breathe and breathe it. (p. 286)

Pearl falls asleep and time passes painlessly, in contrast to the prolonged time of a captive Pearl swinging on the gate at the story's beginning; her journey away from the 'House of Boxes' ends in the 'long room' of the *wharenui*, with adults unconcerned with offices or ironing. They speak without condescension, reassuring her that a little pear juice on her pinafore requires no apology. On the way to the shore, their timely attention continues. Mansfield mirrors the rhythm of the transport in one uninterrupted paragraph at the centre of the story.

Once at the shore, Pearl Button lacks the words to describe it, but she knows it is 'something perfectly different': '"Why," said the woman, "it's the sea"'; she urges the child to see for herself, '"You look again"'

(p. 287). The story so thoroughly succeeds in taking one away from the normative time of the Pākehā adult that one forgets, along with Pearl Button, how long she has been away. Perhaps her preoccupied mother only belatedly notices her absence. At the end, normative time descends with the 'blue men', and the narrative of kidnapping promises to undo Pearl Button's rescue (p. 288).

* * *

The 'company assembled in the Burnell's washhouse' in 'At the Bay' plays out another drama of temporal conflict. The scene begins with liberation from adult control: 'Round the table there sat a bull, a rooster, a sheep and a bee.'[51] Lottie, the youngest, has trouble following the card game directed by high-handed Pip, but the others coax her and their enthusiasm builds: 'it was all they could do not to burst into a little chorus of animals before Pip had finished dealing' (p. 363). Soon, they are so engaged that they do not realise time has passed, until they hear a faint knocking and feel a paralysing fear: 'the quick dark came racing over the sea, over the sand-hills, up the paddock' (p. 363). Pip intensifies their panic with his spider story, but his pose of mastery dissolves as he shares their terror. In one mind, they blame the preoccupied adults: 'Oh, those grown-ups, laughing and snug, sitting in the lamplight, drinking out of cups! They'd forgotten about them. No, not really forgotten. That was what their smile meant. They had decided to leave them there all by themselves' (p. 364). Lottie is first to see the face at the window as something demonic, washed out by failing light, 'a pale face, black eyes, and a black beard'; all scream and rush for the door, but of course, it is only Uncle Jonathan, 'come to take the little boys home' (p. 364).

Where had he been? Their suspicions of adults and fears of an uncanny apparition reflect the divergent experience of time. The reader finds, in the next short chapter, a flashback that tells how Jonathan has lingered in conversation with his sister-in-law, Linda, in the front garden. The children in the washhouse are spared the 'adult gibberish', but the sense of incompatible time remains. The motif of temporal incompatibility weaves together many chapters of 'Prelude' and 'At the Bay'. Self-conscious Aunt Beryl feels doomed to be out of time; she worries she will lose her eligible years sequestered in the country. The relationship of Linda and Stanley Burnell is also beset with temporal conflict. She is child-weary while he remains boyish and ambitious, especially for his long-awaited son. In 'Prelude', the giant aloe, prominent on a mound in the drive, signals another sort of time, indifferent to human time, following its own cycle to bloom every century. Linda smiles one of those adult smiles as she explains this dilatory time to the neophyte gardener, small Kezia, who looks earthward to harvest her blossoms; similarly, Meynell describes her own son Francis at the age of six, 'poring over the ground' and 'familiar with delicate shows and scents'.[52]

The Overlooked Child in 'Sun and Moon'

Mansfield and Meynell treat children as individuals, whom adults patronise at their peril. Meynell's voice, even when confessing to her own false assumptions, provides a protective layer of concern. In 'The Boy', for instance, she exhibits gentle tolerance of her twelve-year-old, who harbours a 'passionate dislike of fuss' and who 'will not endure to be told to do anything, at least in that citadel of his freedom, his home'.[53] Mansfield's stories, to a greater degree, emphasise the fearful isolation and the misunderstanding by adults that can fire a child's revolt. In 'Sun and Moon', Mansfield reveals the child's psyche to be at odds with that of contemporary adults. The parents in the story are not Victorians with stern expectations for propriety from children; rather, they have embraced a modern stance toward childhood that can bring its own brand of misunderstanding and injustice.

The parents in 'Sun and Moon' display a stylish whimsy with the nicknames they give their children. Forgoing sternness until pressed, they belong to the generation Meynell describes in 'Injustice' as 'self-indulgent': 'That children have to be taught self-denial is a truth that the self-indulgent youth, middle-age, and old-age now alive, and having children in charge, would blush to publish.'[54] Meynell also warns against a tendency in the new century to expect too much gaiety from children: 'The child over-amused is in peril of losing amusement itself within his own heart.'[55] Sturdy and taciturn, Sun resists the modern expectation for frivolity. He is not drawn into the party: '"Such a serious little poppet,"' says one guest.[56] His body keeps him on the margin: Sun is literally too heavy to be playfully lifted by the enthusiastic adults. Little Moon is a hit with the guests because she is both lighter and more light-hearted. The only adult Sun likes is 'a little grey man, with long grey whiskers, who walked about by himself' (p. 139).

After the adults have their dinner and the children are allowed to come down, they are expected to show appreciation through childish excitement. What child would not see the remains of the party as a privileged playground? Moon fills the bill as she makes a beeline for the half-demolished gingerbread house. What was earlier a 'beautiful dining-room' registers for her brother as appalling disorder:

> The lovely food [. . .] was all thrown about, and there were bones and bits and fruit peels and shells everywhere. There was even a bottle lying down with stuff coming out of it on the cloth and nobody stood it up again. (p. 140)

The sexual image of the bottle with 'stuff coming out' disgusts Sun. Unaware of the boy's disturbance, the father urges him to scavenge, but he has an unwelcome reaction, a horror only intensified by his sister's enthusiasm: '"Daddy! Daddy!" shrieked Moon. "The little [door] handle's left. The little nut. Kin I eat it?" And she reached across and picked it out of the door and scrunched it up, biting hard and blinking.' Sun can stand no more: '"I think it's horrid – horrid – horrid!" he sobbed' (p. 141). He simply cannot be childish in the whimsical way his sister is. The behavioural antagonism between the two children brings the title 'Sun and Moon' into ironic focus. Instead of equal and complementary deities in the natural universe, they are planets on a collision course that leads to the dominance of Moon.

Moon is not self-aware enough to be a villain, but her tendency to laugh whenever others laugh and her habit of nodding, which is so annoying to her brother, promote her with adults; she is the desirable, playful child. Sun cannot comprehend her flirtatious charm as she resists her doting nurse's attempt to dress her. In her 'fluffy' dress and the 'white shoes with big blobs on them', Moon performs as Sun sits quietly in the Russian suit his mother has chosen (p. 138). The clever Russian costumes are, to the *Ballets Russes* generation, what fanciful fairy costumes were to the Victorians, fashionable affectations imposed on children. Even costumed, Sun cannot equal Moon's performance; he fails to interpret the performative gestures that win adult approval. To him, Moon's cute curtsy is simply dragging 'one of her feet' (p. 138).

Meynell's appeal to take seriously the distastes of children finds a counterpart in Mansfield's sympathetic view of Sun's predicament. He manifests the child's 'fastidiousness that time is slow to cure'.[57] Meynell emphasises Dickens's memory of distaste at the 'omnivorous parent', dramatised in a scene when hungry Pip is forced to witness Mr Pumblechook's gourmandising: 'Here is the injustice, for children have a thousand distastes.'[58] Meynell argues respect for children when they act out: 'even the naughty child is an individual, and must not be treated in the mass'.[59] Mansfield's Sun is the stolid, unglamorous child, who 'doesn't mind people not noticing him – much . . .' (p. 138). Ironically, he must endure distress as a reserved, fastidious child, a child who might have suited the parents of a previous time. His outdated reserve keeps him from living up to the current expectations which Moon, the happy-go-lucky child, readily fulfils. Hers is the stylish personality that appeals to her fashionable modern parents.

Acknowledging Tribalism, Terror and Sorrow

Meynell acknowledges the darker aspects of the child's psyche when she comments on her childhood thrill in 'othering': she recalls a time with her sister, 'two little English girls, who chose to frighten all the children of an Italian village and sweep the hill of them. It was done without malice, but with a horrid sense of dominance.'[60] Meynell compares the girls' assault to an atavistic hunt: 'They joined, they closed upon the quarry, or in open order cut off the escape of scattered fugitives,' and, at the end of this escapade, she and her sister are peculiarly satisfied: 'The two representatives of the predominant race [. . .] sat down in the conquered district, flushed with success.'[61]

The tribalism of children also comes to the fore in Mansfield's 'Prelude', when the Samuel Josephs, neighbours to the Burnells, treat Kezia and Lottie as prey, toying with them on the Burnells' last day in town. When Stan 'foxes' Kezia, tripping her up with a false choice of 'strawberries and cream', his siblings are thrilled.[62] They demonstrate their tribal unity by appealing to their mother for approval: 'Even Mrs. Samuel Josephs, pouring out the milk and water, could not help smiling' (p. 58). In 'The Doll's House', the 'othering' of the Kelvey children is more pervasive. The shunning of the working-class Kelveys is reinforced by the adults, and especially Aunt Beryl, whose officiousness compensates for her own feelings of marginalisation. Kezia is the only child willing to include the Kelveys, but she too takes satisfaction from the superiority of ownership, a sense of dominance, when she shows off the doll's house.

The terror felt by Mansfield's children is more obscure than their tribalism. Meynell's psychology helps to explain Kezia's fear as she leaves her emptied house for the last time and makes a mad dash to Lottie. According to Meynell, children do not need the menace of a specific monster to experience such terror:

> a child who is 'prone to fears' will be helpless under their grasp, without the help of human tales. The night will threaten him, the shadow will pursue, the dream will catch him; terror itself have him by the heart [. . .] Fear knows him well and finds him alone.[63]

Solitary Kezia experiences just such a nameless menace:

> Kezia was suddenly quite, quite still, with wide open eyes and knees pressed together. She was frightened. She wanted to call Lottie and to

> go on calling all the while she ran downstairs and out of the house. But IT was just behind her, waiting at the door, at the head of the stairs, at the bottom of the stairs, hiding in the passage, ready to dart out at the backdoor. (p. 59)

A companion to Meynell's prose statements on terror is her poem 'The Treasure'. It explains that fear is the 'sentinel' and preserver of life:

> What demands that sense of menaces,
> And then such flying feet [. . .]?:
> Life: There's nought else to seek;
> Life only, little prized; but by design
> Of Nature prized. How weak,
> How sad, how brief! O how divine, divine![64]

Kezia's flight manifests fear's preserving role. Meynell's idea of terror as life-preserving connects the mad dash to a later scene, when the decapitated duck makes Kezia frantic for life: 'Put head back. Put head back!' (p. 82). Keeping in mind how fear is to be prized, we can also see how this terror anticipates the touching scene from 'At the Bay', when a slightly older Kezia questions her grandmother directly about death and refuses to accept its inevitability: '"Say never . . . say never . . . say never –"'. A standoff emerges: 'And then she began, very softly and lightly, to tickle her grandma' (p. 358). The tickling leads to gaiety and forgetfulness, the companion treasures of fear: 'Both of them had forgotten what the "never" was about' (p. 358).

Like Meynell, Mansfield portrays the importance of the child's dwelling 'near the ground'. In Kezia's case, both fear and delight are tied to her bodily orientation.[65] Kezia makes three trips, on her first day at the country house, into 'the spread tangled garden' (p. 72). Her tendency to terror leads her to avoid the 'frightening side', where the child's proximity to tree roots makes them appear daunting, 'the marks of big fowls' feet' above the wet clay (p. 72). Her small stature also adds to the splendour of red-hot pokers, 'taller than she', and sunflowers that form 'a tiny jungle', and her lightness allows her to sit on the box border, 'by pressing hard at first it made a nice seat' (p. 72). Kezia learns from ground-level exposure of the pungent, dusty inside, 'sneezing and rubbing her nose' (p. 72).The two sides of the garden, one fearful and the other alluring, convey vividly the ambivalence of childhood as Kezia unknowingly prepares for future loss as well as joy.[66] Kezia exemplifies a version of the Wordsworthian theme, the child collecting a hoard of memories of the earth that she revisits redemptively in adult years when banished, as Meynell describes it, to 'breathing at the levels of the lilac-trees and hawthorn'.[67] Meynell makes a point in 'Real Childhood' of the child's experience of sorrow as well as joy:

> But the cloudy dusk behind poplars on the plains of France, the flying landscape from the train, willows, and the last of the light, were more mournful to you then than you care to remember now. So were the black crosses on the graves of the French village; so were the cypresses, though greatly beloved.[68]

The Shared Project: Paying Back Children

Viola Meynell's praise of her mother's essays applies to Mansfield's stories: 'children all the world over who have been turned into silliness, boredom and sentimentality in admiring anecdote have something repaid to them when childhood comes under shrewd but Exquisite Observation'.[69] In obvious ways, the experiences of Meynell and Mansfield differ: the one ensconced in a traditional marriage and prolific motherhood, the other a Bohemian experimenter whose childlessness may have intensified her interest in children. More fundamentally, they share traits consistent with perspicacity about childhood vulnerability.[70] Meynell was tossed about at an earlier age. Raised in Europe, mainly in Italy, she was nostalgic, like Mansfield, for her non-English childhood. Unlike Mansfield, Meynell returned many times, often travelling with family and visiting family members who remained in Italy. Both Meynell and Mansfield thrilled to danger early in the war: in 1915, they both write of enjoying the appearance of Zeppelins.[71] Mansfield crosses the front lines of battle to visit Carco; when in London during the war, Meynell enjoys the air raids that terrify others.[72]

Both writers reappraise children's relations to preoccupied adults. In her essays, Meynell sometimes implicates herself as the busy adult. The writer who crosses the divide between adult and child depends on clear memories of childhood, and each application of memory comes with the caveat that the writer must render childhood without condescension, respecting difference and not overdetermining the child's attitudes. Mansfield likes to frame her deep dive into memory as contact with a secret self. If she had read Mansfield's stories, Meynell would certainly have placed Mansfield in the same pantheon as Dickens and Stevenson, as a writer gifted with memory and authentic awareness of children and their vulnerability to forgetful or self-absorbed adults.

Notes

1. Vita Sackville-West, 'Introduction', *Alice Meynell: Prose and Poetry* (London: Jonathan Cape, 1947), pp. 7–26 (p. 18).

2. Katharine Tynan, *Memories* (London: Eveleigh Nash & Grayson, 1924), p. 40.
3. Tynan, p. 40.
4. Tynan, p. 40.
5. The essays include memories of her childhood, her own children and even 'sometimes the children's children'; Viola Meynell, *Alice Meynell: A Memoir* (New York: Scribner, 1929), p. 289.
6. Paul Robinson, 'Alice Meynell', in Tracy Chevalier, ed., *Encyclopedia of the Essay* (London: Routledge, 1997), pp. 559–60 (p. 560). Linda Austin describes Meynell's extended influence: 'For at least two decades after her death in 1922, she was treated as a psychological and moral authority on children and child-rearing.' See Linda Austin, 'Self against Childhood: The Contributions of Alice Meynell to a Psycho-Physiology of Memory', *Victorian Literature and Culture,* 34: 1 (2006), pp. 249–68 (p. 250).
7. Sir Henry Newbolt, quoted in June Badeni, *The Slender Tree: A Life of Alice Meynell* (Padstow: Tabb House, 1981), p. 227.
8. Alice Meynell, 'Fairies', in *Childhood* (London: Batsford, 1913), pp. 26–34 (p. 26).
9. Meynell, 'Fairies', p. 28.
10. Meynell, 'Fairies', p. 27.
11. Meynell, 'Fairies', p. 27.
12. Writing to Murry about their financial troubles in 1917, Mansfield knows what will bring reward: 'My serious stories won't ever bring me anything, but my "child" stories ought to and my light ones, once I find a place.' *Letters* 2, p. 75.
13. CW4, p. 102.
14. Claire Tomalin, *Katherine Mansfield: A Secret Life* (New York: Knopf, 1988), p. 59.
15. Viola's cottage was renovated from the cowshed at Humphrey's Homestead. See photograph, Derek Aram, 'D. H. Lawrence: A Digital Pilgrimage', 26 June 2017, available at <https://thedigitalpilgrimage.wordpress.com/tag/greatham/> (last accessed 5 August 2020).
16. Cherry A. Hankin, ed., *The Letters of John Middleton Murry to Katherine Mansfield* (New York: Franklin Watts, 1983), p. 41.
17. Badeni, p. 229.
18. If Murry means Alice, he must mistake her silences and 'extreme modesty' for stupidity. See Badeni, p. 211.
19. Hankin, p. 40.
20. Hankin, p. 41.
21. Meynell's son is Sebastian. Hankin mistakenly identifies 'Bastian' as W. J. J. Sprott, p. 41.
22. Lawrence stayed in Viola's cottage rent-free while revising *The Rainbow,* and Viola typed his manuscript. She writes of Lawrence, 'As his friends [. . .] were frequently lifted into his books, he was a very unsafe person to know'; quoted in Raymond N. MacKenzie, *A Critical Biography of English Novelist Viola Meynell, 1885–1956* (Lewiston, NY: Edwin Mellen Press, 2002), p. 263. In the story 'England, My England', Lawrence 'lifts' the accident with a scythe at Greatham, which crippled Alice Meynell's granddaughter, Sylvia. In revising, he altered events and made the child's ineffectual father responsible for leaving the scythe in the grass. The skewed but identifiable portrait seemed especially cruel after Meynell's son-in-law, Percy Lucas, died heroically at the Battle of the Somme (MacKenzie, pp. 159–64.) Alice Meynell refers back to a 'certain Mr. Lawrence's' stay in a year when writers 'were all over the place': 'If a bomb fell here it would destroy a heap of literature.' Damian Atkinson, ed., *The*

Selected Letters of Alice Meynell (Newcastle upon Tyne: Cambridge Scholars, 2013), p. 370.

23. Anne Olivier Bell and Andrew McNeillie, eds, *The Diary of Virginia Woolf, Volume 3* (New York: Harcourt, Brace, Jovanovich, 1980), p. 251.
24. In a letter to Alice, Everard Meynell jokes about his sister Olivia's 'discarded Morris dresses'. See Viola Meynell, p. 315.
25. *Letters* 1, p. 155.
26. *Letters* 1, p. 155.
27. Badeni, p. 207.
28. Mansfield's writing 'sacrifiged' may refer to a private joke with Murry. It is hard to imagine the 'Tigers', as the two called themselves, approving of self-sacrifice. *Letters* 1, p. 166.
29. Alice Meynell praised Murry's criticism, but writing to playwright Aubone Hare, she suggests Murry is too mild: 'Middleton Murry is *fine*! He might with advantage be shorter and simpler over the excellent thought he has, but how masterly, for instance, is his defence of realistic fiction as a really creative work! But he should, when necessary, be stronger and angrier than he ever is'; quoted by Viola Meynell, p. 330.
30. Meynell, 'Toys', in *Childhood*, pp. 1–5 (p. 5).
31. Meynell, 'Injustice', in *Childhood*, pp. 48–53 (p. 51).
32. Meynell, 'Children's Books of the Present', in *Childhood*, pp. 20–6 (p. 26).
33. Angela Smith, 'Mansfield and Dickens: "I am not Reading Dickens *Idly*"', in Gerri Kimber and Janet Wilson, eds, *Celebrating Katherine Mansfield: A Centenary Volume of Essays* (London: Palgrave Macmillan, 2011), pp. 189–201 (p. 189).
34. Mansfield uses the designation 'pa-man' in her letters to describe a hardy, traditional gentleman, like her own father, who takes pleasure in the role of overseeing and providing. For a full consideration, see Mark Williams, 'The Pa man: Sir Harold Beauchamp', in Charles Ferrall and Jane Stafford, eds, *Katherine Mansfield's Men* (Wellington: KM Birthplace Society with Steele Roberts Publishers), pp. 13–26.
35. Like the Mary of Rossetti's 'Annunciation', she has a 'Very white small face' bathed in moonlight. CW1, p. 170. Further references to this story are placed in the text.
36. CW3, p. 455.
37. CW3, p. 455.
38. CW3, p. 456.
39. Viola Meynell's first chapter of her *Alice Meynell* is 'A Dickens Friendship', pp. 1–12. For Alice's last words, see Viola Meynell, p. 347. Cf. *Dombey and Son*, Chapter XVI, *Project Gutenberg*, available at <https://www.gutenberg.org/files/821/821-h/821-h.htm> (last accessed 18 August 2020). Viola does not note the similarity. I believe it adds to their weight.
40. *Letters* 2, p. 46.
41. Meynell, 'Near the Ground', in *Childhood*, pp. 53–8 (p. 53).
42. Meynell, 'Real Childhood', in *The Children* (London: J. Lane, 1897), pp. 90–5 (p. 92).
43. Meynell, 'That Pretty Person', in *The Children*, pp. 28–36 (p. 28).
44. Meynell, 'Real Childhood', p. 95.
45. Meynell, 'Near the Ground', p. 54.
46. Meynell takes children's beliefs seriously and upbraids J. M. Barrie. He should not expect children to clap for Tinker Bell in *Peter Pan*, as though they believed in fairies: 'all children know the difference between pretending and believing'. See Meynell, 'Fairies', p. 32. On Meynell's resistance to the 'emerging empiricist narratives of

human beings', see Ashley Faulkner, 'The Coronation of the Virgin: Alice Meynell's Typological Critique of Modern Bodies', in *Cahiers victoriens et édouardiens,* 74 (Autumn 2011), pp. 75–88, available at <https://doi.org/10.4000/cve.1048> (last accessed 3 August 2020).

47. Meynell, 'The Man with Two Heads', in *The Children,* pp. 48–52 (p. 51). Francis Meynell recalls his disappointment when his mother opened the cupboard to demonstrate no such 'Man' lived there. *My Lives* (New York: Random House, 1971), p. 19.
48. Meynell, 'Real Childhood', p. 91.
49. Meynell, 'Real Childhood', p. 90.
50. CW1, p. 285. Further references to this story are placed in the text.
51. CW2, p. 361. Further references to this story are placed in the text.
52. Meynell, 'Near the Ground', pp. 54–5 (p. 57).
53. Meynell, 'The Boy', in *The Children,* pp. 72–5 (p. 73).
54. Meynell, 'Injustice', p. 51.
55. Meynell, 'Daily Time', in *Childhood,* pp. 58–65 (p. 63).
56. CW2, p. 139. Further references to this story are placed in the text.
57. Meynell, 'Injustice', p. 48.
58. Meynell, 'Injustice', p. 52.
59. Meynell, 'The Child of Tumult', in *Prose and Poetry: Alice Meynell* (London: Jonathan Cape, 1947), pp. 293–8 (p. 294).
60. Meynell, 'The Stranger's Children', in *Childhood,* pp. 5–15 (p. 13).
61. Meynell, 'The Stranger's Children', p. 15.
62. CW2, p. 58. Further references to this story are placed in the text.
63. Meynell, 'The Man with Two Heads', p. 48.
64. Meynell, 'The Treasure', in *The Poems of Alice Meynell: Complete Edition* (New York: Charles Scribner's Sons, 1923), available at <http://xroads.virginia.edu/~public/FEG/alice/ampoems2.html#085> (last accessed 17 August 2020).
65. Meynell shares Wordsworth's belief in the child's divinity, but she emphasises a small body as the crucial factor in connecting the child to Nature. Linda Austin argues for Meynell's common-sense materialism, in keeping with Victorian philosophers like George Henry Lewes: 'if Wordsworth was for Victorians the chief Romantic chronicler of memory, the self, and childhood, Meynell was his successor', p. 249.
66. Meynell goes so far as to say that the 'low region of the earth air [. . .] has always been *patria*': 'The country that children pore over is surely the country of memories for which men afterwards die'; 'Near the Ground', p. 57. Meynell's *patria* parallels Mansfield's sense of obligation to memorializs her brother Leslie that calls her fiction home to New Zealand.
67. Meynell, 'Near the Ground', p. 54.
68. Meynell, 'Real Childhood', p. 95.
69. Viola Meynell, p. 147.
70. Born forty years apart, on 11 and 14 October, they died within two months of each other.
71. Mansfield sees them in Paris, 'the Ultimate Fish [. . .] flying high with fins of silky grey'. *Letters* 1, p. 159. See also Viola Meynell, pp. 315–16.
72. Viola Meynell, p. 316. On 8 October 1917, Alice Meynell wrote of the air raids: 'I have enjoyed the high excitement [. . .] it was only people with children whose nerve gave way in London'; Atkinson, *Selected Letters,* p. 394.

A NEW STORY

'The Chorus Girl and the Tariff' by Katherine Mansfield

Martin Griffiths

Introduction

In June 2019, I discovered a forgotten piece of prose from 1910, 'The Thawing of Anthony Wynscombe' by Katherine R. Mansfield, which was published in volume 12 of Katherine Mansfield Studies.[1] Since then, I have discovered another story by a 'Katherine Mansfield', very likely the same as the renowned modernist short story writer of the same name. 'The Chorus Girl and the Tariff' ('TCGT'), published here for the first time since 1909, is a sketch rather than a short story – there are no characters – but its attribution to the New Zealand-born writer seems plausible. I traced the story from a vague reference to a sketch by 'Katherine Mansfield' in the November 1909 edition of *The Leavenworth Times* (Kansas) to *The National Monthly*, where the sketch appeared, with the help of the Buffalo History Museum, which holds a complete edition of the latter periodical.

In 'TCGT', a chorus girl complains about increasing taxes, the exhaustion of travelling and the dull humiliation of scratching a living off, and on, Broadway, New York.[2] As a member of 'The Mugnaficent Merry-makers', she positions herself as a thick-skinned suffragette with fading illusions of fame and fortune. Given the subject and the timing of the story's publication, Mansfield's authorship seems plausible: Mansfield was a chorus singer for a few weeks in March 1909 in the north of England and Scotland (with Garnet Trowell and the Moody Manners Opera Company). Indeed, in a letter to Garnet Trowell she exclaims, 'Oh to be in New York.'[3] A further connection between the events in Mansfield's life in 1909 and America occurs in another, much later, correspondence: 'I dreamed last night of Bowden. I was at an opera with you, sitting in a converted railway carriage seat, and I heard Bowden talking of his wife to an American lady.'[4]

Nevertheless, despite circumstantial evidence, the writing is problematic, in so far as the vocabulary is idiomatic in the extreme. The first sentence alone contains four examples of American theatre vernacular or detailed American geography. One word, kimmelweck – a kind of bread roll – is specific to Buffalo, New York, the city that published *The National Monthly* in which the story appears.[5] References, such as 'Klaw and Erlanger' and 'Adolph-Castoria' (variations on the theatrical syndicate 'Erl and Klawlinger' and the hotel 'Waldorf Astoria') and 'one-night-stand' (a stage platform rather than a sexual encounter), have uniquely American connotations. However, the humorous monologue sounds convincingly like the author of 'The Lady's Maid' in the plotless, first-person narrative.[6]

Across the Atlantic

The USA maintained a prominent presence in London news, current affairs and popular culture in the UK at this time. Mansfield even commented on the New York railway system and ex-President Teddy Roosevelt in her pastiche letters to the editor of *The New Age*.[7] American culture and language readily found a place in Mansfield's writing, which included the tropes 'little New York gutter child', 'Put sand on your boots, kid; you're sliding', 'slap up evening dress' and references to American flora and fauna, fabric, cinema, beverages, literature and literary characters.[8]

The representation of American vernacular to the British public – via the press – was aided by popular fictional characters such as 'Mr. Dooley', whose ruminations appeared frequently in *The Westminster Gazette*.[9] American actresses/singers Fritzi Scheff and Anna Held – who are both mentioned in the text of 'TCGT' – were well known to British audiences and assisted in the dissemination of American popular culture and vaudeville theatre.[10] Mansfield liked to associate with singing celebrities, particularly ones of international pedigree: 'Ah! I am in heaven. I have been with Fritz Rupp the opera singer. He has played, sung, acted, spoken. My sadness is gone.'[11] Perhaps not coincidentally, both Fritz, or 'Fritzi', and 'Anna' appear as character names in Mansfield's *In a German Pension* stories.[12]

American contralto Mary Louise Rogers, who toured with Garnet Trowell in the Moody Manners Opera, may have provided the author of 'TCGT' with inspiration for the chorus girl. After appearing in March 1909 with the Moody Manners Company at the Gaiety Theatre in Manchester, Rogers continued the tour to Glasgow, at which point she and Mansfield may have met. On 14 May, Rogers travelled to New York – the state in which she was born and raised – possibly taking 'TCGT' with her.[13] Teresa Carreño, who was also raised in New York, met Mansfield on at least three occasions in London and is mentioned twice in letters by Mansfield to Garnet Trowell;[14] she, too, may have sent the sketch 'home'. After all, Carreño performed in Buffalo at least a dozen times over a forty-two-year period, and the pianist – whose career began in the theatre as an accompanist for singers and stage actresses during the 1870s – gave a concert in Buffalo less than six weeks after the sketch was published there.[15]

Furthermore, Mansfield looked to her sister Vera for assistance in finding publishers for her stories in 1908.[16] Perhaps an approach was made to Vera's fiancé, James McIntosh Bell, later referred to by the sisters as 'Mack'.[17] McIntosh Bell was born in Ontario and studied at Queens' University, Toronto, before 1904. His connection with the United States was strengthened by the doctoral studies he undertook at Harvard University, immediately prior to his arrival in New Zealand in 1905, and travelling between Boston and Toronto, where his parents continued to reside, he would have passed through the border city of Buffalo.

Mansfield's New Zealand

From early childhood, Mansfield was a talented musician, playing equally well on the piano and the cello, and she was a very good singer. She performed as an actress, entertainer and teller of jokes, and aspired to read her stories on the stage. Relevant early influences in her life are evident: the Trowell twins, Arnold and Garnet, together with their father, Thomas – the latter Mansfield's cello teacher – performed with a touring juvenile theatre company, 'Pollard's Opera', in New Zealand, and presented a six-week season in Auckland at Christmas 1898. Repeat performances in Wellington, most likely attended by Mansfield, included *The Gay Parisienne, Djin-Djin, The French Maid, In Town* and *Rip Van Winkle.* While Thomas Trowell was a member of the orchestra and also conducted some of the performances, Arnold Trowell toured as solo cellist for a biograph show – an early form of cinema.

From an early age, Mansfield was familiar with the 'one-man' play or live monologue. In 1900, for example, she attended dramatised readings of Robert Browning and Shakespeare, given by 'New York' actress, Mrs Hannibal A. Williams, in Wellington.[18] Indeed, Mansfield attended Mrs Williams's monologue recital of 'As You Like it' at the Sydney Street

Schoolroom on 11 June 1900. Likewise, Millie Parker, Mansfield's musical companion and friend in Wellington, recalls that the Australian actors, Julius Knight and Bland Holt, and their theatrical troupes were directing advertising at pre-adolescents: 'My first consciousness of the theatre was the little cotton flags bearing the magic device "Bland Holt" which were distributed to us in the school playground on leaving school.'[19] Mansfield even appeared as an extra in a silent movie.[20]

American actors and actresses toured in New Zealand while Mansfield was living there in 1907 and 1908. Charles Waldron, Rapley Holmes and Ola Humphrey – who all appeared on stage in New York between 1904 and 1908 – visited Wellington as part of J. C. Williamson's 'New Dramatic Company' in January 1907. Humphrey, in an interview for the *Dominion*, tactfully refers to Wellington as more than a 'one-night-stand', the latter term perhaps noted and reused by the author of 'TCGT'.[21] Mansfield socialised with international singing star Clara Butt (an English contralto who had toured widely in North America), and probably attended 'At Home' receptions for visiting artists from abroad.

American vaudevillian actor Andrew Mack, with a 'specially selected company of American artists including Mae Stevenson, presented 'Tom Moore' in Wellington during March and April 1907.[22] Mansfield – who attended a lecture on 'Thomas Moore' and mentioned 'Tom Moore' in her 1907 notebooks – may have attended and even met some of the party.[23] Further, Mack was performing in Buffalo, New York, in December 1909, within weeks of the appearance there of 'TCGT'.

The Cotillon series of dances, also known simply as 'The German', feature in 'TCGT' and are as much theatrical as social spectacles. The 'double eight' and the 'revolving star' are mentioned in the story and were dances probably known by Mansfield. In 1908, she attended her sister Chaddie's birthday party, at which 'three figures of the Cotillon' were danced. These included the 'Mirror' dance, in which a mirror discreetly helps the selection of a partner, and a 'Screen' dance, in which the screen obscures all but the shoes of the potential partner.[24]

Vernacular Terminology and Forbes's The Chorus Lady

Tropes, both American and English, that are common to 'TCGT' are likewise evident in other works by Mansfield, adding to the likelihood that the story could be hers. These include 'skate' – meaning derelict person; 'dead' – meaning absolutely; 'blow' – meaning reckless spending or indulgence; 'flat' – meaning dwelling or apartment; 'for instance' meaning for example; 'frizzled' or 'frizzling' – meaning overcooked; 'lines' – in the context of female form, as in 'built on perfect lines'; 'Madge' – a generic name for a female friend; 'stuffy' – meaning claustrophobic; 'pretty' – as a qualifier meaning fairly; 'lobster red' and variants; 'straight' – meaning honest; 'chewing gum' being a form of confectionary; 'berth' – as in the bed or bunk on a railway carriage; '[full of] sawdust' – meaning artificial or decrepit; 'fad' – meaning fashion; 'feed' – in reference to the human consumption of food; and 'neither here nor there' – meaning irrelevant.[25] The phrase 'good things a cooking' – with its Dickensian vernacular[26] – has echoes in Mansfield's letters: 'It's not v. nice to see Mr. and Mrs. Sullivan a-lapping up the cream & licking of their paws'; 'Me – blue cotton kimono & pink slippers afilling of the vases'.[27]

Mansfield was clearly interested in theatre and the dramatic possibilities of converting theatrical conventions, stories, techniques and characters into her own tales. Reusing or borrowing material from real life is an acceptable, even desirable, activity, compared with borrowing from literature or theatre. While Mansfield very frequently based her writing on her own life experience, she did occasionally, it seems, take from other authors; for example, Mansfield controversially appropriated the plot of Anton Chekhov's 'Sleepyhead' for her story 'The Child-who-was-tired'.[28]

Such may also be the case with 'TCGT', for James Forbes's play *The Chorus Lady*, first published in 1906, and 'TCGT' share content to such an extent that one can only conclude the author of the latter borrowed very heavily from the former.[29] Common names and phrases include: 'twenty dollars [pay] per week', 'ferry rides' and 'show girl', and, more tellingly, the two works even share reference to a boy (or man) breaking his neck (or back) in the elevator shaft.[30] The phrases 'spear-carrier', 'grease paint' and 'show ponies' – which the stage version of *The Chorus Lady* and 'TCGT' have in common – do not occur in John W. Harding's 1908 'novelised' version, so one must conclude that the author of 'TCGT' used the stage version as the principal source.[31] A production of *The Chorus Lady* – starring American Rose Stahl – was performed in London in May 1906 and April 1909. That the author of 'TCGT' saw such a live production – or accessed a copy of the play during this time – seems likely. Thus far, then, Mansfield, who is known to have been in London in the relevant months and attended theatre productions in 1909 (see CW1, p. 168, n.3), cannot be ruled out as the author.

Other commonalities of unusual words between 'TCGT' and Forbes's *The Chorus Lady* include 'hostelry' or 'hostelery', 'thermometer', 'skate', 'cinch' and 'punk'. Instead of 'The Moonlight Maids', the name of Forbes's troupe, we have 'The Mugnaficent Merry-makers' – also a variant of 'The Moody Manners' and Hollander's 'Merry Makers', who toured New Zealand in 1908. Both the 'Maids' and the 'Merry-makers' are paid a salary 'per' (a contraction of the phrase 'per week').

American Magazines and Books

Alternatively, a short story version of Forbes's play, which was published in *Smith's Magazine* in December 1907, may have been read by Mansfield in Wellington.[32] Likewise, Grace Luce Irwin's 'Diary of a Show Girl', which was published in March 1909 and serialised in the same year, contains many of the tropes found in 'TCGT'.[33] These include Fritzi Scheff, Coney Island, chorus girl, lobster, little old New York, surface car, Waldorf Astoria, dear old Broadway, chewing gum, merry dancing, [$]18 a week and $20 'per', spear carrier, John D. Rockefeller, old beau, cinch and a-coming. Perhaps Mansfield used this as a source.

Evidently, Mansfield developed literary aspirations from New York magazines; she writes, 'O I have a glorious subject for a Vignette – have you the Smart Set asked the girl in the bookshop.'[34] The autobiographical story 'Toots' contains a scene in which the character, Pip, opens a large package of 'English and American magazines'.[35] Further, Mansfield sent, or rather had sent by S. S. Koteliansky, at least one story to the *Smart Set.*[36] Mansfield appears to have absorbed literary phrases from such American magazines: 'And my room here is so nice. It's like a wild west cabin': 'I bought a poun a ba-kin | and fried it in a pan | But nobody came to e-eat it | But me-e and my young man!'[37] Likewise, the author of 'TCGT' may have borrowed the acronym 'N. G.' and the term 'gazaboo' from Dorothy Dix's *Fables of the Elite*, stories from which appeared in the *Smart Set.*[38]

New York actors and actresses frequented the pages of popular literature. Elizabeth Robins's 'Come and Find Me' – a text which introduces issues of the working woman, as well as examples of American vernacular – was not only read by Mansfield but effusively praised in her notebooks.[39] We can see Robins's influence in Mansfield's 'The Young Girl', in which Mrs MacEwen 'from New York' commands attention, despite her absence. MacEwen is mentioned several times but, for the reader and for the 'stage johnnies', she never appears.[40] Likewise, Florida N. Baxter, a character in Mouche's 'A Flirtation' (a story sometimes attributed to Mansfield), is a superior version of the 'coarse' Lulu, 'who sang badly in a foolish operetta at the theatre'. Florida is, not surprisingly, determined to be a celebrity singer, authoress or 'society leader'.[41]

A search for specific Americanisms in the works of Mansfield uncovers many more or less relevant examples. Amongst the former we might include 'straight' as a synonym for 'honest': 'that's straight' in 'TCGT'. According to Ohsawa, this usage occurs no less than seventeen times in Mansfield's stories.[42] The phrase 'down dear *old* Broadway' [my italics] appears once in 'TCGT', and in her book review 'Lions and Lambs' Mansfield cites 'little *old* New York' [my italics], the exact phrase that appears in the Harding version of Forbes's *The Chorus Lady*.[43] Finally, 'TCGT' contains hints of Mansfield's shorthand: for example, the dropped apostrophe and frequent use of a dash.

Conclusion

Mansfield associated New York City with actors and actresses throughout her short life. Even as late as 1921, she was still connecting the East Coast city with theatre: 'I note that Bertha [Herbert] sells slips, tuniques and cossaques at a li'l shop in New York. It being the pantomime season I shall make the joke . . . I expect they are *all slips*.'[44] New York celebrity contralto Mary Louise Rogers and virtuoso pianist Teresa Carreño could easily have provided examples of American slang to a young Katherine Mansfield, as could McIntosh (Mack) Bell, Charles Waldron, Rapley Holmes, Ola Humphrey and Andrew Mack. On multiple occasions, in both New Zealand and England, the New Zealand-born writer had opportunity to absorb and imitate American culture.[45]

The lone voice, or the voice of the lone traveller, occurs again and again in the fiction of Mansfield. In the stories 'Miss Brill' and 'The Lady's Maid', themes of social isolation are scrutinised or laid bare by the monologue technique. Broadly speaking, Mansfield's use and development of the monologue revolutionised the direction of the modernist short story. Specifically, the lone voice emphasises the impoverishment and exploitation of many of Mansfield's characters. In this regard, 'TCGT' fits nicely into the writer's œuvre. Yet where Mansfield approaches lost innocence by way of unrealism – a woman becomes a 'girl', a man becomes an animal, a domestic room becomes a stage – the author of 'TCGT' treats it in a relatively high-handed and flippant way. However, Mansfield was, at least during the early part of her career in London, capable of such high-handedness.

The emphasis on the word 'girl' in 'TCGT' – which appears seventeen times as 'chorus girl' and thirty-three times in total – signals the loss of innocence that one might ascribe to an aspiring theatre actress. Notwithstanding that repetition is a common technique amongst many of Mansfield's works, it is notable that we have precedence: the word 'girl' is used by Mansfield twenty-six times in the contemporaneous 'His Sister's Keeper' (1909). In Mansfield's relatively brief story 'The

Little Girl' (1912) – which provided the title of an American edition of Mansfield's stories – 'little girl' is repeated nine times and 'girl' twelve.[46]

Mansfield had a desire to reach an audience in America.[47] By 1923, and within a year of its publication, *The Garden Party and Other Stories* had been reprinted once in the UK and seven times in America.[48] Further, an interest in American culture, theatre, literature and travel are all evident in Mansfield's writing. According to Gerri Kimber, Mansfield had already read the American poet Walt Whitman and 'The American Diary of a Japanese Girl' before she arrived in London in August 1908.[49] Finally, if 'TCGT' was written by a non-citizen (what American would mistakenly attribute 'N.G' and 'P.X' as synonyms for A.M. and P.M?) – then Mansfield is as good a candidate as any, and aspects of subject, biographical opportunity and stylistic preference are valid supporting evidence for attribution to the New Zealand-born author.

Notes

1. See Martin Griffiths, 'A Mysterious Lost Story by Katherine Mansfield', in Enda Duffy, Gerri Kimber and Todd Martin, eds, *Katherine Mansfield and* Bliss and Other Stories, Katherine Mansfield Studies, vol. 12 (Edinburgh: Edinburgh University Press, 2020), pp. 123–34.
2. Katherine Mansfield, 'The Chorus Girl and the Tariff', *National Monthly: A Magazine For Democratic Men and Women*, Buffalo, NY, November 1909, pp. 215–16.
3. Draft of a letter to Garnet Trowell, 28–30 April 1909, *Letters* 1, p. 91. The letter – written in Brussels, the same city in which American male suffragist 'Guy' (a fictional character in 'Being a Truthful Adventure' [1911]) appears – refers to Garnet in the American vernacular as 'brother'. Mansfield also refers to the New York 'town' of Hiltonville 120 miles from Buffalo, in her story 'The Aloe' (1915). See CW1, p. 512.
4. *Letters* 1, p. 166. Mansfield married George Bowden in March 1909.
5. The reference to 'three kimmelwecks and a cent's worth of mustard' corresponds with Mansfield's comment in a letter to Garnet Trowell (September 1908, *Letters* 1, p. 62): 'Would you like me to cut some sandwitches, and I promise not to forget the mustard.' The date of the letter suggests that the sketch was written by Mansfield after she had returned to London. However, there are reasons to suggest the story was conceived earlier, perhaps when Mansfield was in New Zealand.
6. The narrator refers to herself in the third person as well.
7. Katherine Mansfield, 'North American Chiefs', CW3, p. 384, and 'A Paper Chase', CW3, p. 383.
8. 'Elsie Lindtner', CW3, pp. 432–3 (p. 433); 'In Confidence', CW2, pp. 31–6 (p. 32); see also a letter from Mansfield dated 21 January 1917, *Letters* 1, p. 294.
9. Dooley is a fictional character in Finlay Peter Dunne's *Dissertations by Mr Dooley* (London: Harper and Bros, 1906).
10. Fritzi Scheff was sometimes, as in the case of 'TCGT', spelt Fritzy Scheff.
11. CW4, p. 55.
12. Elsa, in Mansfield's 'The Advanced Lady', refers to her fiancé Fritz as 'Fritzi', and the character Anna appears in 'At Lehmann's' and 'A Birthday'. See *In a German Pension* (London: Swift, 1911).

13. On the same day, a notice in *The Sun* places Anne Mukle, pianist and proprietor of Beauchamp Lodge, London – where Mansfield had recently resided – in New York. See 'Notes of Musical Events', *Sun*, 14 March 1909, p. 7, and Antony Alpers, *Katherine Mansfield: A Biography* (London: Jonathan Cape, 1954), pp. 66–7.
14. *Letters* 1, pp. 64, 65 and 69.
15. For a period in the early 1880s, she sang professionally and even formed her own opera company alongside her then-husband, baritone Giovanni Tagliapietra. Tagliapietra's brother, Arturo, whom Carreño married in 1902, came to New Zealand with the pianist as her manager in 1907 and probably met Mansfield in Wellington, or perhaps in London in 1909.
16. *Letters* 1, p. 53.
17. See *Letters* 4, p. 309.
18. See letter to Murry, 25 April 1920, *Letters* 3, p. 291, and Alexander Turnbull Library (ATL) Eph-A-DRAMA-1900.
19. Interview with Margaret Parker, *Dominion*, 4 April 1964 (ATL MS-Papers-5303-1).
20. See letters to Bertrand Russell, *Letters* 1, pp. 293–4. See also Kathleen Jones, *Katherine Mansfield: The Story-Teller* (London: Penguin 2010), p. 138.
21. 'Social and Personal', *Dominion*, 29 May 1908, p. 5.
22. 'Andrew Mack as Tom Moore', in 'Amusements', *New Zealand Times*, 1 April 1907, p. 6.
23. The lecture is mentioned in the *New Zealand Times*, 14 May 1907, p. 6. See also CW4, p. 26. Mack attended a dinner of 'enthusiastic admirers' in Wellington on 1 June 1907. See 'Notes by Lornette', *New Zealand Mail*, 5 June 1907, p. 26.
24. For details of the Cotillon, see *How to Lead the German* (New York: Dick and Fitzgerald, 1895). See 'Ladies Column', *Evening Post*, 13 July 1907, p. 15.
25. Also 'cambric roses' [or 'paper flowers']; 'shrump' or 'shrimp' – meaning small person; 'turn in' or 'turned in' – meaning go to bed; 'dump' or 'dumped' – meaning to leave, or drop off, such as at the railway station; 'in fact' to precede an emphatic statement; 'rheumatism' – in relation to walking; and 'kid' – meaning child. Mansfield, in a note dated 1 February 1915, writes, 'Life was like sawdust and sand' (CW4, p. 157).
26. Mark Tapley, quoting the captain of 'The Screw', says, 'you were always a cooking for everybody'. Charles Dickens, *Life and Adventures of Martin Chuzzlewit* (Philadelphia: T. B. Peterson, 1844), p. 213.
27. See *Letters* 4, pp. 260; 261.
28. Elisabeth Schneider, 'Katherine Mansfield and Chekhov', *Modern Language Notes*, 50: 6 (1935), pp. 394–7.
29. A reprint of the 1906 stage version is found in James Forbes's *The Famous Mrs. Fair and Other Plays* (New York: George Doran, 1920), pp. 17–92. See also John W. Harding's novelised version of James Forbes's *The Chorus Lady* (New York: Dillingham, 1908).
30. One might infer that the author of 'TCGT' borrowed from the Forbes/Harding book too, given that the elevator incident is in this novelised version, but not in the stage play. However, an improvised aside by Crawford (perhaps played by the actor Wilfred Lucas in a live production) may have been included in a 'working' copy of the script and thus included in the book.
31. In 'TCGT', the author refers to 'old Broadway'. Similarly, in the book review 'Lions and Lambs', Mansfield cites 'little old New York' (CW3, pp. 508–9 [p. 508]). Although the author of the book under scrutiny is by an American, the phrase seems, at first glance, to be Mansfield's own (that is, not a quote from the book). However,

the exact phrase appears in the Harding version of James Forbes's *The Chorus Lady* (p. 237).

32. James Forbes, 'The Chorus Lady', *Smith's Magazine* (New York), December 1907, pp. 423–70.
33. Grace Luce Irwin, *Diary of a Show Girl* (New York: Moffat, Yard and Co., 1909).
34. CW4, p. 56.
35. CW1, pp. 13–22 (p. 20).
36. *Letters* 1, p. 152.
37. *Letters* 4, p. 288.
38. 'N. G.' is short for 'No Good', and *Fables of the Elite* was a collection of stories serialised in various American magazines.
39. CW4, p. 91.
40. Mansfield uses the derogatory phrase 'Johnny' twice in 'Millie' (CW1, pp. 326–30) and in a letter to Richard Murry, c. 26 December 1921, *Letters* 4, p. 354.
41. 'A Flirtation' by 'Mouche', CW2, pp. 523–9.
42. Ginsaku Ohsawa, ed., *A Katherine Mansfield Dictionary* (Tokyo: Bunashobo-Hakubunsha, 2002).
43. Harding, *The Chorus Lady* (p. 237). See also CW3, pp. 508–9, p. 508.
44. Letter to Anne Drey, 24 December 1921, *Letters* 4, p. 349.
45. KM's impersonations of Hollywood actresses are reported in an interview with Anne Estelle Rice. See 'Memories of Katherine Mansfield', *Adam International Review*, ed. Miron Grindea, 300, pp. 76–85 (p. 78).
46. Katherine Mansfield, *Something Childish and Other Stories* (London: Constable, 1924).
47. Mansfield expresses her desire to be published in American magazines in a letter to J. P. Pinker, 16 August 1921, *Letters* 4, p. 263.
48. Ian Gordon, *Katherine Mansfield* (London: Longmans, 1963), p. 15.
49. Gerri Kimber, *Katherine Mansfield: The Early Years* (Edinburgh: Edinburgh University Press, 2016), p. 247; Gerri Kimber, 'Tea, Zen and *Cosmic Anatomy*: The Mysticism of Katherine Mansfield', in *Turnbull Library Record*, 48: 1 (January 2016), pp. 21–35.

'The Chorus Girl and the Tariff'

Katherine Mansfield

If you've got the price of a Coney Island free lunch that you want to risk in reckless gambling, you can bet your stake that things would be different if I was the leader of the House majority, (whatever that is) instead of only being head spear carrier in Err & Klawlingers Mugnaficent Merry-Makers, I'd give some of those law makers a rehearsal that would make their hair stand on end. I'd put them through the amazon drill – that's what I would – and I'd have them evolute the double eight and swing around the revolving star until their empty old heads were dizzy and then some.[1] I'd make them get up at four – P.X. – in the morning after having turned in at three – N.G. – the night before, and make them eat a one-night-stand breakfast at a fourth rate hotel and then wait around in a dreary way station for the five o'clock train that never showed up until eight.[2] And all this time I'd set the thermometer at about six below. Then I'd bump 'em around on a rickety old train until seven o'clock that night and dump them off at the station of another one-night-stand town just seventeen minutes after the hotel bus driver had become tired of waiting for the train and gone back to the hotel – yes they call 'em hotels though where they get the license to the name is more than I can tell. And then I'd make 'em hike two miles through the snow to the hostelery and I'd fix it so that they got there just after the supper dishes was cleared away. And then I'd have the landlord hustle around to get up a good feed and I'd have the smell of those 'good things a cooking', just permeate the whole structure. And when the whole bunch got their mouths good and watery, then I'd trot in the stage manager and I'd have him say, 'Scoot for the show house, there, the whole blamed bunch of you. If we don't make the eleven-thirty train out of here tonight we miss the next stand. No time for supper now. Curtain goes up at seven-thirty'. Yes, that's what I'd do. And a whole lot more. I'd make those frizzled up old shrumps – Ah! but what's the use. I'm dead sick of it all. Honest to mush, if I had a handkerchief I'd cry.

The chorus girl has no bed of roses. Often she doesn't even have an upper berth in a sleeper and has to catch what sleep she can in a stuffy and draughty day coach. I believe I'd rather be a wash-woman or a female blacksmith – almost. Of course, in some ways the chorus girl has it on some folks – even on John D. Rockefeller. For instance, Jawn had to start to work at three dollars a week.[3] A chorus girl starts at fifteen. But there her superiority ends. She never gets more than eighteen no matter how long she stays in the business. And look what Jawn get [*sic*] now – something like one thousand dollars a minute. And besides he never had to wear tights. He never had to stand for hours at a time in the outer offices of managers, only to be told to call again the next day. He never had to walk the streets weary and footsore looking for work and not knowing where to lay his head. He never lived for six days on three kimmelwecks and a cent's worth of mustard. Yes, we have our troubles – us chorus girls. We have troubles enough without having a bunch of doughheads that call themselves our Great Fathers sitting up nights in Washington thinking of things on which to revise the tariff upwards in order to make it harder for the poor chorus girl. Oh! wait until women can vote! There'll be some doings. Ham sandwiches and mutton broth will be in the free column then – they'll be given away at every corner and every hotel will contain seventeen free rooms for chorus girls out of jobs. There'll be no tariff on chewing gum and lobsters will be on the free list. You know the kind of lobsters that I mean; the kind that turn red when you boil 'em – not the sort that turn yellow when you roast 'em.

Being in the chorus was no cinch before they revised the tariff – upwards. Now its – its – its [*sic*] what General Sherman said war was.[4] I couldn't bring myself to write that word. I said it once and that was bad enough. Honest to goodness Madge, they have put a bigger duty on everything that we wear; our shoes, our gloves, our underskirts, and our silk tights. It's a fright. Stockings are getting so high it takes a giant to climb into them and a millionaire to buy them. Everything has been revised upwards but our salaries. There seems to be a general tendency to remove all protection from these and let them go as low as they like. Stick to the washtubs girls. If there is any generous landlady paying you six bucks and eats a week, to wait on table from 11 to 2, stand by your job. If you know of any good, respectable family that wants a nice, clever, blond haired upstairs girl, drop me a wire. I've about come to the conclusion that shaking a broom ain't much harder than carrying a spear. And what's more you can do it all in one place. You don't have to ride a couple of hundred miles between performances. And the clothes is easier to get.

To land a job in the chorus a girl has to have a good nerve. She has to have a good voice. And what's more she has to have a good – that is there has to be enough of her to fill out a pair of tights. The nerve part is important. So is the voice. But that other part – oh my. What I mean is this. A girl with a good figure and a poor voice often slides into the chorus – a girl with a good voice and a poor, scrawny figure, never. What's that, you say you've seen lots of 'em that way on stage? Well they weren't that way when they joined. They just got that way from overwork. Did you ever notice the horses that used to pull the surface cars down dear old Broadway?[5] Did you ever see them when they came in from the West – all sleek and smooth and fat – fresh from the farms and fields? And then did you notice them six months after? My how thin and tired and punk they looked. The hardships and work of the big city has ground the very life out of them. And its [*sic*] the same with the chorus girl only she has the advantage of the make-up, and the spotlights, and wigs and the padding to help her out. If the tariff on lumber raises the price on sawdust I don't know what some of us poor old skates will do.

A regular chorus girl starts in at fifteen dollars per week. To get this fifteen she has to have a voice worth about twenty-five per and figure worth double that. Then if she's a good chorus girl and tends to business she gets a raise to eighteen dollars the second year. If she stands five foot, seven in her stockings and is built on perfect lines, she stands a good show of becoming one of the leaders. She takes her stand at the end of the first row and marks the time for the other girls to march by and takes the initiative in the drills. For this she gets twenty dollars. Sometimes, if a chorus girl stands in with the manager, she gets a job as mistress of the wardrobe in addition to her chorus position. This pays her an additional twenty-five per and puts her all to the cream. There I knew it. I knew I'd lapse into dressing room slang again. I'm with the girls so much – and they're a good bunch too – that I just can't help it and those who read this article must excuse me. I've had a good education at that, but I guess nobody will rise higher than her surroundings. At least no chorus girl. But let's see; where was I? Oh, yes, talking about salaries. The chorus is divided into three sections – the 'regulars', the 'ponies' and the 'shows'. The regulars get the least pay and the shows the most. The ponies are the little girls, those wild things who are always rushing in and rushing out again. They are required to be good dancers and they mostly get about twenty-two or twenty-five dollars a week. The manager prefers pony girls who can sing. The show girls get from thirty to thirty-five a week and some of them even more. There are some show girls who never leave Broadway and who have as many regular devotees as Anna Held and Fritzy Scheff.[6] They don't need to have any voice. Its [*sic*] the looks that count with them. They must be tall and stately and must know how to wear their clothes as if they were to the manor born. Some of 'em look like queens, don't they? Did you ever notice the second one from the left end in the show that I am with? Yes, the brunette; the one with the poise of an empress and those languidly intelligent eyes. Looks like a woman who could move worlds, don't she? Well she don't know beans. She has to sign the receipt for her pay with a cross. That's straight. You can't tell a girl's schooling by her stage presence.

It is the ambition of every chorus girl to become a star, just as it is the ambition of every boy to become a policeman. Not very many succeed though. It's easier to raise the duty on wearing apparel than it is to raise ones self [*sic*] from the level on which you start. Most careers are like many flying machines. They don't go up. And few chorus girls marry. I sometimes wonder why this is. I think it is partly because we are seldom in one place long enough to give any man a chance to propose and partly because some chorus girls behave so giddily as to bring disrepute to the class as a whole. But I want to tell you right here Bo – and you can put a heavy line where I say it – that the man who gets any of the girls in my company will be picking up a treasure. They're all wool and a yard wide. At least Florence Pattengill is. I think she admits to sixty-eight around the waist.

Of course the life of even a chorus girl has its bright moments. When we take a walk up Broadway at night for instance. And on those rare occasions when we get a night off. We have to use all kinds of subterfuges and plan all kinds of tricks to fool the stage manager. And he's usually a pretty wise gazaboo, too.[7] Any man who can manage a stageful of chorus girls has got to be wise. But, as I say, our real happy times are when we have a day off. Then we can do just as we like – we are free. Free from the everlasting jangle of the tunes that we have heard every night in the whole run of 765 performances, free from the petty gossip of the dressing room and the smell of grease paint. Free from all the taint and glare of the artificial life that we lead in canvas cities and pasteboard forests where cambric roses climb paper machie tree trunks and where an electric moon smiles down on a lovelorn tenor whose ardent and tuneful adoration is poured out more for the benefit of the audience than for the edification of the fifty-eight-year-old milk-maid who joins him in the duet. And if I may digress, will you pardon me if I ask you whether you knew that the very silken wig which he wears costs more since the tariff was revised. And so do the plum colored tights that he sports with such ill grace. But smile out, gentle reader. It ain't his fault that his mother allowed him to walk too soon. And glance at the aged milk-maid. Watch her as she skips nimbly down the path. If you had rheumatism as badly in the knees as badly as she has, you'd make a face too. But that is neither here nor there. Note the pretty shoes she wears. Note the dainty gloves. Note the lingerie she displays when she climbs the shaky barnyard fence. Protected, every bit of it, by the upward revision of the tariff. Why since this duty business, became a fad actresses can't even afford to have their diamonds stolen. In fact many of them can't have diamonds. They wear paste. It's tough enough on the stars, but think how it hits us poor chorus girls who have to buy our own stage shoes, gloves and stockings out of our munificent weekly stipend of eighteen dollars.

But as I said before, we forget all this when we have our occasional nights away. Ah! then we enjoy ourselves! No, we don't go to the Adolph-Castoria and blow ourselves.[8] What do we do? Why we stay at home mostly. Maggie Finsterbach – her that carries the spear next to me – likes to get away so that she can take her kids for a ride in Central Park.[9] Yes, sure she's married. She's only twenty-two and a fine looking girl who won't reach the sawdust stage for some time yet. Her husband died. My, but that girl does hustle, taking care of her kids until the last minute, and then rushing down to the theatre, and making up and going on for three hours, only to jump into her street clothes with her grease paint still sticking to her, and dashing madly away for an uptown car, that will carry her back to home and kids. And there's Kit McGinn. You've often seen me with her. She spends her days off with her old mother. They live in a flat on the tenth floor and the only time the old McGinn Dame gets to the street is when Kit has her annual day off. She gets a rig then and takes the old woman for a drive. And there's 'Noodles' Miller. We call her Noodles because she is the slipperiest thing you ever saw. My, but that girl can lie. She used to tell us that she spent her afternoons off, away in the country with her millionaire beau. But don't she, you say? Naw. Do you know what she does? Well, she gets the eight-year-old crippled kid of her oldest sister who married a drunkard, and takes him for a ride on an East River Ferry. That's what she does. And myself? O, I ain't had a day off in so long that I forgot what I did do. No, it is not because I don't stand in with the manager. You see the last time I had a chance to get away, was just when this crippled nephew of that Miller liar fell down the elevator shaft and near broke his back and I let her get away in my place to sit up with him. And the time before that – let me see – oh, yes, that old McGinn Dame had a stroke and I told Kit she could go. And the time before that – yes I remember now – Maggie Finsterback's oldest got the pneumonia and I said she could have my day. I guess I'll have to get those law fellows to pass a law revising upwards the tariff on good nature. I think I need the protection.

(First published in *The National Monthly*, 1909, Buffalo, NY, pp. 215–16.)

Notes

1. The 'Amazon drill' is an exercise from Genevieve Stebbins, *The Genevieve Stebbins System of Physical Training* (New York: Edgar S Werner, 1898). A spear carrier is a minor actor or singer.
2. P.X. (Post-Exchange) and N.G. (No Good) are American military slang acronyms: 'Mr Barton Wilkinson had ambitions, too. One of them was to find the prettiest chorus girl in New York [. . .] "Say", said this aristocratic young man to his chum one evening, in Monroe, "come over with me to New York tonight". | "What for?" | "Society Swirl". | "N. G.," said the other; "I've seen it."' From 'The Vengeance of Veronik', by William Hamilton Osborne, *The Smart Set*, vol. XX, 4 December 1904, p. 77. See Griffiths's essay in this volume: "'The Chorus Girl and the Tariff" by Katherine Mansfield', pp. 127–34.
3. Jawn – refers to John D. Rockefeller (1839–1937) – a word popularised in *Mr Dooley's Opinions*, by F. P. Dunne (Toronto: Copp, Clark, 1902).
4. General William Sherman (1820–91) publicly declared that war was 'Hell'.
5. A surface car is a cab or taxi.
6. Fritzy (Fritzi) Scheff's career spanned the genres of opera, theatre and cinema, and she always retained her native Austrian accent, despite living most of her life in New York. Anna Held – who appeared in London during the 1909 season of 'Miss Innocence' – tended towards light theatre.
7. Gazaboo refers to a man, boss or person of authority. A popular 1908 show title *The Runaway Girls* featured 'the main gazaboo' skit as the opening act.
8. To 'blow' is to spend money recklessly.
9. Central Park, being the main recreational area in the centre of New York City.

CREATIVE WRITING

SHORT STORY

'Mr. Brill'

Michael Hoover and Daniel Humberd

A centennial homage to Katherine Mansfield and her classic short story, 'Miss Brill'

The afternoon was brilliantly fine, the crystal blue sky marred only by the occasional cloud casting its shadow on the park below. Mr. Brill stood absorbing the view from his apartment window, consciously ignoring the lingering musty smell of disturbed soil coming from the old suit tossed upon the bed. It needed to be sent to the cleaners, but he had been putting it off for days now. It seemed all he had been doing lately was staring out of this window at the world, trying to figure out where exactly he belonged in it now. With a deep, resigned sigh, Mr. Brill made a decision. He trudged to the kitchen, returning to the bedroom with the rubbish bin. His first target was the pair of scuffed black shoes, polished only for special occasions. There wouldn't be any more of those – into the bin they went. Next he gathered up the old suit and stuffed it inside, perhaps a bit more angrily than needed, which is why he heard the rattle from the jacket's inside breast pocket. Mr. Brill paused, pulled the jacket from the bin and reached into the pocket to retrieve a memory. In his hand was a mahogany chess piece, or rather a single piece broken in two, a hand-carved queen and her broken crown. Mr. Brill remembered clearly the night she had been broken, the anger and fear and self-pity that had broken her, and the shame that had led him to scour the floorboards to recover her tiny crown. But he hadn't the heart to glue her pieces back together – she was broken, and so was he. He had instead slipped her into his jacket pocket that night and tried his best to forget about her.

With the broken queen in hand, Mr. Brill made another decision. He returned to the kitchen, grabbed a chair and carried it to the bedroom closet. Standing on the chair, he pulled a worn yet beautiful chequered wooden box from under a collection of dusty scarf boxes. Laying the wooden box on the bed, he opened it to reveal a near-complete set of carved wooden chess pieces, one half in the purple heartwood of mahogany and the other in a brilliant white maple. Each piece sang its own tune to him, reflecting the myriad hours he had spent shaving miniscule bits away until they were uniform. Yet each piece was a unique individual, even if he alone could distinguish one's individuality from the rest. Mr. Brill gently placed the broken queen and her crown into the box with the rest of the pieces and snapped the brass clasp closed. Before second thoughts could change his mind, he threw on the musty suit jacket, picked up the box and left the apartment.

He was immediately pleased he had worn the jacket, his breath puffing the slightest hint of white vapour into the refreshingly crisp air around him. As he walked the familiar path to the park, he noticed the brisk weather hadn't impacted the number of people hanging around. In fact, there were enough people that he was momentarily worried that their 'special' seat would be taken, but he found his worry unwarranted as he rounded the last corner and saw the empty stone table waiting for him. The bushes around the area had grown since he was last here – the landscaping season had ended weeks ago.

In a matter of minutes, the box was opened chequered side up, the pieces were set and he stood looking down, the broken queen in his hand. With a sigh, he placed her on the board, slipped her crown into his jacket pocket and took a seat behind his maple army. As he considered his first move, he noticed a snobbish young couple off to one side, casting furtive glances and gestures in his direction, coupled with little murmurs and laughs. Mr. Brill paused a moment to look himself over, noticing for the first time what others might see: a lonely old man in a frumpy suit jacket, playing a silly game by himself. He grunted with lack of concern for their imposed vanity and opened the game with his king's pawn.

Mr. Brill stood and shuffled around the stone table, taking a seat behind the broken mahogany queen. As he studied the board in silence, he glanced again at the couple. They were no longer casting looks in his direction. Bundled close against the light chill, they seemed wholly focused on each other, whispering and laughing – perhaps new or soon-to-be lovers, taking the time to get to know one another before moving things further along. Mr. Brill remembered the time in his life when he had done the whispering, trying to elicit those same little laughs. His memories of those times were few, but those he had were cherished. He smiled wistfully as he responded by pushing the mahogany king's pawn forward.

The maple army countered this preliminary advance by sending out its knights . . . first one, then the other, each movement eliciting a matched response by the mahogany force. The two sides' centremost pawns stood face to face now, their knights providing a covering overwatch of the front lines and its flanks. Sitting behind his maple army, Mr. Brill decided the time for positioning was over. He slid his maple king's pawn diagonally forward to push the mahogany queen's pawn off its space. A worthy sacrifice.

'Mummy, what's that smell?' a little girl asked her mother as they passed close to the stone table. Her mother shushed her, casting a sidelong glance and sour expression at Mr. Brill as they hurried past. He pretended not to notice. Children often spoke when they had no place to, and he refused to be bothered by the opinion of a brat and its brood mother. As he watched them recede, a flash of colour caught his eye on the short retaining wall they passed. Mr. Brill scowled at the graffiti some other young brat had left behind. This park was one of his favourite places, and he felt a flash of anger at the defacement of a place meant for everyone to enjoy. Selfish obnoxious children, that's what they were. Still, as he stood again to move to the other side of the table, Mr. Brill sniffed surreptitiously at his jacket collar and recoiled a bit at the stench. He gave a derisive snort; he was wearing his rubbish bin jacket. Of all the jackets in the apartment, why had he chosen this one?

He sat for a long moment on the mahogany side and studied the board, losing himself as he admired the pieces. If someone asked why he had felt compelled to carve the set, he wasn't sure that he could provide a meaningful answer. It had come about almost accidently. When closing up his shop one night, he had found the first small piece of maple on a table in the corner, left behind by some unknown patron. It was a curious thing to find in a bakery, and he had absentmindedly slipped the wooden block into his pocket with the intention of throwing it away. But later that night, as he was emptying his pockets and winding his watch, he had discovered the piece of wood again. As he studied its delightfully swirled woodgrain, something from inside the block had called to him, if only he would take the time to draw it forth. With painstaking precision and patience, he had used the tip of his penknife to work the grain, and from the block a shape had emerged. A pack of coarse sandpaper later and the first of the maple pawns appeared. He picked that first pawn up from the board – he could always pick it out, though to anyone else it looked identical to the rest. But he had held that pawn for countless hours – the first attempt always takes the longest – and now he admired his work and felt the satisfaction of creating something beautiful.

Mr. Brill was returned from his reverie by an overanimated conversation. The young lovers on the nearby bench were gone, supplanted by a pair of genteel ladies, a lifetime of stories written in the lines on their faces. They both wore their Sunday best, blue and red floral smocks with fine shoes and stockings, bundled against the cold in puffy down jackets. They reminded him of her. He didn't want to listen to their conference, desperately didn't want to intrude, but they were speaking so loudly that he couldn't help himself. It was a silly conversation, inexplicably skittering from buttons to telephones to online shopping. Mr. Brill had never been one for socialising. He much preferred the solitude of his quiet living room, or in an earlier era, the oven room of his bakery; safe spaces away from the prying eyes and ears of any who might cast judgement. He returned his attention to the game, avenging the lost pawn with his mahogany knight, purposely losing it to its maple twin before ending the series of exchanges by pushing his broken queen forward into the fray.

He shuffled back around to the maple side again. Mr. Brill found himself staring at the board, unable to decide how best to counter the gambit the mahogany army was driving at. The broken queen now controlled the centre of the board, and he did his best to consider how to drive her back before she could trap him. Something new was distracting him, though. He realised it came from the obnoxiously bright-coloured headphones on the teenager who had wandered to his side of the park and started pacing in circles nearby. His bobbing head was down, fingers tapping furiously at his phone. How could he think straight enough to do anything with that music blaring so loudly in his ears? Didn't he know the damage he was causing? Of course, no one could tell the teen otherwise; children tend to think only in the present. The kid was certain to regret his lack of forethought when he couldn't hear the high notes any more, but that would likely be decades from today.

Another couple passed by then, clearly locked in an argument but pretending that they weren't. Their anger bubbled just under the surface. 'Calm down, it's not a big deal,' he was saying, but his words only served to enrage her further. 'Don't tell me to calm down. I hate when you tell me to calm down,' she replied, her facade of normality beginning to crumble into unabated anger. The man looked lost, unsure of what to say to make things right. Mr. Brill brought his maple bishop out to threaten the broken queen in an attempt to push her back behind her lines. But the broken queen didn't respond the way he intended, instead moving to take up position behind her remaining knight, still maintaining control of the centre of the board. He castled his maple king, moving him away from conflict. As the couple walked away, Mr. Brill took the opportunity to move back around the table. As he again took a seat behind the mahogany side, he furtively watched the man slouch his shoulders, hanging his head. 'I'm sorry. I wasn't thinking.' By then they were too far away for Mr. Brill to hear her reply, but he saw the woman's arm snake around the man's waist in a clear sign of forgiveness. He had been in the man's position before – had even said those very words and elicited the very same response. It took real effort to work out the kinks, to listen to each other's complaints and compromise on solutions. In the end it had always been worth it.

He had lived nearly his entire life alone. There had been flings in his youth, but he had always found himself chasing, rather than being chased. Besides, even from adolescence he had led the life of a baker, a scion of the sunrise, leaving no time for evening carousing – the time when most youth is spent. On his nineteenth birthday his parents had gifted him a set of blackout curtains for his new efficiency apartment. At the time he had secretly scoffed at the idea of receiving curtains as a birthday gift, but they had quickly become one of the few things he used on a daily basis. Mr. Brill could now see the wisdom behind the gift. He had eventually taken over his father's bakery, and then, eventually, the comparatively voluminous apartment above it – the one in which he had grown up. It already had blackout curtains.

But in all his life he could never find the time to build more than a scant handful of meaningful relationships. Those he had were all gone now. He had never found the time to keep up the chase, and so the chase had left him behind. Indeed, he had lived nearly his entire life alone, not exactly lonely, but never quite happy in his solitude either. Mr. Brill never understood how the rest of the world seemed to flow by so effortlessly, like a dance on a stage, like choreographed chaos. He brooded on their deft interactions, watched them float along like ballet dancers, swaying to and fro between friends and lovers with an ease that he had never managed to master. It had made him turn inward on himself, and what he saw inside made him all the more bitter to what he saw outside. So he put his head into his craft, did his best to ignore the outside world, instead creating little things of ephemeral beauty that were meant to be enjoyed only once.

The teen with the headphones had wandered away again, and Mr. Brill took another long look at the graffiti on the wall, cocking his head as he studied its form. He could see this was more than a vandal's signature, more than a foolish, 'I was here.' It was a simple image: a broken lightbulb, its tungsten filament still aglow. But its colour was vibrant, the lines clean and purposeful. There was a three-dimensional aspect to it that made the glass shards of the broken bulb seem to push forth from the wall. It was clear there was meaning behind the image, even if he couldn't immediately parse it out. Mr. Brill gave a quiet smile. It was a fleeting artistic statement; the city was sure to scrub the graffiti off the wall at some point. He looked down at his chess set, his own only lasting work of art. The pieces weren't what any would call exquisitely crafted; they were clearly made by the hand of an amateur, and so he had always been reticent to share it with others. Yet this graffiti artist's creation had been shared with the world, regardless of what the world might think. Mr. Brill had shared his creation with only one other person.

It had started with a slice of honey-cake – or rather, with the intention of one, a Sunday ritual unexpectedly broken. His mention of it the next time he saw her had generated a cascade of apologies, though this hadn't been his aim. He had been genuinely curious, had grown accustomed to her visits, became concerned when she didn't arrive to claim the slice he specially withheld for her on every Sunday. She hadn't known he would sometimes bake an entire cake for the single slice he knew she would take home, or that her Sunday visits were the highlight of his week. His curiosity had started a conversation. Her weekly visits became more frequent. The growth of their affection hadn't felt like a chase; it was organic, mutual. He invited her to play chess; she had never played, so he taught her about thrusts and parries, shared with her the pieces he had spent countless hours crafting. She invited him to share a bench in the park; he had never watched the crowd, so she taught him about the elaborate play, shared with him what she had been so reluctant to share with her students. After a lifetime of solitude they had found each other. In watching the crowd with her on Sunday afternoons, he had learned to see the world from a new perspective. Sometimes they would play chess together in the park, though he would usually win those games; she would be too distracted by the play going on around her to offer a fair challenge.

Their marriage had been a struggle at times. They were both stubborn – and he tended toward obstinance, which had led to some calamitous fights – but his adoration for her had only grown with each passing year. And then, she was gone. It seemed only a moment had passed between sitting beside her as the doctor gave his diagnosis, and standing beside her grave as she was lowered into the ground. Mr. Brill plucked the broken mahogany queen from the board, turned her in his hand, studied the irregular fracture at her top. She had always preferred to play with the mahogany side; she loved its rich colour, the pattern of its grain. He had gone home only for a minute, just to pick up a fresh change of clothes, and was on his way back out of the apartment when he got the call. The chess set had been sitting on the kitchen table, a half-played match still splayed across the board. He had struck out in his grief, dashing the pieces to the kitchen floor. It was only later, upon cleaning up the mess, that he discovered he had broken one of the pieces.

Mr. Brill pulled the tiny crown from his jacket pocket and fit its matching wound to the top of the broken mahogany queen, holding the pieces together to make her whole. He then picked up the white maple queen and held the two opposing pieces side by side, studying them intently. He could fix her to be just like her maple twin, glue the broken pieces back together, but that wouldn't heal the trauma she had sustained as a result of his grief. She would always bear the imperfect jagged scar across her crown.

Just then, the tiniest of raindrops splashed on the back of his hand. Mr. Brill looked up from his daydreaming; he hadn't noticed the darkening clouds rolling in. The match unfinished, Mr. Brill quickly slid the chess pieces on to the tabletop, flipped the board over and began packing the pieces back inside. He lingered on the broken queen and her crown, considering for just a moment before packing the queen into the box and slipping the broken crown back into his pocket.

* * *

On his way home, Mr. Brill stopped at the bakery downstairs to purchase what had become their usual Sunday treat. He dropped his keys in the fluted dish on the table just inside the apartment door, laying the broken mahogany crown in alongside them. He placed the chequered box back in its usual place on the coffee table and took off his jacket, hanging it on the doorknob to be taken to the cleaners in the morning. He then made his way to the kitchen with the small package from the bakery. Mr. Brill grunted disappointment that the slice of honey-cake didn't have an almond, but he decided that was alright. He couldn't always expect it to be an almond Sunday.

The bakery's new owner clearly took pride in her work. The slice didn't have the same texture that his recipe had – it wasn't as moist, had a spongier feel. But the rendering was just as meticulous as any he had ever created, the white sugary glaze dripping just slightly over the edge, each of the eight delicate layers perfectly even with just the slightest crunch to the browned crumble crust. The balance of the smoky-sweet, caramelised honey and the savoury saltiness of the almond buttercream was rich and intoxicating, and before Mr. Brill was quite finished revelling in each bite, the evanescent delicacy before him was gone.

CREATIVE ESSAY

The Life-Affirming Words of Katherine Mansfield in a Time of Pandemic

Monica Macansantos

Near the beginning of her story 'Prelude', Katherine Mansfield makes one brief mention of Quarantine Island, in Wellington Harbour. The Burnell family are moving from their house near the centre of town to a more sprawling property in the country, and Lottie and Kezia, the two youngest daughters, are the last to leave. It is evening when they set out on a buggy sent for them, and it is the first time they have been out this late; excitedly, they turn back towards the neighbourhood where they have spent their entire lives, noticing how much smaller these familiar houses seem in the darkness, before seeing the stars in the night sky and the moon hanging over the harbour. It is at this point that they notice Quarantine Island's lighthouse shining in the middle of the bay.

Though Mansfield does not dwell on this detail – choosing instead to follow the girls as their buggy reaches the top of a hill, before they lose sight of the harbour altogether – the image of a lone, shining island in the middle of a glimmering bay anchors the rest of this scene, for it is where the overarching sense of hush evoked by the night sky, the city lights, the stars, the moon and the gold-tinged waves comes to rest.

* * *

I probably wouldn't have recognised Mansfield's Quarantine Island as the Matiu/Somes Island I knew from my Wellington days if I hadn't visited the island myself during my first year in New Zealand, and if my then boyfriend and I hadn't found the old cemetery for victims of the Spanish flu pandemic near its tiny port. One has to veer slightly away from the main trail encircling the island to find the cemetery, tucked behind native bush. Some of its headstones are so tall that they tower over the scrub grass, and if one cares to have a look at these headstones, one will notice the names of siblings, and their ages, etched in the order of their deaths. Many of the dead were children, and I wonder how it felt for my boyfriend, who had emigrated from the Philippines with his family at the age of nine, to stumble upon the graves of these children, who had likewise arrived in this country with their parents, only to meet their deaths before their ships could dock in Wellington. Some died within the same day, and some within the same week; some had parents whose names accompanied theirs on their family headstone, which also bore the name of the ship that had carried them to this small island on the other side of the world.

'There were so many incurable diseases back then, so people died young,' I remember my boyfriend saying, as we stared at these names, these dates belonging to a distant time. The unrelenting sunshine of that day made us feel as though these tragedies belonged to a faraway era, and within the safety of the present we dedicated a brief moment of silence to the dead. But soon we were making our way back to the main trail, towards the island's summit, where our eyes ached just by staring at the endless, glittering water, as we talked about a future that seemed just as bright when glimpsed from afar.

* * *

Visible from much of the city and the surrounding hills, Matiu/Somes Island is an everyday sight for Wellingtonians, occupying a permanent, though peripheral, presence in their lives. Even before the Spanish flu pandemic of 1918, the island was used as a quarantine station for immigrants from Europe entering New Zealand on board infected ships. Judging by her gentle description of the island in 'Prelude', I can imagine Mansfield growing up in its proximity, finding its presence quietly reassuring even when glimpsed from afar, in spite of its reputation for harbouring foreignness and disease.

Perhaps it was my nostalgia for New Zealand that led me to pick up my second-hand copy of Mansfield's selected stories when much of the Philippines was placed in lockdown. I was about to leave for an artists' residency in Japan when the airports were closed, and in a single day our movements became regulated and monitored in ways I never could have imagined just a few days before. Our neighbourhood had a speakerphone broadcasting orders from neighbourhood officials to stay at home; whenever we left our neighbourhood to buy groceries or medicine, we had to pass by the *barangay* office and tell them where we were going before we could be issued a quarantine pass. Checkpoints were everywhere, with armed police inspecting our quarantine passes before allowing us to proceed. I'd be buying imported chocolates to cheer myself up, only to overhear the grocery clerk telling her boss on a walkie-talkie what I was up to, and what I was purchasing.

At home with my mother, our days grew simple, unburdened of priorities that seemed to belong, as time wore on, to a different life. My thoughts were no longer directed towards a future that grew vague and uncertain as time passed, but towards the present and the everyday as I strove to maintain my own sanity within the confines of domestic life. In New Zealand, a country I had left a year and a half before for many different reasons, there were no such restrictions put in place yet, and my mind would often return to what my life was like two years ago, before I came back to a country slipping deeper into authoritarian rule.

I had picked up a copy of Mansfield's selected stories at a second-hand bookshop in Wellington shortly after had I defended my PhD thesis at Victoria University, intending to read it upon my return to the Philippines. Her patient, detailed style felt ponderous, however, and I had quickly moved on to contemporary fiction while promising myself that I'd eventually give Mansfield another go, once I had the time for her. It was this quarantine, in the end, that would force me to slow down, to pay attention to her words, while the threat of disease kept me rooted in my childhood home, unable to flee.

As the streets of our neighbourhood emptied out, the sound of birdsong began to emerge through the growing hush that seemed to hold us still. I began to sit on our front balcony in the mornings, reading Mansfield's stories while pausing every now and then to observe native birds flitting through our bougainvillea bushes, and tiny green buds emerging from the bare branches of our guava tree, which had appeared to be on the brink of death before lockdown began. Life continued at its usual pace in our garden, urging bougainvillea blossoms forth from their branches, drawing butterflies and birds to the trees and bushes surrounding our house.

Like life in our garden, Mansfield's stories unfold at a leisurely pace, taking in the way light falls across a lawn or gleams through morning mist, or the way a flower with a tiny tongue at its centre seems to be so lovingly shaped that it is 'such a waste' for it to wither and fall on to the ground. One of my writer friends once told me that reading Mansfield's work was an unpleasant experience for many Kiwis, who were forced to read her stories in high school, and I can see why her work would tax a young person's patience. Mansfield's stories draw their narrative pacing from the normal, unhurried pulse of everyday life, and one must recalibrate one's sense of narrative time in order to appreciate the description of 'a green wandering light playing over' a cup of coffee, or of a café proprietor whose longing pose beside a window seems to have become an unconscious habit of hers. I can imagine her stories being tossed aside these days by editors of literary journals due to descriptions and scenes that may feel laboured, inessential or overindulgent to a contemporary reader. Accustomed to trimming away what we deem unnecessary in the service of efficient, 'urgent' storytelling, perhaps we have lost the capacity to appreciate the rewards of a meandering description of a beach, or of a room in an abandoned house.

Mansfield's stories require a childlike sense of wonder to find magic in details that grown-ups often take for granted, such as the little almond doorknob in a gingerbread house that a young boy cannot stop thinking about in 'Sun and Moon', or the little lamp inside a doll's house that Kezia can't stop describing to her schoolmates in 'The Doll's House'. In a time when we are forced to slow down, to think in the present tense instead of hankering for what is not in front of us, I wonder if Mansfield is the writer we need right now, when our future feels uncertain and the present is all we can truly claim for ourselves.

* * *

'Prelude' was written a few years before the Spanish flu pandemic, but the story takes place much earlier in time. Inspired by her brother's visits to her London home, Mansfield began to write about her childhood in New Zealand, and time and distance were enough to soften her memories of a homeland whose narrow-mindedness and provincialism she had once chafed against. The Burnells closely resemble her own family, the Beauchamps, who also moved their young family from a smaller house in town to a larger property in the hills of Karori. Kezia, the more observant and imaginative of the three sisters in the story, may be Mansfield herself. Mansfield's antipathy towards her family, expressed overtly in her letters, is absent in 'Prelude', while appearing in a gentler form in the subsequent stories she wrote about the Burnells, such as 'At The Bay' and 'The Doll's House'. Her depictions of family life are loving and detailed, employing the smallest of gestures, mannerisms and endearments to paint a portrait of the Burnells that radiates with a quiet longing for the innocence of childhood and the safety of home.

Leslie, Mansfield's younger brother, was among the many young New Zealand men conscripted by the British to fight in the First World War. Leslie had many opportunities to visit his sister in London while he trained as an officer in England, and the memories they shared during his visits awakened a longing for her homeland, and her youth, that found full expression in a story, 'The Aloe', which was to become 'Prelude'. Her disappointment in her family and homeland was indeed justified: her parents did not exactly appreciate her literary ambitions, and her mother, worried that Mansfield was exhibiting signs of same-sex attraction, once sailed all the way from New Zealand to England to take her to a small town in Germany, where she allegedly underwent what is now known as gay conversion therapy. But Mansfield adored her brother, and the childhood they shared was, by all accounts, a happy one. Much of Mansfield's earlier fiction was set in Europe, but Leslie's visits offered her the possibility of reclaiming a past that was lost to her when she left for England, and of recreating in her fiction a cherished New Zealand that she could claim for herself.

It was grief, in the end, that fuelled her completion of 'Prelude'; Leslie was killed in Belgium in October 1915. She began writing an earlier version entitled 'The Aloe' after Leslie died, and I can imagine the urgency she felt as she wrestled with the permanence of her brother's death and the loss of a shared past. Reading 'Prelude' in 2020, in the midst of a pandemic that has made me contemplate the nearness of death in ways I never thought were necessary, I feel as though the story taunts mortality by showing what death cannot fully take away: the Wellington of Mansfield and her brother's childhood is intact, as is the feeling of childhood innocence that remains unmarred throughout the story by the petty squabbles and concerns of adults. Death, in the form of a duck's surprise slaughtering in front of the children or the image of Quarantine Island shining at night, hovers in the periphery, but does not bring this story, with all its disparate and fascinating characters, to a complete pause.

* * *

The unending tragedies playing on a reel before us as we consumed the news in recent months made the unusual stillness that filled our days feel immobilising. While I was reading Mansfield at a leisurely pace on our balcony, doctors were dying of the disease; their beaming faces would flash on our TV screen as we learned about their ages, their specialties, their tireless work on the front lines until they themselves fell ill. There was a cardiologist admired by many in his field; a *barrio* doctor who had dedicated his entire career to serving the poor; a paediatrician who had closely monitored the disease's spread in the Philippines before she herself fell ill; and a paediatric surgeon, the only doctor in the Philippines capable of separating conjoined twins, who loved riding his motorcycle around the countryside whenever he had a free day. There was a husband and wife, both doctors, who fell ill and were kept apart from each other as they fought for their lives; the husband fought hard before succumbing to the disease because he was afraid there would be no one else left to care for his autistic son.

Meanwhile, our President would deliver meandering late-night speeches peppered with insults and threats, aimed at those who dared break the quarantine. In one speech, he told the police to shoot violators; the next day, a man who had lost his patience at a checkpoint and fought with the police was shot dead. In another speech, the President proclaimed that the doctors who had died on the front lines were lucky to be able to die for their country, adding, 'If it's your time to go, then it's your time to go.'

A flight evacuating a COVID-19 patient to Japan burst into flames during take-off in Manila, killing everyone on board. A young doctor was on this flight, and shortly before boarding he told his friends on social media that he couldn't wait for this pandemic to end. He was my age, and just a year younger than Mansfield herself when she died of tuberculosis at thirty-four.

It was at this point that I began to wonder if it was possible to grow numb from despair.

* * *

Mansfield was diagnosed with tuberculosis near the end of the First World War. Her doctor advised her to give up her writing so that she could live a longer life, thinking it was best for her to reserve her bodily strength for fighting the disease. Her writing took up much of her energy, but it was something she was unwilling to surrender in order to live. Giving death full control over her life was a kind of death in itself, and it wasn't the kind of life she wanted. In her earlier work, death hovers at the corner of one's eye, a constant yet peripheral presence in the lives of her characters, who have grown indifferent to its shadows despite its occasional and brief intimations. Most of the time, the brightness of life is an overwhelming presence in itself, especially for the children in her stories, who are just beginning to come into cognisance of the world in which they live. Death is a part of this world, but life, in its infinite brightness, simply outshines it.

It was during this period, in which she travelled from resort town to resort town in Europe in search of a cure for her illness, that Mansfield turned again towards her childhood in New Zealand, which seemed far removed from the darkness and pain that now overshadowed her life. She wrote vividly about her homeland during this time, most notably in her stories 'At the Bay' and 'The Doll's House', in which the Burnells appear, as well as in the loosely autobiographical 'The Garden Party', which takes place in her childhood neighbourhood of Thorndon. Absent from these stories is the kind of cynicism one would expect from a writer who knows she will die young. The same sense of childhood wonderment present in her earlier work suffuses the descriptions and characterisations in these later stories. Her impending death may have given her a greater urgency to record life as it presented itself to her, to preserve its sharpness and vividness in her writing, even as death, which was finally impossible to ignore, asserted its presence more clearly in her work. It is referenced in a conversation Kezia has with her grandmother in 'At the Bay', in which she asks why her Uncle William died young, before wondering aloud if everyone has to die. And in 'The Garden Party', Laura directly confronts the indifference of her wealthy family when a workman is killed in an accident just below their garden – she is told that their garden party must go on, and that they cannot allow the death of a man they don't know to ruin their happiness.

Society's inability to accommodate grieving and loss also comes to the fore in her later work. In 'Life of Ma Parker', an old servant mourning the death of a beloved grandchild finds no solace in her writer employer's voyeuristic interest in her suffering, while in 'The Fly', a businessman is unexpectedly forced to reckon with his grief over losing his son six years before, and without a proper outlet, he finds a fly on his desk that he slowly tortures to death. There also seems to be a greater amount of honesty surrounding casual cruelty in Mansfield's later work: in 'The Doll's House', for instance, she unflinchingly portrays the cruelty of children in the schoolyard as they gang up on the daughters of a washerwoman. Insulting the Kelvey girls by telling them they're going to become servants when they grow up gives the other girls such a rush that 'never did they skip so high, run in and out so fast, or do such daring things as on this morning'. Cruelty seems to co-exist more closely with innocence and goodness in her later work, to the point that these qualities can exist in a single character: the Burnells' Aunt Beryl, for instance, is shown to be a sensitive and perceptive woman in 'At The Bay', while in 'The Doll's House' she shoos the Kelvey sisters away from the Burnells' front yard 'as if they were chickens', having caught Kezia showing them the doll's house that was never meant for their eyes. Guarding one's innocence against the cruelties of the world, which is a recurring theme in Mansfield's earlier work, becomes a seemingly impossible undertaking when these cruelties have existed all along within ourselves.

And yet there remains a certain optimism in her later stories that allows for the celebration of goodness in the face of cruelty, even when it is tempting to be cynical about the lasting effects of kindness in a cruel world. The girls in 'The Doll's House' ostracise the Kelvey sisters because they are told by their parents not to play with them, and their parents, who look down on Mrs. Kelvey and suspect her husband is in jail, view the Kelveys' 'moral dereliction' as a contagious disease that their children could contract through close association. It is Kezia's innocence that renders her immune to the prejudices of her parents and peers, allowing her to invite the Kelveys to her family's front yard, where the doll's house is on display, because she doesn't see why the Kelvey sisters shouldn't see this precious little house with its treasured little lamp she has told the entire school about. In the end, it is Kezia's kindness that the two girls remember, not 'the cross lady': they trade smiles by the side of the road after Aunt Beryl shoos them away, and our Else says, 'I seen the little lamp.'

* * *

My small moments of joy in this difficult time are often accompanied by guilt, since I am not on the front lines of this pandemic, where the real battles are being fought. I am fortunate to count myself among the middle class of a third world country during a lockdown that has become increasingly punitive towards the poor and has left many of its citizens to starve. It is indeed tempting to give in to a creeping sense of futility when none of us knows when this pandemic will end, and when it continues to take the lives of the best and kindest among us.

But I also think about the way Mansfield lived in the presence of death, and how a recognition of her own mortality allowed her to write honestly about death, even as life, and human kindness, continued to shine through her work. I find it difficult to ignore the light her stories have given me access to during this pandemic, especially when the alternative is to give in to the nihilism and callousness perpetuated by our President in his nightly speeches. I want to honour the lives of these doctors and nurses who have died fighting this pandemic, but I cannot give in to despair, because if their deaths are to have any meaning, this world, for which they sacrificed their lives, must contain some kindness in it, some light.

* * *

As I seek to tread carefully between joy and mourning through this pandemic, wishing to honour both without negating either feeling, I wonder if it is possible to find sanctuary in my own happiness without becoming numb to the tragedies taking place around me. Guarding my own happiness is the only way I can persevere, but how do I do this without pushing away my grief, which is also necessary for my healing?

Among the stories I've read by Mansfield, 'The Garden Party' is the one which has given me the most solace in the midst of death and despair. A worker is killed in an accident below the Sheridans' garden, and while Laura feels it is inappropriate to continue with a garden party her family has been preparing for weeks, her sister and mother dismiss her plea. Mrs. Sheridan tells her, 'People like that don't expect sacrifices from us. And it's not very sympathetic to spoil everybody's enjoyment as you're doing now,' while her sister Jose says, 'You won't bring a drunken workman back to life by being sentimental.'

Despite Laura's protests, the party goes on as planned, and while Laura continues to think about the dead man, whose family inhabits one of the 'little mean dwellings' on a street leading up to their house, she also basks in the perfection of the afternoon as she receives compliments for her beauty from guests and enjoys the music played by a hired band, whose cheery sound she had worried would bring pain to the dead man's grieving widow. After their guests leave, Mr. Sheridan mentions the man's death and the family he has left behind, and is immediately censured by his wife: '"My dear", said Mrs. Sheridan, holding up her hand, "It nearly ruined the party. Laura insisted we should put it off."' For a passing moment, even Laura finds her father tactless for mentioning the man's death, quickly catching herself when her mother comes up with the idea of collecting leftovers from the party in a basket for the grieving family, in addition to some arum lilies, because 'People of that class are so impressed by arum lilies.'

Carrying the basket, Laura descends the hill towards the dead man's house, and while she had merely intended to leave the basket outside his door, to her horror she is pulled inside when his family answers the door. While the Sheridans are determined to keep the squalor of the impoverished neighbourhood near their property at bay, the dead man's family seems intent on bringing Laura into their world and exposing the rawness of their grief to her. Even as Laura tries to escape, the dead man's sister invites her into the bedroom where the dead man is lying, drawing away the sheet covering his face for Laura to see:

> There lay a young man, fast asleep – sleeping so soundly, so deeply, that he was far, far away from them both. Oh, so remote, so peaceful. He was dreaming. Never wake him up again. His head was sunk in the pillow, his eyes were closed; they were blind under the closed eyelids. He was given up to his dream. What did garden-parties and baskets and lace frocks matter to him? He was far from all those things. He was wonderful, beautiful. While they were laughing and while the band was playing, this marvel had come to the lane. Happy . . . happy . . . All is well, said that sleeping face. This is just as it should be. I am content.

'It was simply marvellous,' Laura tells her brother upon her return. She tries to explain what she has just glimpsed, but no words can capture what she has understood about life just by looking at the dead man's face.

She has seen life's beauty in its fullest form, and she has also felt its ache.

(A version of this essay appeared in New Zealand's *The Pantograph Punch* on 10 June 2020.)

CRITICAL MISCELLANY

The Paper Knife – Patrick White and Katherine Mansfield

Oliver Stead

Many scholars of Patrick White will know of the Australian writer's fascination with Katherine Mansfield, but I suspect fewer scholars of Mansfield will be aware of the powerful influence exerted by the New Zealand-born writer on the Australian.

On 2 January 1972, by then a strong contender for the Nobel Prize in Literature, Patrick White wrote from his Sydney home to the Chief Librarian of the Alexander Turnbull Library in Wellington that he was gifting to the library a paper knife, formerly owned by Mansfield. He would be sending it in the care of his friend, Desmond Digby, who was returning to New Zealand to visit his family in Auckland, and would be paying Wellington a visit. 'Dear Sir', he wrote,

> When I was in Wellington some years ago Antony Alpers gave me a paperknife which had belonged to Katherine Mansfield, and which he had been given by L.M. I was going to leave the paperknife to the Alexander Turnbull Library in my will, but as I may not die for some time yet, and the paperknife is such a small object it could easily get lost or stolen, I would rather let you have it now.[1]

If readers will excuse a personal digression, it intrigues me that White donated the knife (I am continuing to call it a knife because Mansfield herself did, in a letter to John Middleton Murry[2]), at the same time that the Stead family was on its way to Menton, so that my father, C. K. 'Karl' Stead, could take up the Katherine Mansfield Fellowship for 1972. I was eight. While in Menton we were visited by the Fellowship's founders, Celia and Cecil Manson, and other literary New Zealanders. I remember that a lot of Karl's conversations with my mother, Kay, and others involved a mysterious person called 'LM'. 'KM' and 'LM' became inextricably linked in my mind during that year, long before I

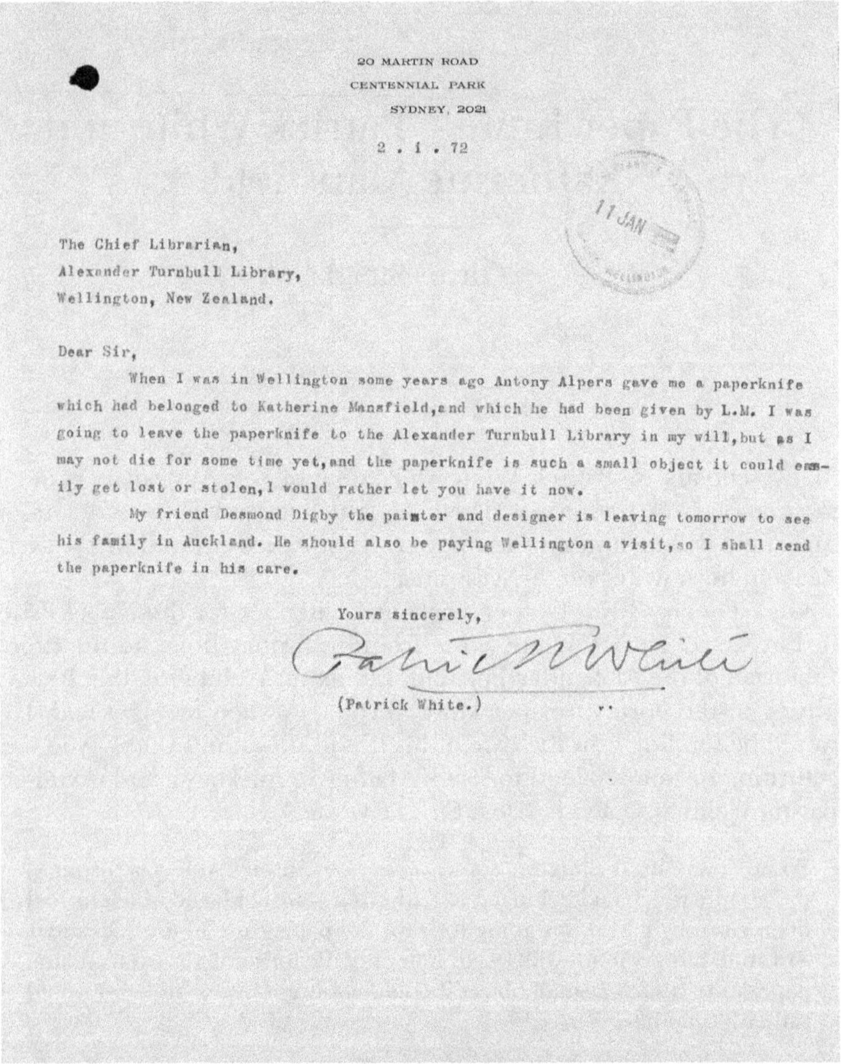

20 MARTIN ROAD
CENTENNIAL PARK
SYDNEY, 2021

2 . 1 . 72

The Chief Librarian,
Alexander Turnbull Library,
Wellington, New Zealand.

Dear Sir,

When I was in Wellington some years ago Antony Alpers gave me a paperknife which had belonged to Katherine Mansfield,and which he had been given by L.M. I was going to leave the paperknife to the Alexander Turnbull Library in my will,but as I may not die for some time yet,and the paperknife is such a small object it could easily get lost or stolen,I would rather let you have it now.

My friend Desmond Digby the painter and designer is leaving tomorrow to see his family in Auckland. He should also be paying Wellington a visit,so I shall send the paperknife in his care.

Yours sincerely,

Patrick White

(Patrick White.)

Figure 2. Letter from Patrick White to Chief Librarian, Alexander Turnbull Library, 2 January 1972. Alexander Turnbull Library Katherine Mansfield Closed file TL 2/15. Photograph courtesy of Alexander Turnbull Library. Permission to reproduce courtesy of the Patrick White Estate and Alexander Turnbull Library, National Library of New Zealand.

had any real understanding of who they were or what their relationship might be. Back home in Auckland, I recall my eye being drawn often to the spines of several first edition volumes of Mansfield's writings on the family bookshelves, including *In a German Pension*, a title I found intriguing. I don't know whether this was because the books looked inherently interesting to me, or whether they had come to acquire a talismanic significance due to Karl's preoccupation with them. Later still, aged perhaps between ten and twelve, I began to read Mansfield, struck by the vivid images, the wide-eyed, observant character of Kezia, and the very sinister story 'The Woman at the Store'. In these features Mansfield's stories functioned in the manner of 'young adult' fiction for me – much more so than Karl's novel, *Smith's Dream*, which I found unsettling, or, even more disturbing, Henry Miller's *Tropic of Cancer*, *Tropic of Capricorn* and *Sexus, Nexus and Plexus*, Allen Ginsberg's *Howl*, William Burroughs's *Naked Lunch*, Jack Kerouac's *On the Road*, Norman Mailer's *The White Negro* and Thomas Pynchon's *The Crying of Lot 49*, all of which I encountered on those same shelves, much too young, and found apocalyptic.

Fast forward some three-plus decades to 2010, when, as Exhibitions Curator at the National Library of Australia, I first became aware of the knife. This talisman I encountered while researching White for a 2012 exhibition commemorating the one hundredth anniversary of his birth. I was fascinated by the greenstone-handled knife with its connotations of New Zealand and its association with Mansfield. I first learned of the knife through reading David Marr's magnificent twin tomes, *Patrick White: A Life* and *Patrick White: Letters*,[3] my interest intensified through the same wistful nostalgia for my home country I had felt as a child and as a teenager, jogging along behind Karl on the Mansfield trail, with my family in France and London. I wanted very much to use the knife in the exhibition as a symbol of White's fascination with Mansfield's stories, letters and journals, and their profound influence on his own fiction and correspondence. I liked the idea that the knife might add a Kiwi element into an international story which was becoming overwhelmingly Australian in the telling. So I was dismayed to find, rather too late, that the knife was not, in fact, in Canberra but in Wellington, at the Alexander Turnbull Library, part of the National Library of New Zealand. The reason for this oversight lay in my reading of *Patrick White: A Life*, in which David Marr describes the knife, stating that 'it remained among [White's] most valued possessions'.[4] Marr was evidently not aware of White's gift to the Turnbull when writing his biography. I therefore assumed, wrongly, that the knife resided in the 'realia' collection of Australia's National Library, along with Patrick's glasses. By the time I realised the knife was actually at the Turnbull, it was too late to request its loan for an exhibition already overfreighted with loans.

Later still, in my present role as Curator, Drawings, Paintings and Prints at the Turnbull, I had my first proper encounter with the knife, in the flesh as it were. Because my role entails looking after the quaintly called 'Curios' collection, I also took on the day-to-day housekeeping and administration of other three-dimensional items of Mansfield memorabilia in 'Curios', including her chair, typewriter, items of her clothing, and two locks of hair purporting to be hers. After thirteen years of repatriating human remains in a previous curatorial role, I viewed the hair somewhat circumspectly. But now I had a chance to investigate the knife and its extraordinary provenance more closely.

What could be the background, context and possible motivations for White's presentation of the knife to the Alexander Turnbull Library in 1972? White's letter to the Turnbull's Chief Librarian, A. G. Bagnall, suggests that serious concern for the safety of the object was one motivation. David Marr notes that, at the time, White was very concerned about the possibility of items going missing from the house at 20 Martin Road, Sydney, which he shared with his partner, Manoly Lascaris.[5] He and Manoly had recently returned from an extended tour of the USA and Europe, and White was apoplectic to discover items missing from the property, which had been tenanted in their absence. At more or less the same time, White had learned that the whole area around Martin Road, on the fringe of Centennial Park, was to be bulldozed to make way for facilities needed, should Australia be successful in its bid to host the Olympic Games. He was concerned about what might happen to his extensive collection of Australian paintings, if he and Manoly were forced to move.

In 1972, White also knew that he was a serious contender for the Nobel Prize in Literature, and was corresponding extensively with the Swedish critic Ingmar Björkstén, who was lobbying for him to win the prize. That year, his nomination was pipped at the post by that of Aleksandr Solzhenitsyn, but he expected to be nominated again the following year. In 1973, his nomination won a narrow victory over that of Saul Bellow, the citation curiously mentioning his introduction of a 'new continent' into literature.[6] In years to come, White would champion, unsuccessfully, a nomination to be made for the New Zealander Janet Frame, of whom he had written in 1963 to Ben Heubsch of the Viking Press, New York, that her novel *Owls Do Cry* had 'bowled him right over', making him feel that he had always been 'a few steps out from where I wanted to get in my own writing'.[7] In the same letter, he mentioned his correspondence with Antony Alpers and talked about the 'despair and confusion under the simple, uncomplicated New Zealand surface'. 'I shouldn't be surprised if any New Zealander took a gun to his neighbour,' he opined, going on to say that he laughed when the Queen referred to New Zealand as 'this happy country' in a speech she had recently made in Auckland.[8] In gifting the paper knife to New Zealand, he may have been affirming his own hard-won literary accomplishment and survival as an Australian author, and also acknowledging the many literary friends he had made in New Zealand through his cousin, Margaret (Peggy) Garland, née Withycombe.

White's first encounters with Mansfield's fiction took place in 1930, at the family home of Lulworth, Sydney, on his return from the UK, where he had been a pupil at Cheltenham College. His mother, Ruth, had a volume of Mansfield stories on her shelves, and he quickly became a 'passionate admirer' of them, especially 'At the Bay'.[9] He was also intrigued by Mansfield's connections to D. H. Lawrence, whose writing he also admired, enjoying the evocation of New South Wales scenery in *Kangaroo.* Mansfield also had relatives among the Beauchamps of Sydney, providing an Australian connection for White to savour.

Mansfield's influence on White's fiction has been widely noted. Without going into a detailed critical comparison of their respective works, one has only to think of the similarities in *mise-en-scène* evident in Mansfield's 'The Garden Party', for example, and the opening scenes of White's novel *Voss,* which involve a garden party, to recognise the literary debt owed by the Australian writer to the New Zealander.

White was already writing novels when he left Australia again for university at Cambridge in 1932. While studying, he read Mansfield's letters and journals, published in 1927 and 1928, and was intrigued by her unflattering portrait of Lawrence.[10] In 1934, he made a literary pilgrimage to Zennor, where Mansfield and Murry had stayed with Lawrence and his wife, Frieda. When he got back to Cambridge, he submitted poems to the *London Mercury* and was thrilled to have them accepted. So White earned his literary début in the journal that had published Mansfield and Lawrence before him.[11] In Germany in 1936, White journeyed to Rügen and the *Schloss* of Mansfield's cousin, Elizabeth von Arnim, whose writing he also greatly admired.[12]

In 1961, White and Lascaris were living together on their lifestyle block, or smallholding, called Dogwoods, at Castle Hill outside Sydney. A frequent correspondent and occasional visitor was his first cousin, Peggy Garland. British-born Peggy was then living rather unhappily in Wellington with daughters Tanya and Sally, and sons David, Nick and brain-damaged Philip, who needed much care. All would soon leave the family home in Kilbirnie. Peggy found strength in adversity as a beloved friend of Wellington's leading intellectual families, many of whom became lifelong correspondents.[13]

Five years earlier, Peggy's philandering husband, Tom Garland, a doctor and pioneering medical administrator, had returned to the UK, leaving Peggy and the children behind in Wellington. To ease her stressful domestic situation, Peggy found a congenial lodger in the New Zealand scholar and author Antony Alpers, whose 1953 biography of Mansfield, published by Knopf, was considered the most significant of its time.[14] In the course of many years of research, Alpers had acquired several pieces of Mansfield memorabilia, befriending Ida Baker – L.M. – from whom he had acquired the paper knife in appreciation of his work.[15] Preparing to leave permanently for Britain herself, Peggy was keen for White to visit her in Wellington before her departure. He arrived by air in March 1961. The visit inspired him to write some letters which, to a New Zealander, reveal an uncanny, almost prescient insight into the Kiwi zeitgeist, all the more extraordinary considering the brevity of his visit. Wellington, he informed Ben Heubsch, 'makes Australia seem like a rubbish dump, and yet with all this unspoiled beauty there are the most astonishing outbreaks of human violence and youthful degeneracy'.[16] To Frederick Glover he wrote,

> Peggy's lodger, Antony Alpers [. . .] went out of his way to show me a lot of interest. He took me to the various houses in which KM had lived. The family seems to have gone through a series of increasingly impressive colonial mansions. The house of *The Garden Party* was particularly fascinating. Antony took me to the Turnbull Library, and we looked at a lot of original letters and notebooks, some of them not normally produced (Katherine had a rather hectic purple-ink phase while a girl in Wellington), and when I left he presented me with a little paper-knife in greenstone and silver, rather *fin-de-siècle* in style, which had belonged to her.[17]

If White was fascinated by Mansfield's letters, he was also a little repelled. To Marshall Best he declared, 'letters are the devil. I always hope that any that I have written have been destroyed [. . .] Katherine Mansfield is a good example of the letter-writer traduced,' observing that her letters and notebooks reveal her as a 'monster of sensibility and egotism', but he confessed to being intrigued by the 'private, sometimes automatic outpourings'.[18] Alpers remained friends with White and stayed with him and Lascaris in Sydney on several occasions.

White's encounter with Mansfield's letters and notebooks at the Turnbull had lasting consequences for his own notes and correspondence. Having decided to leave Dogwoods in 1964, White ordered Lascaris to burn much of his manuscript material, evidently to avoid leaving a legacy of the kind of monstrous 'sensibility and egotism' he had seen in Mansfield's material at the Turnbull. According to David Marr, 'a bonfire of letters and manuscripts burned for two days in a pit behind the house before the two men left'.[19] Years later, White would declare, in a letter to the director-general of the National Library of Australia,

> I can't let you have my 'papers' because I don't keep any. My MSS are destroyed as soon as the books are printed. I put very little into notebooks, don't keep my friends' letters as I urge them not to keep mine, and anything unfinished when I die is to be burnt.[20]

Yet after White's death, these claims turned out to be not entirely true – he left a substantial legacy of manuscripts and letters, now in the National Library of Australia.

But to return to the knife. White's gift to the Turnbull Library was both generous and emblematic. But how was it received? Chief Librarian A. G. Bagnall's rather less than effusive reply to White's letter is as follows:

> Dear Mr White,
>
> I was most interested to receive your letter of 2 January in which you kindly advise that you are sending across to us per Mr Desmond Digby a paperknife which had belonged to Katherine Mansfield, given to you by Antony Alpers. Coincidentally, L.M. through our Manuscripts Librarian Mrs Margaret Scott, who has been working on Mansfield material in France and England during the last year, has presented the library with K.M.'s typewriter, while Antony Alpers has arranged with someone in California to let us have a doll which she gave to a friend leaving New Zealand over sixty years ago. So this is indeed the season of homing Mansfield relics. Your thoughtful action is much appreciated.[21]

There are some suggestions in notes among the Turnbull's internal files that Bagnall was, in fact, less than enthusiastic about receiving 'relics' into the library's collection. The doll that he mentions is the charming 'hussif' (housewife) doll, intended for use as a needle holder, that a young Kathleen Beauchamp made in 1901 or 1902 for her teacher, Rebecca Howell, who was leaving New Zealand for the United States. According to the provenance note in the library's catalogue record for the doll, Rebecca Howell gave it to another pupil called Emma Knox some time before September 1956, and the doll 'later became the property of Wellington Girls' College'.[22] The doll was finally donated to the Turnbull by Wellington Girls' High School in 1991. There is no mention in the record of Alpers's unsuccessful efforts to interest Bagnall in the doll. At some point, though, the hussif doll did come into Alpers's possession. On 5 April 1972, in a postscript to a letter penned from Queen's University, Canada, to Margaret Scott, he mentioned the doll, and said that it would be coming to the Turnbull Library in his trunk.[23]

None the less, the Turnbull *was* receiving relics directly from

L.M., most recently Mansfield's tiny, beautiful Corona typewriter. A typewritten library internal memo dated 20 February 1972 lists these, ironically, with the typewriter repeated at the bottom of the list in ballpoint, because it arrived, distressingly late, in a separate shipment:

> Articles received from Miss Ida Baker
> Complete first draft of her book Katherine Mansfield: The Memories of LM (Many variations from the published version).
> Typescript copies of 9 letters from S.S. Koteliansky to Ida Baker. (Originals in Berg Collections, New York Public Library.)
> One original letter from S.S. Koteliansky to Ida Baker (missed when the others were sold).
> Ida Baker's pocket diary for last months of KM's life.
> Photocopy of KM's inscription in the copy of Bliss which she gave to Ida Baker on publication.
> KM's copy of Of the imitation of Christ given to her by her cousin Jinnie Fullerton when the latter was trying to convert KM to Roman Catholicism. Contains KM's pressed wild flowers picked on walks in the S. of France.
> Negatives of photographs of KM most of which have never been printed.
> Sundry letters to Miss Baker.
> KM's handbag mirror, silk fan, fruit knife, Chinese jacket, brooch, typewriter, small leather purse, etc.
> Photocopy of Brave Love and Notebook manuscripts.
> KM's typewriter.[24]

LM had given the fruit knife to Margaret Scott personally. In April 1970, Scott wrote to Cherry Hankin:

> I'm sorry you were here a bit too soon to see the gift I received from Ida Baker yesterday. It is a little green pocket knife which KM always carried in her handbag and used for fruit and for sharpening pencils when travelling. It smells of tobacco. It will end up in the Turnbull collection of Mansfieldiana, of course, but at the moment I am enjoying the feeling that it is mine.[25]

In the end, though, Scott gave the green, Bakelite-handled knife not to the Turnbull, but to the Katherine Mansfield Birthplace Society.[26]

What was the significance of the paper knife to Mansfield? We do know something of this from a letter she wrote to Murry in 1919:

> Your life is so dreadfully hard I feel – I ought to give you all that's fair – L.M. has gone off to 'look' at 'Bawdygerra' as she calls it & wont be back till evening so I'm quite alone. Now I've come in to get out of the glare and am sitting in my room – Your spectacle case is on the mantlepiece. On the table with the Russian bottle & Ottoline's book & the green paper knife is your spoon I don't use it. I cant have it washed and polished here. I only eat fairy soup out of it.[27]

Clearly, the paper knife was of great sentimental value to Mansfield. While researching this essay, I decided to see if I could identify its manufacture. This turned out to be much easier than expected. From 1903 to 1905, the combination bookmark and paper knife turns up with startling regularity in illustrated advertisements placed by Stewart Dawson & Co, jewellers, in New Zealand newspapers. Using a surprisingly effective 'simple-stupid' approach, I typed 'greenstone bookmark' into *Papers Past,* the digitised newspaper website of the National Library of New Zealand.[28] Not only did I get a number of direct hits providing illustrations of the knife, but I found its price, 4/6, and learned that, for the same price, one could obtain a similar button hook. The price is modest for this 'nice present to send Home' (that is, the UK, always referred to as 'Home' by early colonials). Within the same frame, a pair of elegant gold sleeve links is illustrated, in different styles. These could be had in 9 carat for 21 shillings, or 45 shillings for 15 carat. Grouping these items together was evidently effective advertising, as, under the heading 'Presentations', the *Otago Daily Times* for 16 May 1904 reports that an appropriately named Mr Studd was the recipient of links and bookmark, in honour of his recent 'mission' in Dunedin:

> In compliance with the wish of the choir and workers of his recent mission, Mr Studd was photographed with them in First Church grounds on Saturday afternoon. An adjournment was then made to the Young Men's Christian Association Hall, for a farewell praise and prayer meeting. Before separating, Mr WL Logie [. . .] was asked to be spokesman and make a small presentation to Mr Studd. This took the form of a set of gold-mounted greenstone sleeve-links and a silver paper-cutter and bookmark with greenstone handle.[29]

In view of the suggestion of the jeweller that the paper knife would make 'a nice present to send Home', and the actions of Mr Logie and the choir and workers of the mission in farewelling Mr Studd (who, no doubt, was going Home), it would seem likely that Mansfield's own combination paper knife and bookmark in silver and greenstone was given to her as a parting gift and memento of New Zealand, before she left for Home, either in 1903 or in 1908. As she matured, it must have become for her a potent symbol of her expatriate identity.

Certainly, the paper knife held sentimental value for others in the colony. The *New Zealand Herald* for 11 March 1905 carries a 'lost and found' notice for one lost in Auckland: 'LOST, near Queen-street. A silver-mounted Greenstone Combined Paper Knife and Bookmark. Reward. – A.S. Patterson & Co., Custom-street'.[30] This notice reminds me forcibly of the 'immemorial' notice in the shop window of 'At the Bay':

Figure 3. Illustrated advertisement for Stewart Dawson & Co, *Otago Witness*, 12 August 1903 Issue 2578, p. 18. Ref: N-P-2165-18. Photograph courtesy Alexander Turnbull Library, National Library of New Zealand.

LOST! HANSOME GOLE BROOCH
SOLID GOLD
ON OR NEAR BEACH
REWARD OFFERED[31]

Similarly, it conjures up the notice, 'in a deep black frame' above Fenella's grandpa's bed in 'The Voyage':

Lost! One Golden Hour
Set with Sixty Diamond Minutes
No Reward is Offered
For It Is GONE FOR EVER![32]

Coda – Patrick White in Menton

In 1976, Patrick White and Manoly Lascaris toured the South of France, armed with an edition of the letters and journals of Mansfield as a travel guide. He thought her 'very good on the feel and the look of that part of the French coast, and her rather dreadful outpourings helped me when I was gathering material for the French section of *The Twyborn Affair*'.[33] They visited the Villa Isola Bella in Menton, where they were welcomed by Katherine Mansfield Fellow Michael King. During their visit, King contrived, with great difficulty, to have White meet the deputy mayor of Menton in an attempt to influence the French authorities to restore funding to the Mansfield Fellowship, which had been cut off due to New Zealand protests against French nuclear testing in the Pacific. At the formal reception, the deputy gave a florid speech and White was invited to respond. As King described it, White said 'clearly, in his beautifully modulated voice, "Actually this sort of thing gives me the shits."'[34] Not surprisingly, French funding for the Fellowship was not restored as a result of White's visitation in Menton.

In 1980, the Viking Press in New York brought out *The Life of Katherine Mansfield,* Antony Alpers's long awaited improvement on his 1953 *Katherine Mansfield: A Biography.* On the jacket cover, verso, was a typically pithy vote of praise from White:

> A skilful unravelling of the web of literature, deceit, friendship, and feud till now clinging to Katherine Mansfield. A New Zealander himself, Alpers is well equipped to interpret the childhood idyll; but he is equally good on the brittle bitcheries of Garsington and Bloomsbury, and the stations of Katherine Mansfield's European purgatory in her trial by tuberculosis and early death at Fontainebleau.[35]

Figure 4. Photographer unknown, Patrick White and Michael King at the Villa Isola Bella, Menton, 1976. National Library of Australia, Patrick White Papers, MS9982 File 30 Box 2. Photograph courtesy of National Library of Australia.

Notes

1. Patrick White to A. G. Bagnall, 2 January 1972, Alexander Turnbull Library (ATL), Katherine Mansfield Correspondence, Closed file TL 2/15.
2. *Letters* 3, p. 51.
3. David Marr, *Patrick White: A Life* (Sydney: Random House Australia, 1991). David Marr, ed., *Patrick White: Letters* (Sydney: Random House Australia, 1994).

4. Marr, *A Life*, p. 376.
5. Marr, *A Life*, p. 507.
6. Marr, *A Life*, p. 535.
7. Marr, *Letters*, pp. 218–19 (White to Ben Heubsch, 17 February 1963).
8. Marr, *Letters*, pp. 218–19.
9. Marr, *A Life*, p. 100.
10. Marr, *A Life*, p. 122.
11. Marr, *A Life*, p. 123.
12. Marr, *A Life*, p. 145.
13. Diane Beatson and Peter Beatson, eds, *Dear Peggy: Letters to Margaret Garland from her New Zealand Friends* (Palmerston North: Massey University, 1997).
14. Antony Alpers, *Katherine Mansfield: A Biography* (New York: Knopf, 1953).
15. I have been unable to confirm the date of L.M.'s gift of the knife to Alpers; nevertheless, White's 1972 letter to the Turnbull Chief Librarian does confirm that Alpers told White he was given the knife by L.M.
16. Marr, *Letters*, p. 183 (White to Ben Heubsch, 15 March 1961).
17. Beatson and Beatson, p. 63 (White to Frederick Glover, 5 April 1961).
18. Marr, *Letters*, p. 185 (White to Marshall Best, 7 April 1961).
19. Marr, *Letters*, p. 266.
20. Marr, *Letters*, p. 492.
21. Patrick White to A. G. Bagnall, 2 January 1972. ATL, Katherine Mansfield Correspondence, Closed file TL 2/15.
22. ATL, Curios-028-047, available at <https://tiaki.natlib.govt.nz/#details=ecatalogue.77287> (last accessed 28 September 2020).
23. Antony Alpers to Margaret Scott, 5 April 1972. ATL, Katherine Mansfield Correspondence, Closed file TL 2/15.
24. ATL, Katherine Mansfield Correspondence, Closed file TL 2/15.
25. Margaret Scott to Cherry Hankin, 20 April 1970. ATL, Katherine Mansfield Correspondence, Closed file TL 2/15.
26. Katherine Mansfield Birthplace Society, Ref. KMBS 1067.2. Laurel Harris, Mary Morris and Joanna Woods, eds, *The Material Mansfield: Traces of a Writer's Life* (Auckland: Katherine Mansfield Birthplace Society and Random House New Zealand, 2008), p. 82.
27. *Letters* 3, p. 51.
28. National Library of New Zealand, *Papers Past* website, available at <https://paperspast.natlib.govt.nz/> (last accessed 28 September 2020).
29. *Otago Daily Times*, 16 May 1904, available at <https://paperspast.natlib.govt.nz/newspapers/ODT19040516.2.45?query=greenstone+bookmark&snippet=true> (last accessed 28 September 1920).
30. *New Zealand Herald*, 11 March 1905, available at <https://paperspast.natlib.govt.nz/newspapers/ODT19040516.2.45?query=greenstone+bookmark&snippet=true> (last accessed 28 September 1920).
31. Katherine Mansfield, 'At the Bay', in Vincent O'Sullivan, ed., *The Complete Stories of Katherine Mansfield* (Auckland: Viking, 1988), p. 229.
32. Katherine Mansfield, 'The Voyage', in O'Sullivan, p. 330.
33. Marr, *A Life*, p. 567 (White to Alan Williams, 2 September 1979).
34. Marr, *A Life*, p. 569, n. 25; p. 708 (Michael King to David Marr, 7 October 1989, 'quoting from a letter of August 1976').
35. Antony Alpers, *The Life of Katherine Mansfield* (New York: Viking, 1980).

Appearances Matter: Katherine Mansfield and the Photographic Record

J. Lawrence Mitchell

Kathleen Beauchamp's contemporary, Canadian Marion Ruddick, left a now well-known eye-witness account of how shamefully the ten-year old was greeted by her mother just back from nine-months abroad in 1898: 'Well, Kathleen, I see you're as fat as ever,' she said by way of greeting.[1] The surviving photograph of Mansfield at about that age really does not support the put-down, though the remark itself has sometimes licensed critical acquiescence. Antony Alpers, in many ways a sympathetic biographer, set the tone with: 'Family snapshots of the time show a solemn little podge, dressed identically with her sisters and wearing a resentful frown behind her steel-rimmed glasses.'[2] Kathleen Jones sees the young Mansfield as 'plumper than her sisters' and describes 'the stubborn, direct gaze scowling at the observer from family photographs'.[3] In fact, what definitively distinguished Mansfield from her sisters was that she alone among the children wore spectacles.[4] It is unlikely that Annie Beauchamp's comment was out of character and Mansfield, no doubt, endured many such remarks in private.[5] Hardly surprising, then, that she came to see herself as an outsider and an 'ugly duckling', like Juliet, who 'lived in a world of her own' in the early (1906) autobiographical story by that name.[6] Hardly surprising, too, that, for Mansfield in adulthood, appearances had come to matter a lot. She was always fastidious[7] about her appearance, and obviously took great pains about the way she dressed and how she styled her hair; but, at the same time, she was something of a shape-shifter, a chameleon who could baffle friends with her ability to transform herself.[8] Many years after her death, Richard Middleton Murry, her brother-in-law, still recalled the impression she made: 'Katherine was a head-turner. The mode from Paris, the brown velvet jacket with silver buttons, the short skirt, the coloured stockings, the Spanish–Japanese hair-do, the high heels, the immaculate turnout.'[9]

The many surviving formal studio portrait photographs of Mansfield speak directly to her desire to control her self-image – how she wanted to appear to her distant family in New Zealand and Canada, to friends, to lovers and to the world at large.[10] Unfortunately, much remains uncertain (or unaddressed) about important aspects of these images – the original photographer and/or studio, the location, the date, the *raison d'être* for the photograph – and this essay takes advantage of the availability of now published letters to help resolve some of the issues. Inevitably, of course, some photographs have been lost or did not survive. Pat Lawlor, for example, mentions a conversation with Mabel Tustin, a contemporary of Mansfield's, in which she said that Eric Waters 'had unintentionally destroyed interesting photographs and papers of Katherine Mansfield interest, possibly also a beautiful miniature of her grandparents'.[11] And if George Bowden, Mansfield's ill-served first husband, was ever the recipient of a 'special' photograph of his wife, it has left no trace. Yet about one portrait photograph in particular we know a good deal, though no print or negative has yet been located in any of the major archives – the 'birthday' photograph Mansfield sent Garnet Trowell in 1908.

The story begins with a letter from Garnet in mid-September, to which Mansfield replied on 17 September 1908. Her reply (headed 'Midnight') is worth quoting at length:

> My dearest, I opened your letter just now and the three photographs fell into my thrilled and happy hands – Now you are framed on my writing table – you are on a little low shelf by my bed [. . .] so your face shall be the last thing I see when I blow out the light [. . .] I think they are splendid – they are you. I've been trying to tell you which one I like best, but each one I look at is so precious that I really cannot [. . .] I must send you one next month of myself [. . .] but funds won't permit until October.[12]

Then, on 2 October 1908, she reported, 'Today I had my photograph taken for you – but the proofs do not come until next week, and I shall send you copies the week after.'[13] Finally, on 12 October 1908, she wrote from St John's Wood, where she was staying with the Trowell family: 'Histed is sending you one of my photographs to arrive on my birthday. Après tout, my darling, my birthdays belong to you. So I send this remembrance.'[14] Luckily, Garnet Trowell preserved these letters from Mansfield, so we know exactly the date on which the portrait was made, as well as the photographer – Ernest Walter Histed (1862–1947), whose studio at 42 Baker Street claimed to be 'Under Royal Patronage' and who catered to celebrities.[15] If we believe anything of Histed's magniloquent claims for his 'photographic studies from life', the portrait

Mansfield sent her lover must be accounted a great loss. He boasted that 'the character of the sitter is brought out by the artist in a manner which has, up to the present, only been possible in a painting'.[16] But why was the photograph not preserved along with the letters? Could it have been deemed a necessary sacrifice at the time of Garnet's marriage in 1923 or perhaps at his death in 1947?

After the ill-fated collection of short stories, *In a German Pension* (1911), Mansfield's next collection of stories did not appear until 1920. A favourable review of the two little publications *Prelude* and *Je ne parle pas français* in the *Times Literary Supplement*[17] prompted publisher Michael Sadleir to write to John Middleton Murry, expressing Constable's wish to 'publish a volume of Katherine's stories', as well as a new edition of *In a German Pension.*[18] Murry forwarded the letter to Mansfield, enquiring about her ongoing discussions with a different publisher, Grant Richards, and suggesting an opportunity to negotiate advantageous terms for publication. Soon thereafter, he secured a £40 advance on 15 per cent royalties from Constable for what would become *Bliss and Other Stories.* Sadleir had also expressed his willingness to include 'some little drawings by Anne Rice', and Murry took it upon himself to agree.[19] Perhaps remembering the difficulties over J. D. Fergusson's line drawings for *Prelude,* Mansfield summarily dismissed the plan, saying 'Anne's drawings don't matter.'[20] After he had read the book manuscript, Sadleir sought some changes. He judged 'The Wind Blows' to be 'on the trivial side' and specified six 'excisions' he wanted in 'Je ne parle pas français'.[21] These Mansfield vehemently resisted at first, insisting 'Ill never consent. Ill take the book away first.'[22] Yet the next day she conceded: 'I feel I was too undisciplined about my story & Constable. I leave it to you.'[23]

By late 1920, publication was imminent and Mansfield gratefully acknowledged Murry's efforts on her behalf: 'a thousand thanks for managing the Constable affair'.[24] Meanwhile, Clement Shorter, editor of *The Sphere,* had approached Constable with a request for a photograph of Mansfield to accompany a preliminary announcement of the book. Since she was still in Menton (France), the request was, quite reasonably, sent to Murry, who had been representing her literary interests. 'In all innocence', he recalled years later, he gave them a photograph that he 'particularly treasured' and still thought of as 'a beautiful photograph of her as she was in 1913'.[25] Unfortunately, when Mansfield received a clipping of the announcement from her press agency (dated 6 November 1920), she was furious at the photograph selected and fired off a protesting telegram to her husband,[26] followed by letters to him and to Michael Sadleir on the same day. Her language is extravagant –

she wants the photograph burned; it is 'a hideous old photograph' that makes her appear to have 'beastly eyes & long poodle hair & a streaky fringe', she complains to Murry;[27] and it is 'like a turnip or even a turnip manqué', she tells Sadleir.[28] In fact, by any measure, it is an attractive portrait from the Adelphi Studio on the Strand (London), created well before illness had taken its toll on her appearance. She is shown as fuller in the face, with a more traditional hairstyle, and wearing the green-stone earrings her mother had given her on her nineteenth birthday.[29] Antony Alpers said the photograph showed her 'in good health, if a trifle sulky' and suspected it was merely 'an *apparent* provocation' for her outburst.[30] To be sure, such an innocuous photograph hardly seems to warrant her multiple protests and overwrought reaction, and others in the family cherished it. In 1930, her sister Vera even commissioned a hand-coloured copy as a present for their father.[31] Yet, upon Mansfield's initial verbal assault, Murry was 'dumbfounded' and found 'the violence of Katherine's reaction almost incomprehensible except as a psychological effect of her pthisis', as he later reflected.[32] What especially galled him at the time was his wife's suggestion that he knew that she 'hated this thing. And you did possess other photographs of mine that you knew I did not mind.'[33] This is one of those not infrequent 'misunderstandings' between the 'two tigers', as they were sometimes known, in which, for once, Murry seems unjustly maligned.

A more plausible explanation for Mansfield's unhappiness with the repudiated photograph emerged in a subsequent letter. She reminded her husband that she had been 'ill for nearly four years – and I'm changed changed – not the same',[34] thereby seeming to intimate that the experience of life – indeed, the suffering – from which her work had grown needed to be reflected in her appearance. To Constable, she wrote acidly that, 'Instead of advertising *Bliss,* it [the photograph] looked to me as though it ought to describe How I Gained 28lb in One Month.'[35] There may also have been some feelings of guilt or embarrassment, since the photograph so innocently chosen was evidently the very one Mansfield had sent Francis Carco in anticipation of their brief dalliance, fictionalised in her story 'An Indiscreet Journey' (1915), as Murry much later surmised.[36]

Hastily, Mansfield sent Sadleir a substitute, a recent photograph in postcard form, 'in case anyone should ask my publishers for a more-or-less likeness'.[37] She had, as it happened, visited a local studio on 4 November to have her photograph taken as a surprise for her husband and recounted the experience for him: 'The photographer took off my head & then balanced it on my shoulders again at all kinds of angles.'[38] The following day, she added: 'Ill post you my photos on Wednesday

[November 10]. One is looking bang at you *like you asked for* [my italics] and one half-bang.'[39] With these specifics, we can confidently identify and date the 'bang' photograph as the head-and-shoulders shot that she sent Sadleir for publicity and which was subsequently used on the Constable dust-jacket, and the 'half-bang' photograph as the one she would send to Knopf in New York. The couple had obviously discussed getting an up-to-date portrait photograph of her and Murry had expressed his preference for a full frontal shot, one 'looking bang at you'. But the results were not yet available when Murry was asked for a publicity photograph.

A few days after Mansfield's request to Sadleir to keep the new photograph for future publicity purposes, she sent a telegram with a quite different, and far bolder, request: 'COULD YOU ARRANGE FOR NEW PHOTOGRAPH ALREADY SENT BY ME TO APPEAR ON WRAPPER OF BLISS BLOCK WILL BE SUPPLIED BY MURRY'.[40] Here, surely, she is explicitly asking for a design feature the publisher had never contemplated and that is nowhere broached in surviving correspondence. Constable was an old and well-established firm – once Sir Walter Scott's publisher, and in Mansfield's day, George Bernard Shaw's and Walter de la Mare's. Constable dust-jacket designs were decidedly conservative, even staid. So, the now rare *Bliss* dust-jacket (white printed in black; not seen by Mansfield bibliographer B. J. Kirkpatrick), with a large photographic head-and-shoulders portrait of the author on the upper jacket must be seen as both a concession to the author and an innovation by the publisher. Significantly, none of Mansfield's subsequent first editions with Constable included any such treatment.

By 23 November 1920, Mansfield had received Murry's letter 'enclosing the cover of Bliss', about which she was remarkably non-committal, even contrite: 'Thats alright. Thank you for sending it to me.'[41] Apparently, Murry had sent the upper jacket alone with the crucial photograph rather than the entire dust-jacket; or perhaps the blurb had not yet been composed. But when the book arrived, Mansfield was also caustic about the way Constable had advertised her work on the inside front flap: 'the bit about "women will learn by heart and not repeat" – Gods! Why didn't they have a photograph of me looking through a garter!'[42]

This *Bliss* photograph would eventually reappear as a frontispiece to the second volume of *The Letters of Katherine Mansfield* (1928),[43] albeit misdated as 1921, and on the dust-jackets of the cheaper *Constable's Miscellany* series from September 1928 onwards. But it is hard not to conclude that, without the contretemps just described, the original dust-jacket of *Bliss* would have been as plain and unadorned as later ones were – unless one counts blocks of text as adornment, as in *The Garden Party* (1922) and *The Doves' Nest* (1923). Had Constable been planning to use a photograph in the first place, they would surely, by this stage, have had one available to give to Clement Shorter. Biographer Claire Tomalin is thus clearly mistaken in claiming that 'Katherine was now quarreling with Murry by post again, the ostensible reason being his giving Constable a photograph she disliked for the jacket of her forthcoming book.'[44] Kathleen Jones obviously relied upon Tomalin's account in her brief but erroneous allusion to the matter: 'John supplies Constable with the wrong photograph for the cover of *Bliss*.'[45] The request was for a publicity shot for a magazine, *not* a portrait for the publisher to use on the book. Given the current ubiquity of Mansfield portraits on dust-jackets and as frontispieces, it can be difficult to grasp just how unusual the *Bliss* dust-jacket was in 1920.

Some comparisons may be helpful. Virginia Woolf sat for a number of notable portrait photographers (George Charles Beresford in 1902; Man Ray in 1934; and Gisele Freund in 1939) and had her own press (Hogarth Press), but not until the American (Harcourt Brace) edition of *A Writer's Diary* in 1954 does her photograph appear on a dust-jacket (and then on the back);[46] and no image of D. H. Lawrence appeared on the dust-jackets of his books until his new publisher (Knopf, of course) chose one for *St Mawr* (1926). In the UK, one of the earliest author portraits on the upper jacket is that of a youthful Robert Graves on *Goodbye to All That* (1929), published by Jonathan Cape, with a dust-jacket designed by Len Lye and photography by Alfred Cracknell.

Mansfield's dissatisfaction with her husband's alleged 'carelessness' prompted her desire to 'put my work and publicity in the hands of an agent', and she mentioned J. B. Pinker as perhaps 'the best man'.[47] Because she wanted to have some 'reserve stock to offer him', it would not be until late 1921 that she actually agreed to terms with him,[48] though she had, by then, been using the Curtis Brown Agency to place some stories and to look into being published in America. As she explained to Murry: 'I feel I may make enough money in America to free myself to make money.'[49] So it seems likely that Curtis Brown played some role in steering her to Alfred Knopf, though Mansfield corresponded with Knopf directly too. In a talk he gave at the Grolier Club in 1948, Knopf recalled that, in 1912, he 'first met – perhaps *saw* would be more accurate – Haldane MacFall, Frank Harris, Katherine Mansfield . . . and other writers' in Dan Rider's bookshop in St Martin's Lane, London.[50] In short, she would have been a not unfamiliar face and name to him by 1920. Initially, Knopf imported sheets of *Bliss* from Constable for an American issue in late February 1921 – a strategy that led Mansfield to suggest that he was 'a little bit unduly pessimistic' and to offer to send him some of 'the particularly favourable notices'.[51] Fortunately, the book was well received (especially by Conrad Aiken),[52] and some time in 1923 (probably August) a *bona fide* American edition appeared. A year later (September 1924), the *Bliss* dust-jacket could boast its 'eighth large printing', and Knopf must have felt that the 'small advances' Mansfield secured from him were good investments after all.[53] Unlike Constable, Knopf, himself an amateur photographer, embraced the idea of a photographic dust-jacket for all five of Mansfield's short story collections, as well as for her poems, her so-called 'journal' and her letters. He utilised the sideways pose (Mansfield's 'half-bang') from the same studio sitting as the Constable version, and this photograph had been inscribed at the foot 'Faithfully yours/Katherine Mansfield' – suggesting that she selected this version specifically for her new publisher. Here, as elsewhere, Mansfield seems to invest her portraits with singular significance and to distribute them strategically. Did she ask Knopf to feature the inscribed photograph on the dust-jacket, as she had asked Constable to feature the other one? Or did Knopf simply modify the Constable format and stick with it, happy also to include the imprimatur of Mansfield's inscription?[54]

By 1927, Mansfield had been dead for more than four years and her anxieties about how the world saw her were no longer an issue. Unrestrained by authorial qualms, Knopf was thus empowered to move beyond a single image of the author to a photographic record of aspects of her life that could complement the potpourri of verbal fragments and notes that constituted the *Journal of Katherine Mansfield* (1927). Ironically, Murry's original favourite had pride of place as the frontispiece, followed by twelve other full-page photographs: Mansfield reclining on a bed in her Arabian shawl, in a deckchair, in a fur-trimmed coat, her brother Leslie in uniform, her maternal grandparents (Joseph and Margaret Dyer) on their wedding day, Mansfield and Murry in London and in Menton, and so on; and the buff dust-jacket, printed in black, is dominated by the now familiar 'half-bang' portrait of Mansfield, grown in size. This same, more expansive, version of the portrait appears on the slip-case of the two-volume *Letters* (1929), also apparently not seen by Kirkpatrick. Yet none of these photographs was included in the British (Constable) edition of the *Journal*. The difference in editorial judgement between the American and British publishers provokes some questions. Was it Murry's original plan to include photographs with the text for Constable (his own compilation, after all) – a plan perhaps thwarted by Sadleir's opposition? Or did Knopf take the initiative, looking for a way to transform a dubiously cohesive text into something more substantial? We can only speculate, but Knopf's burgeoning interest in photographic portraits could have been a factor.

Murry must have been solely responsible for dating and labelling the photographs used in the Knopf *Journal* (1927)[55] and, as was too often the case, his memory failed him. In his introduction, for example, he says that *Bliss* was published 'at the beginning of 1920';[56] in fact, it was not published until December 1920, as he should have known, given his role in the negotiations. More serious were his multiple mistakes in identifying the photographs. The 'hideous old photograph' was made the frontispiece for the *Journal*, and there dated '1914';[57] the 1910 photograph by Ida Baker (opposite page viii) of Mansfield reclining on a bed in her 'Arabian shawl' in Rottingdean, Sussex, was dated '1908';[58] the photograph of Mansfield's brother, Leslie, in uniform (opposite page 34) was labelled 'Chummie' October, 1915', though he had left for Flanders with his regiment on 26 September and was killed on 6 October 1915. Most pertinent here, however, is the dust-jacket photograph, also reproduced internally (opposite page 196), where it was labelled 'Montana [Switzerland], 1921'. Both the place and the year are wrong – this is one (the 'half-bang' version) of the two photographs Mansfield had sat for in Menton, identified in her letter of 6 November 1920 and sent to Alfred Knopf in New York.[59] Unfortunately, Murry had confused it with another, not entirely dissimilar, head-and-shoulders shot taken in Montana a year later. There, Mansfield sat for what she planned as 'a new press photo' to go with her forthcoming second book, *The Garden Party and Other Stories*,[60] and sent the results to Pinker, her new agent: 'I enclose two photographs of myself in case the press or the publisher would care for them.'[61] Soon after, she sent a copy to painter Dorothy Brett for her reaction: 'Here's a new "press" photo. Is it any good? Its like me, so M[urry] says. "The spit of you." Do you think it would go all right on a cover?'[62] Here we have evidence that Murry had seen and approved the image – perhaps more tactfully than truthfully – and that, once again, Mansfield wanted her photograph to be featured on the Constable dust-jacket. Nothing came of this idea, and the conventional dust-jacket of *The Garden Party*, embellished only with snippets of praise, must have been a disappointment. Two weeks later, in a birthday letter to her sister Jeanne (Renshaw), Mansfield included a postcard version of the Montana photograph, inscribed 'Your sister "K"',[63] along with her story 'At The Bay' in the forthcoming issue of the *London Mercury* [January 1922]. Another postcard went to Anne Drey, with a long and oddly self-conscious inscription that suggests ambivalence about the photograph: 'This is called: "Dreaming of Paris and Anne". The photographer has enlarged it & put it in his window; people cry so frightfully they have to be just led away.'[64] In the Alexander Turnbull Library, it is inadequately recorded, given available documentary evidence, as being 'taken by an unidentified photographer, probably in 1921 or 1922, possibly in Paris, France'. No, it is unquestionably from Montana-sur-Sierre, Switzerland, and must date from after Mansfield's move to Montana in May 1921 and before she sent a copy to her agent in September.[65]

For the most part, Knopf's early issues and editions shared the dust-jacket design, the two-colour title-page layout with the borzoi logo, and the green cloth bindings with a printed cream label on the spine, but all relied upon the same photograph that Mansfield had sent to Knopf.[66] The dust-jackets generally differed in colour; for Knopf, colour itself was always an important design feature. The *Bliss* dust-jacket (not seen by Kirkpatrick) was mustard-yellow and printed in brown; thus the portrait itself was brown. By contrast, *The Little Girl* dust-jacket (again, not seen by Kirkpatrick) was pink (which faded badly over time), and printed in black and white. Other Knopf authors of the period were given similarly eye-catching colour combinations, though none of them included a photograph as part of the presentation. Robert Graves's poems, *Country Sentiment* (1920), for example, sported blue cloth boards and a yellow dust-jacket printed in blue; E. M. Forster's novel, *Where Angels Fear to Tread* (1920), had orange cloth boards printed in blue and a cream dust-jacket printed in brown; and Carl Van Vechten's essays, *In the Garret* (1920), had black paper-covered boards with printed blue label on the front board and spine and a yellow dust-jacket printed in red.

The Canadian book market for British and American books was quite small, and Canadian issues or editions from the first half of the twentieth century present numerous bibliographical problems. Mansfield's books were published by Macmillan of Canada, typically from imported British (that is, Constable) sheets, and in numbers small enough to make them scarce today. The four short-story collections (*Bliss, The Garden Party, The Doves' Nest* and *Something Childish*) all appeared as Canadian issues – that is, they were printed and bound in the UK with conjugate cancel-title leaves. The first three volumes appear to have been issued at about the same time and reviewed together; Kirkpatrick dates them 'late 1923 or January 1924', and the latter date would be consistent with the 1924 implementation of the Canadian Copyright Act of 1921. Yet the copy of *The Dove's Nest* [*sic*] examined records 'First published, June 1923 [Constable date]/Reprinted, August 1923 [Macmillan date]'. All three books featured an attractive binding quite unlike the sober Constable bindings – red cloth boards stamped in gold on the spine, with top edges gilt, and Mansfield's monogram in gilt at the right foot of the upper cover – no doubt at the behest of Macmillan's energetic young leader, Hugh S. Earys. The dust-jackets are uniformly ochre, printed in black (though Kirkpatrick says 'dark green') and manifestly modelled after the Knopf dust-jacket design, including the 'half-bang' portrait of Mansfield on the upper jacket. Earys was very much taken with the distinctive Knopf style and wrote him a fan letter: 'You are doing something unique in publishing.'[67] For reasons that are not clear – perhaps cost – the Canadian issue of *Something Childish*, which appeared in late 1924 or early 1925, has none of the appeal of the earlier collections – it merely replicates the Constable edition's sober grey–blue binding and dust-jacket in every detail except the publisher's name. For a short time, then, Canadian issues of Mansfield's books – with American-inspired dust-jackets that drew attention to an author whose appearance, ironically, had always been a source of personal anxiety – seemed poised to emulate the success of the boldly colourful Knopf editions.

Notes

1. 'Incidents in the childhood of Katherine Mansfield', Alexander Turnbull Library (ATL), MS Papers 1339; cited in Antony Alpers, *The Life of Katherine Mansfield* (New York: Penguin Books, 1982), p. 16. As Gerri Kimber observes: 'The psychological effects of such a comment on KM cannot be underestimated.' Gerri Kimber, *Katherine Mansfield: The Early Years* (Edinburgh: Edinburgh University Press, 2016), p. 68.
2. Antony Alpers, *Katherine Mansfield: A Biography* (New York: Alfred A. Knopf, 1953), p. 47.
3. Kathleen Jones, *Katherine Mansfield: The Story-Teller* (Edinburgh: Edinburgh University Press, 2010), p. 16. Comments of this sort ignore the fact that smiling in photographs was simply not a cultural practice – especially in formal portraits – until well into the twentieth century. Moreover, none of the members of the Beauchamp family smiles in any of the many family photographs in the ATL.
4. There appear to be no photographs of her as an adult wearing spectacles. The question is: had she outgrown the need for them? Or did she simply avoid being photographed wearing them?
5. There was also another very public rebuke when Annie arrived in London in 1909 and objected to the expensive new black hat KM had bought for the occasion: 'Why child! What are you wearing? You look like an old woman in that' (Alpers, *Life*, p. 93).
6. CW1, p. 38.
7. Gillian Boddy says, 'one of her most characteristic qualities was a strong sense of fastidiousness', and offers some persuasive evidence in support of the claim. Gillian Boddy, *Katherine Mansfield: The Woman and the Writer* (New York: Penguin Books, 1988), p. 116.
8. George Bowden recalled that when he met Mansfield for a second time at a musical party, 'he was astonished to find her appearance quite different. This time she was dressed "more or less Maori fashion", with some sort of scarf or kerchief over her shoulders' (Alpers, *Life*, p. 87).
9. 'Katherine Mansfield', *Radio Times*, 4 July 1973, p. 54; cited in Jeffrey Meyers, *Katherine Mansfield: A Biography* (London: Hamish Hamilton, 1978), p. 61.

10. Setting aside childhood photographs and two or three passport shots, there are more than a dozen manifestly studio-quality photographs that KM sat for between 1906 and 1921.
11. Cited in P. A. Lawlor, *The Mystery of Maata* (Wellington: The Beltane Book Bureau, 1946), p. 16. Mabel Tustin 'attended school' with Mansfield, presumably in Wellington.
12. *Letters* 1, pp. 59–60. Mansfield seems not to have been at all self-conscious about telling Garnet of the privileged placement of his photograph, despite the fact that she knew – and he must have known too – that it replaced one of his twin brother, Arnold ('Tom'), that had been there while she was a student at Queen's College. Tom had transferred his affections to another Queen's College resident, Gwen Rouse.
13. *Letters* 1, p. 63.
14. *Letters* 1, p. 69.
15. In Harriet E. Smith, Benjamin Griffin, Victor Fischer, Michael Barry Frank, Amanda Gagel, Sharon K. Goetz, Leslie Diane Myrick and Christopher M. Ohge, eds, *Autobiography of Mark Twain*, vol. 3 (Oakland: University of California Press, 2015), p. 505. Samuel Clemens reports that, on 10 August 1907, 'Sat 22 times for photographers, 16 at Histed's.'
16. Advertisement, 'Under Royal Patronage', *Westminster Review Advertiser*, November 1908, p. 7.
17. Cherry A. Hankin, ed., *Letters Between Katherine Mansfield and John Middleton Murry* (New York: New Amsterdam Books, 1991), p. 261.
18. See *Letters* 3, p. 206, n. 2.
19. Hankin, pp. 269–70.
20. *Letters* 3, p. 211. Anne Estelle Rice (1877–1959) was an American artist, associated initially with J. D. Fergusson in Paris, who met Mansfield in 1911 and contributed illustrations to *Rhythm*. She and Mansfield became good friends, and in 1918 Rice (by then married to Raymond Drey) painted the well-known portrait of Mansfield in a 'brick red frock with flowers everywhere'. *Letters* 2, p. 245.
21. Hankin, p. 301.
22. *Letters* 3, p. 274.
23. *Letters* 3, p. 274.
24. *Letters* 4, p. 92.
25. John Middleton Murry, ed., *Katherine Mansfield's Letters to John Middleton Murry 1913–1922* (New York: Alfred A. Knopf, 1951), p. 595. There is no little difference of opinion about the date of the photograph. In his 1927 edition of the *Journal*, Murry himself dated it '1914'. John Middleton Murry, ed., *Journal of Katherine Mansfield* (New York: Alfred A. Knopf, 1927), frontispiece. Scholars have opted for either 1913 (for example, Alpers, *Life*, p. 321 and *Letters* 4, p. 110) or 1914 (for example, Jones, p. 388, without discussion). Boddy dates it 1915 (p. 6). Other photographs of Mansfield present similar unresolved problems.
26. *Letters* 4, p. 110.
27. *Letters* 4, p. 110.
28. *Letters* 4, p. 111.
29. Chaddie Beauchamp to Sylvia Payne, 14 October 1907 (Alpers, *Biography*, p. 89); reprinted in Laurel Harris, Mary Morris and Joanna Woods, eds, *The Material Mansfield* (Auckland: Random House, n.d.), p. 43.
30. Alpers, *Life*, p. 321.

31. B. Bennet Alder was the colourist. The ATL description of this hand-coloured sepia photograph is 'watercolor over photograph 95 × 70 mm on oval card in silk-lined folded blue morocco case' (Curio–018–011). It was donated to the ATL by Harold Beauchamp in 1938.
32. Murry, *Letters to JMM*, p. 595.
33. *Letters* 4, p. 115.
34. *Letters* 4, p. 114.
35. *Letters* 4, p. 116.
36. See F. A. Lea, *The Life of John Middleton Murry* (London: Methuen, 1959): 'she might have had it taken for Carco' (p. 80). Colin Middleton Murry confirmed this view for Meyers (pp. 205, 285).
37. *Letters* 4, p. 111.
38. *Letters* 4, p. 101.
39. *Letters* 4, p. 102.
40. *Letters* 4, p. 115.
41. *Letters* 4, p. 118.
42. *Letters* 4, p. 137.
43. John Middleton Murry, ed., *The Letters of Katherine Mansfield*, 2 vols (London: Constable, 1928).
44. Claire Tomalin, *Katherine Mansfield: A Secret Life* (London: Penguin, 1988), p. 213.
45. Jones, p. 388.
46. That is not to say that Virginia Woolf's dust-jackets, embellished with the unconventional designs of her sister Vanessa Bell, were not ground-breaking in their own way.
47. *Letters* 4, p. 115.
48. See *Letters* 4, pp. 137, 263, 268.
49. *Letters* 4, p. 136.
50. Alfred A. Knopf, 'Some Random Recollections', in *Portrait of a Publisher* (New York: The Typophiles, 1965), pp. 3–25 (p. 6).
51. *Letters* 4, p. 160.
52. 'Miss Mansfield is brilliant – she has, more conspicuously than any contemporary writer of fiction [. . .] a fine, an infinitely inquisitive sensibility.' Conrad Aiken, 'The Short Story as Poetry', *Freeman*, 3 (11 May 1921), p. 120.
53. See Alfred Knopf, 'Publishing Then and Now, 1912–1964', in *Portrait of a Publisher*, p. 44.
54. Mansfield had a penchant for signing or inscribing her portraits, almost from the outset. Before she returned to London in 1908, she sent Ida Baker a photograph of herself on the front porch of 75 Tinakori Road, inscribed 'Kåthie'; and the 1906 portrait from Brussels – across which she wrote 'Mes mains dans les vôtres' – was also sent to Ida Baker, according to Alpers (*Biography*, p. xv), *not* to 'Tom' Trowell, Mansfield's first love, and seemingly a more likely recipient.
55. Murry, *Journal* (1927).
56. Murry, *Journal* (1927), p. xii.
57. Not 1913, as he stated in 1951.
58. The Rottingdean photograph of 1910 suggests that Mansfield was re-enacting a line ('Bind it about your head and throat') from her poem 'The Arabian Shawl', one of a number of poems written during her relationship with Garnet Trowell in 1908–9. Jones describes the shawl as 'a black and silver Egyptian shawl' (p. 83).
59. Jones erroneously labels this 'Katherine's last photograph' (between pp. 384 and 385). In fact, the 1921 portrait from Montana-sur-Sierre appears to have been the last.

60. In *Material Mansfield* (p. 76), the studio is identified as G. Brise, Photo-Hall, Montana.
61. *Letters* 4, p. 281. ATL (1/2–148257–F) is the film negative. Mansfield sent her sister a print. ATL notes that 'this photograph was published in a promotion for her book, *The Garden Party*'.
62. *Letters* 4, p. 288.
63. Katherine Mansfield Birthplace Society (KMBS) Collection 0224, in *Material Mansfield* (p. 76).
64. *Letters* 5, p. 15.
65. Boddy includes a copy of this photograph from the Harry Ransom Humanities Research Center (HRHRC, University of Texas at Austin) collection and misdates it '1922, Paris', presumably on the authority of the ATL description.
66. The *Poems* were given a somewhat different treatment, in that each impression had unique paper-covered – often batik – boards.
67. This letter is reproduced in *The Company They Kept: Alfred A. and Blanche W. Knopf, Publishers*, An Exhibition Catalog compiled by Cathy Henderson and edited by Dave Oliphant. HRHRC, p. 216.

REVIEW ESSAY

'A widening circle of connectedness' in Mansfield Studies

Jenny McDonnell

Kostas Boyiopoulos and Michael Shallcross, eds, *Aphoristic Modernity: 1880 to the Present* (Leiden: Brill, 2020).

Claire Davison and Gerri Kimber, eds, *The Edinburgh Edition of the Collected Letters of Katherine Mansfield: Volume 1. Letters to Correspondents A–J* (Edinburgh: Edinburgh University Press, 2020).

Aimée Gasston, Gerri Kimber and Janet Wilson, eds, *Katherine Mansfield: New Directions* (London: Bloomsbury, 2020).

Alice Kelly, *Commemorative Modernisms: Women Writers, Death and the First World War* (Edinburgh: Edinburgh University Press, 2020).

David Trotter, *The Literature of Connection: Signal, Medium, Interface 1850–1950* (Oxford: Oxford University Press, 2020).

In their introduction to *The Edinburgh Edition of the Collected Letters of Katherine Mansfield* (Volume 1), the editors discuss the 'constellatory nature' of letter-writing (p. 5) and the non-linear patterns and forms that Mansfield's letter manuscripts frequently present. Phrases appear diagonally and vertically in margins and other blank spaces; postscripts, addenda and illustrations intersect with the main body of the text; and at times, communication even continues beyond the immediate confines of the letter, spilling out on to sealed envelopes and perhaps exposing the contents to unintended readers on the way through the postal system. For Mansfield, letters may have served an additional constellatory function, as a means of locating herself in space and time as she navigated her way through life. 'We are all sailors, bending over a great map', she wrote to Dorothy Brett on 14 February 1922 (p. 442), and the process of writing and receiving letters came to play a key role as Mansfield charted a course from Wellington to London and throughout Europe. Her correspondence marks the extent of her increasingly peripatetic life, as each move brought with it a new postal address; it also records her frustrations with the limits of standardised time (in her frequent dismay at postal delays), while also invoking cyclical and repetitive temporal patterns as a means of organising life. The same letter to Brett, for example, attests to her belief that 'one ought to link up all one's projects as much as possible with the earth's progress', as '[w]e are more alive' at the beginning of spring and autumn than at any other time (p. 442). Each letter establishes a point of connection within her personal and professional communication networks, while each missing, unsent or destroyed letter suggests a gap or interruption in these networks. As a body of work, Mansfield's letters may themselves be regarded as forming a kind of constellation, producing patterns and points of reference by which readers might navigate new understandings of her life and work. In different ways, these principles inform all of the work under consideration in this review, presenting new approaches to Mansfield's writing that repeatedly generate points of connection, communication and dialogue across space and time.

This is immediately apparent in Claire Davison and Gerri Kimber's new edition of Mansfield's letters (with editorial assistance from Anna Plumridge), the first in a planned series of four volumes, which reorients her writing in a number of key ways. Based on extensive archival work, the Edinburgh Edition of Mansfield's letters presents new transcriptions of the surviving manuscripts, and incorporates some previously undiscovered material. In retranscribing the manuscripts, the editors prioritise the original text, choosing 'never to edit "silently"', and leaving Mansfield's own grammatical errors and omissions intact without identifying them with 'the rather didactic, condescending and intrusive editorial "[*sic*]"' (p. 4). Instead, these letters are supplemented by substantial scholarly supporting materials, including a series of biographical essays of varying lengths that contextualise Mansfield's relationship with each correspondent, and informative footnotes and annotations throughout. Together, these new transcriptions, contextual materials and annotations amount to an admirable demonstration of scholarship, which is cross-referenced with the Edinburgh Editions of Mansfield's fiction, poetry, critical writings and diaries, and will be of huge benefit to future researchers. The editors' emphasis on the letters as material artefacts is especially welcome, including their frequent descriptions of the manuscripts' compositional layout, which are intended as signposts to point 'a future scholar interested in epistolary praxis in the direction of the archives' (p. 5).

The most immediately striking innovation in this new edition comes with its rejection of the strictly linear arrangement that has been favoured in previous publications by John Middleton Murry, Vincent O'Sullivan and Margaret Scott. This 'traditional' linear structure is initially acknowledged in a useful chronological list at the beginning of the volume, but thereafter, letters are grouped and presented alphabetically according to correspondent. This allows for a focus that is 'less about Mansfield's life chronology, more about her specific personal interactions and what happens to these over time with each person in a widening circle of connectedness' (p. xviii), as Ali Smith puts it in her insightful foreword. Instead of a singular metanarrative that builds inexorably to Mansfield's death, then, the collection presents a series of micro-narratives that have no definite beginning or end. This draws attention to 'the ways lives connect, the life in that connecting' (p. xviii), even perhaps suggesting the rhizomatic nature in which these lives and letters intersect. In turn, this structure helps to highlight Mansfield's performance of different registers and voices in her varied relationships in ways that Davison and Kimber suggest are in keeping with her consideration of the 'writing self' as multiple, 'allowing for those "hundreds of selves" and their individual voices to shine through' (p. 6).

The collection begins with an October 1921 letter to the American writer Conrad Aiken, and ends in May 1922 with a single letter to Hugh Jones (the young son of Alice Jones, former administrator for the *Athenaeum*). The 600 pages in between move backwards and forwards in spatio-temporal terms, so that 'time becomes spatial, dimensional' (Smith, p. xviii), and includes letters to some of the most significant figures in Mansfield's life, including Ida Baker, Dorothy Brett and (collectively) the Beauchamp family. (The highly anticipated Volume 2 will bring together Mansfield's correspondence with recipients from K to Z, while the remaining two volumes will comprise her extensive assortment of letters to John Middleton Murry.) Although the letters are presented as discrete sections, the process of reading the collection as a whole invites the reader to detect echoes and patterns across Mansfield's correspondence, perhaps noting the subtle repetitions in her descriptions of a Parisian flower-shop in letters to John Galsworthy (p. 550) and William Gerhardi (p. 575), or the poignant effects generated by a strictly alphabetical arrangement of the Beauchamp family correspondence. Here, the last letter to her sister Jeanne in February 1922 concludes with an oblique reference to her remembrance of their late brother's birthday (p. 266), and immediately gives way to a section on Leslie Beauchamp that includes Mansfield's only surviving letter to him, written shortly before his death in 1915 (p. 272).

Each section in the volume inevitably culminates in a 'final' letter, which marks the end of the extant correspondence with each individual recipient; however, these do not generate a sense of definitive, absolute closure, as each ending is invariably followed by the beginning of a new exchange with another recipient at a different point in Mansfield's life. Moreover, the substantial supporting materials frequently open the letters up to dialogues with other texts and archives: for example, in Sydney Janet Kaplan's illuminating insights into Conrad Aiken's short story, 'Your Obituary, Well Written' (pp. 15–17), or in Gerri Kimber's intriguing essay on Amy Barkas, based on archival research in the Alexander Turnbull Library (pp. 177–8). Even the letters that contain the greatest potential for finality – those written by Mansfield on or about 31 December 1922, shortly before her death – disrupt any clear-cut sense of resolution when read in this way. This is particularly apparent in a remarkable trio of letters to Elizabeth von Arnim, Ida Baker and Dorothy Brett, all of which contain monetary transactions of different kinds. An air of finality might haunt the letter to von Arnim, in which Mansfield repays a substantial debt of £100 (pp. 63–4). However, this is undercut by the sense of potential that informs the gift of 100 francs just to '[p]lay with' (pp. 175–6) in the unsent letter to Baker (discussed at length by Ali Smith in an essay in *Katherine Mansfield: New Directions*), and is entirely undone in the letter to Brett, in which Mansfield incurs a fresh debt by asking her friend to buy her some necessities, offering assurances that she will 'send [. . .] a cheque by return' to cover the costs (pp. 496–8).

Collectively, the letters to Ida Baker and Dorothy Brett amount to more than one-third of Volume 1 – a figure that could have been even larger, were it not for Baker's destruction of Mansfield's early letters at her request in 1918, often regarded as an act of dutiful devotion to her life-long friend. One of the most interesting effects of encountering Baker's letters again in this new arrangement, though, sees the emergence of an alternative image of 'the most reliable, proactive and also *modern* of Mansfield's long-term friends, as she zigzags back and forth across the Channel and fits in extended travels of her own on the way', as Davison and Kimber note in their introduction (p. 9). Reading these letters and annotations back to back (rather than spread out across the five volumes of O'Sullivan and Scott's edition), it is possible to conjure up hints of Baker's voice in Mansfield's direct responses to the questions, anecdotes and even, at times, rebukes that may have appeared in her friend's letters; on 14 June 1918, for example, Mansfield writes

'Youre not just an agency to which I apply for pills and cigarettes, free of charge – though your whole letter was concerned with trying to make me believe that's what Ive brought our "relationship" to' (p. 82). The publication of one side of a written correspondence will inevitably produce gaps and absences – a feature that recurs throughout the entire body of Mansfield's letters – but within these spaces it is nevertheless possible to detect traces of the absent recipient, in a process that Smith describes as 'return[ing] the life threefold to the old artefact of the letter: the life of the writer, the life of the person to whom she's writing, and finally the life of the times both people inhabited' (p. xvi).

Another striking example of this process may be found in the group of letters to Vera Beauchamp that appears roughly halfway through the volume, occupying the final slot in a sequence devoted to Mansfield's correspondence with the Beauchamp family. The majority of the letters to Vera date from 1908, providing a rare, immediate insight into Mansfield's early life (in particular, her encounters with literature, music and culture, as is apparent from the wealth of allusions included in this heavily annotated section). The visions of intellectual and sisterly camaraderie that are evoked in these letters contrast sharply with the sense of distance in later letters to Vera; this is replicated in the formal neatness of the later correspondence, as Anna Plumridge suggests (p. 274), and in references to Vera throughout the collection: for example, in letters to Charlotte Beauchamp dating from the early 1920s. The textual encounter with the Vera of 1908 *after* she has already been introduced as a seemingly minor figure in the mature Mansfield's life provides a flashback to a very different relationship, and is all the more powerful as a result.

These spatio-temporal shifts recur throughout the collection, so that '[i]n her letters, time opens. Round them a community opens, takes shape around her' (Smith, p. xviii). In this volume in particular, the community that emerges is frequently made up of women. Although the list of correspondents from A to J is quite evenly split in terms of gender, the sheer quantity of letters to female friends, family members and acquaintances far outweighs those by the male figures included in this volume. Several are known for their own significant literary and artistic achievements (such as Elizabeth von Arnim and Beatrice Campbell, née Elvery). Other intriguing, marginalised figures also emerge from the background, such as Alice Jones, a representative example of the 'emerging secretarial profession' that helped facilitate early twentieth-century literary production, as Claire Davison discusses in her eloquent introductory essay (pp. 619–20). In this way, the volume frequently foregrounds various interactions between networks of early twentieth-century women, by bringing Mansfield's private letters into a public sphere – a process that always presents ethical challenges, and 'entails a sense of intrusion, almost a breach of trust', as the editors acknowledge in their introduction (p. 1).

A number of letters included in the volume actually disrupt a clear distinction between public and private (neatly represented by Mansfield's habit of continuing to compose letters on the outside of already sealed envelopes, as mentioned above). Perhaps most notorious are the 'letters' to Francis Carco, the originals of which were destroyed but which can be reconstructed from Carco's incorporation of them into *Les Innocents* and *Montmartre à vingt ans* (pp. 514–16). Like O'Sullivan and Scott, Davison and Kimber have reclaimed these letters for Mansfield, offering new revisions and translations that enact an ongoing negotiation of public and private textual space. Likewise, the letter to Laura Bright (Mansfield's godmother, and later stepmother) occupies an uncertain position between public and private correspondence. It presents an account of London life shortly after the outbreak of the First World War, and was published in 1914 as an unsigned letter from 'a correspondent' to 'a Wellington resident' in the Wellington *Evening Post* (pp. 499–500); whether this publication was prompted by Mansfield herself or by Bright seems unclear.

As well as illustrating the potential tension between public and private in Mansfield's letters, the 1914 publication of her correspondence with Bright also helps highlight an idea that the editors of this new edition seek to demonstrate – namely, that the letters themselves have literary 'value' and therefore merit further sustained, critical investigation. In *Commemorative Modernisms*, Alice Kelly undertakes precisely this kind of close interrogation of a selection of Mansfield's letters as a form of war writing – one that was produced within the 'putatively private space of the letter', but which Mansfield was aware could always be exposed to readers other than the intended recipient, given 'the contemporary threat of censorship and the likelihood of her letters being published posthumously' (p. 126). In doing so, she positions Mansfield within another community of women writers in order to explore their reactions to the huge changes in the cultures of death, private memorialisation and public commemoration that the First World War precipitated. In addition to Mansfield's war-time letters, Kelly explores a diverse selection of works, '[r]eading "modernist" writers alongside non-modernist writers, and "war writers" alongside non-war writers, [. . .] in keeping with a wartime and postwar literary culture where these distinctions did not exist' (p. 240). Working with an array of archival and primary materials (including memoir, journalism, fiction, and visual and material cultures), as well as substantial secondary and contextual sources, Kelly presents a compelling commentary on the ways in which women writers bore witness to the war dead. These writings, produced by civilians and participants in the war effort alike, reflect 'varying degrees of proximate and distanced encounters with death, both geographically and temporally' (p. 4). Kelly also emphasises the ways in which these writers frequently crossed generic boundaries, and includes the eye-witness accounts found in nurses' narratives and Edith Wharton's reportage and propagandist fiction; the experimentation with avant-garde and abstract modes in Mansfield's epistolary output and H. D.'s fiction; and finally, representations of post-war commemorative cultures in fiction, with a particular focus on writings by Mansfield and Virginia Woolf.

Kelly structures her study along spatial and temporal lines, beginning with those accounts that were produced in closest proximity to the war effort, in both geographical and chronological terms: the nurses' memoirs that reveal the inadequacy of Victorian mourning rituals and commemorations as a means of confronting the devastating impact of mass death. In her sensitive analysis of these texts, Kelly detects 'writing which registers the shock of the war dead, but doesn't yet know what to do with it' (p. 40), before discussing another proximate response to the war in the form of Edith Wharton's 'uncomfortable propaganda'. The final chapter focuses on the aftermath of the war, revisiting familiar texts by both Virginia Woolf (*Jacob's Room* and *Mrs Dalloway*) and Mansfield ('The Garden Party' and 'The Fly'), and placing them in dialogue with work by E. M. Forster, Rudyard Kipling and Christopher Isherwood. In these analyses, she explores the ways in which these writers addressed post-war commemorative cultures, including 'the ongoing identification and burial of bodies; the question of locating and visiting the dead; and the building of local and national memorials' (p. 196).

The writers and texts discussed in the middle section of *Commemorative Modernisms* occupy a more ambiguous position in terms of their temporal and geographical proximity to the war. In this section, Kelly draws on Allyson Booth's concept of 'civilian modernism' in a discussion of H. D. and Mansfield's use of 'hybridised figurative language' (p. 124) in writing about a war through which they lived without fully witnessing it first-hand. Both writers were directly and indirectly affected by the events of the war, as each suffered the loss of a brother to the conflict, and experienced air-raids (and, of course, Mansfield also made a trip through war-time France in 1915 for the encounter with Francis Carco that inspired 'An Indiscreet Journey'). Kelly demonstrates that these war-time contexts converged with individual bodily traumas in the form of H. D.'s experience of a stillbirth and Mansfield's diagnosis with tuberculosis, so that both writers came to employ depictions of the body as an abstract representation of war trauma. Kelly explores three groups of Mansfield's war letters in detail, dating from March 1915, March 1918 and July to December 1919, tracing the evolution of war discourse in her writing, and her frequent appropriation of war tropes in writing about her illness. Thus, she argues that Mansfield's experimentation with oblique expression and figurative language was honed in her war letters. These 'overlapping discourses of the war, illness and mortality' (p. 146) reached their fullest expression in the 1919 letters that coincided with Mansfield's overt call for contemporary writers to confront the war (for example, in her public and private comments about Woolf's *Night and Day*), and anticipated her own turn to the indirect representation of the war and its aftermath in a number of stories. As previously noted, Kelly goes on to discuss a selection of these stories in the final section of *Commemorative Modernisms*, but she also makes a particularly persuasive case for the critical interpretation of Mansfield's letters, concluding that there is clear evidence that, '[r]ather than being ancillary writings [. . .], letters may actually be where modernist experimentation took place' (p. 146).

Kelly's reading of Mansfield's letters alongside the varied modes of war-time writing also raises intriguing questions about the ways in which traditional and new media were used for the purposes of commemoration and memorialisation in response to the First World War. Her interrogation of H. D.'s engagement with contemporary new technologies (specifically, cinema) is especially striking in its attention to the inherent spectrality of film and newsreels as commemorative media, since 'what we see on the screen must, by necessity, already be past' (p. 180). A similar sense of space–time disruption also informs her discussion of the ways in which the seriality of Mansfield's letters functions as a 'means of marking time, measuring progress, and implying continuity' (p. 122). In this reading, Kelly draws on Liz Stanley's work to establish that letters are informed by 'temporal and spatial interruptions between the writing and the reading of a letter' (quoting Stanley, p. 127), so that the act of reading (or rereading) a letter will always disrupt a clear-cut distinction between past, present and future.

In the opening essay of *Katherine Mansfield: New Directions*, Ali Smith describes the sensation of reading manuscripts by Mansfield and other writers in terms that also overtly evoke a sense of time travel: 'like a portal, it opened to a connecting force, one that moved from actual hand to actual hand down through time and up through time simultaneously' (p. 16). This implied erasure of spatio-temporal boundaries in Smith's account makes for an appropriate point of departure from which to consider a collection of essays that envisions 'travelling with Mansfield without borders' (p. 7), as Aimée Gasston describes it in her perceptive introduction. Co-edited by Gasston, Gerri Kimber and Janet Wilson, *Katherine Mansfield: New Directions* brings together fourteen essays from emerging and established scholars and is divided into four sections on 'Form and force'; 'Mansfield's modernisms'; 'Literary influence and life writing'; and 'Social and domestic transactions'. The collection amply demonstrates the potential for new readings of Mansfield's life and writing, and in different ways, these essays set out to explore 'new routes, bifurcating, splitting, flitting, perhaps forging ahead, perhaps returning and looking again' (Gasston, p. 1). The collection looks back to forge links between Mansfield's writing and ancient texts (as in Erika Baldt's essay on the revision of the Orphic mysteries in 'Bliss' and 'An Indiscreet Journey'); looks forward to identify dialogues with later writers (as in Kathleen Jones's discussion of Mansfield's influence on Philip Larkin and Yiyun Li); and looks again at Mansfield's relationship with her near contemporaries (as in Nick Hocking's reading of 'Psychology' with reference to Henri Bergson's *Laughter*). Gasston further links these 'new routes' with the 'roots' that generate the 'Signes of Spring', discussed in Smith's opening essay. This pun might once more suggest an associative link to the entangled roots of the rhizome, a fitting image for Smith's digressive, playful and expansive essay, which speaks to the ways in which Mansfield's writing can 'reveal links between disparate-seeming things' (p. 14). In fact, Smith's essay suggests points of connection and patterns that reverberate across the collection as a whole, as well as linking back to the new edition of Mansfield's letters in subtle ways.

At the heart of Smith's essay, as previously noted, is a close reading of Mansfield's 'final' letter to Ida Baker, which illustrates its status as 'an astonishing literary work itself' (p. 17). She also highlights the letter's existence in a series of transcripts, typescripts and manuscripts that reveal the persistent playfulness and slippages of Mansfield's language, and which prompt a disruption of spatio-temporal boundaries in the act of reading it – the sense that 'whatever answer there'd be to this letter or card is still to come, hasn't happened yet, is still waiting to happen, even though I'm sitting in the British Library literally a hundred years later to the day 12 June 1918' (p. 21). This focus on 'the talismanic nature of what writers leave behind themselves' (p. 14) in her encounters with the archives provides one example of the ways in which Smith's essay resonates across the collection as a whole. Her haunting descriptions of Mansfield's manuscripts – the 'aged envelope', 'the thinness and lightness of the different papers', 'the ghosts of Mansfield's paperclips' that suggest 'the metal of time' (pp. 20–1) – echo the emphasis on materiality in the new edition of the letters, and also speak to the ongoing, crucial engagements with archival material that continue to generate new critical readings and rediscovered sources.

Chris Mourant's engaging essay draws on the archives of the Shakespeare & Co. Lending Library to identify the books that Mansfield borrowed and read during her stay in Paris in 1922, in order to explore her intellectual engagement with American modernist writers, journals and the marketplace; he further posits that her 'retreat' to Fontainebleau at the end of the year should not be read as a rejection of literary ties, but in fact 'cannot be disentangled from her reading at this time' (p. 106). Whereas Mourant offers new insights into the final months of Mansfield's life, Gerri Kimber proposes a reconsideration of a significant figure from the beginning of her career. In particular, Kimber turns to archival material in order to present a revised portrait of George Bowden, Mansfield's first husband, through a comprehensive overview of the Bowden papers in the Harry Ransom Center and the Alexander Turnbull Library, focusing on what Bowden himself termed the pair's 'happy if short intellectual comradeship' (p. 175). Bowden (a singing teacher and elocutionist) also plays a key role in Katie L. Jones's persuasive examination of Mansfield's early practice of recitation and vocal performance as evidence of her efforts at establishing her voice within the public sphere between 1908 and 1909. In this way, Jones make a strong case for Mansfield's engagement with the London literary marketplace *before* she began regularly publishing poetry and prose in the journals and magazines in which she would ultimately create a lasting name for herself.

By contrast, the *absence* of voice is central to Ruchi Mundeja's astute examination of Mansfield's 'ventriloquizing of characters' silences', and the ethics involved in '[i]nscribing the silences of the disempowered' (p. 61). In particular, Mundeja focuses on Mansfield's narration of characters that are marginalised in terms of class, a thread that is picked up in a later group of essays by Alex Moffett, Ann Herndon Marshall and Janet Wilson, all of which consider Mansfield's depiction of capitalist structures, class, labour and economic exchange. Again, each of these might be seen as intersecting in different ways with a 'root' from Smith's opening essay, which suggests that Mansfield's writing 'demand[s] that we pay attention to what we're made of, that we perceive our roles in the social and historical structures that form us and which we form' (p. 13). Moreover, her commentary on the economic transactions in Mansfield's last letter to Ida Baker shares a particular resonance with Wilson's nuanced analysis of Mansfield's 'Economic Women', 'whether as consumers, labourers, sellers or debtors' (p. 203).

This focus on materiality manifests itself in another way in Smith's categorisation of Mansfield's letters as 'extraordinary, vital, literary/psychological/theatrical/intimate artefacts' (p. 25) that record and recreate '[t]he aliveness of all things' (p. 28), from the 'signs of spring' that Mansfield seeks in her final letter to Ida Baker (p. 18), to the bird-song that she transcribes as a 'two-note musical sequence' in a 1903 letter to Sylvia Payne (p. 25). A focus on the non-human and natural world also informs two particularly memorable contributions to the collection. Enda Duffy's wide-ranging consideration of representations of snow within work by Mansfield, James Joyce and what Gasston terms 'a constellation of other global and modernist reference points' (p. 4) undertakes a thought-provoking interrogation of the limits of modernism. In another fascinating essay, William Kupinse focuses on the ambiguous descriptions of the plant at the centre of 'Prelude', which displays features of both the aloe and the agave, and addresses the various gendered, colonial and ecocritical implications that each plant might generate in analysing the story. Coincidentally, both plants are also characterised by their rhizomatic roots, perhaps encouraging us once more to seek new links and points of connection of the kind that Smith identifies in the experience of reading Mansfield's letters – 'the level of nerve-end involvement that reading her letters had once more visited on me' (p. 15). Her empathetic response to Mansfield's work is prompted here by concern about the fate of another non-human agent, Wingley the cat, as Mansfield contemplated whether or not he should be euthanised rather than endure the disruptions of her own nomadic lifestyle; reassuringly, the new edition of the letters can offer confirmation that Wingley did eventually find a new home in Sussex with Ida Baker's aunt (n. 9, p. 97).

As previously noted, Mansfield's letters frequently reveal such gaps and absences, a feature that is also found throughout her suggestive and elliptical fiction. This is discussed in detail in Elleke Boehmer's contribution to *Katherine Mansfield: New Directions*, which draws on relevance theory and cognitive linguistics in a close reading of the ellipses that readers must negotiate in interpreting Mansfield's work. Boehmer focuses on the use of 'under-specification' in a selection of stories to consider the extent to which 'seeming gaps in meaning are in fact full of meaning' (p. 38), and identifies comparable strategies at work in Ali Smith's fiction. These principles of suggestion and indirectness proved especially appropriate for Mansfield's practice of the modernist short story – what Gasston terms her 'hymns to brevity' (p. 1) – a form that is characterised by compression, fragmentation and open-endedness. Similar structural attributes and temporal disruptiveness can also be associated with an alternative mode of writing that Mansfield practised early in her career, and which forms the subject of another recent collection of essays: the aphorism.

In their introduction to *Aphoristic Modernity: 1880 to the Present*, co-editors Kostas Boyiopoulos and Michael Shallcross identify some features of the modern aphorism, including its 'interplay of continuity and rupture, permanence and ephemerality' (p. 6), and 'its open-ended generosity of meaning' (p. 15) as a response to and product of modernity. This collection of essays stems from a 2015 conference at the University of York, and includes broad-ranging commentary on the aphoristic mode in writing by Oscar Wilde, Wyndham Lewis, Jorge Luis Borges, Samuel Beckett and others, as well as entertaining and informative discussions of contemporary meme culture in an essay by Francesca Coppa, and Stevie Smith's exploitation of the 'aphorism's capacity to interrupt' (p. 159), as discussed by Noreen Masud. Mansfield's own early practice of the aphoristic form is discussed in an essay by Chris Mourant, which presents a comparative reading of Mansfield's 'Bites from the Apple' and Edwin Muir's 'We Moderns', both of which were composed for the *New Age* and can be placed in dialogue with other writings produced for and published in the journal during the same era. Thus, his analysis of the text draws attention to the inherently dialogic nature of both the aphorism and the magazine format, arguing that Mansfield's experimentation with this fragmentary, suggestive form may have played a key role in her development as a modernist writer. In keeping with Mourant's other work (including his recent monograph, *Katherine Mansfield and Periodical Culture*), the essay also reveals the value of archival work for analyses of Mansfield's writing, and is prompted by his discovery of the typescript of 'Bites from the Apple' in 2012. This is one of several significant archival finds to have appeared in recent years – a process that continues to uncover new material, as is further apparent in the inclusion of a number of new letters in the Edinburgh Edition.

While Mourant's essay is the only one in the collection that directly addresses Mansfield's practice of the aphoristic form, Maebh Long's essay is also worth singling out for its innovative and exciting exploration of a link between 'the formal, textual structure of the aphorism [and] the geographical reach and fluidity of the archipelago' (p. 191) to propose a model for rereading modernism and modernity in global terms that disrupts the long-standing binaristic structure of the metropolitan centre and the periphery. Long demonstrates the extent to which both aphorisms and archipelagos are characterised by disrupted borders, fluidity and multiple perspectives, features that are also shared with

Deleuze and Guattari's rhizome, to which 'there is no stable beginning or end, but a multiplicity of points that can connect to any other point' (p. 197). Like the constellation and the rhizome, then, the archipelago might provide a useful reference point when considering Mansfield's own border-crossings and disruptions of linear spatio-temporal models in her practice of the short story and other forms, and also in the non-hierarchical arrangement of the new edition of the letters, which generates multiple points of connection across her writing.

Finally, islands and archipelagos also make an appearance in David Trotter's absorbing study of *The Literature of Connection*, as one of several models of global 'connectivity' that reveal the ways in which the world became connected and networked throughout the century that led up to the digital age. Trotter explores 'the transformation of connective relationships of all kinds – economic, social, political, cultural, erotic, affective – brought about [. . .] by the widespread introduction in the period between 1850 and 1950 of new (near-instantaneous, real-time) techniques and technologies of telecommunication' (p. 1). These connective relationships were made possible by three key elements, which form the subtitle of the study, and through which communication is enabled: signal, medium and interface. The book is divided into two sections, the first of which traces different scenes of communication in a Victorian to modernist 'British' literary tradition, focusing on writers such as Thomas Hardy, Joseph Conrad, Wyndham Lewis, D. H. Lawrence, Mina Loy and Mansfield; section two looks further afield at work by August Strindberg, Franz Kafka, African–American popular and literary culture, and post-war spy narratives. In different ways, Trotter suggests that these texts reveal 'the romance of connectivity' (p. 11), depicting characters that seek to make contact and transmit messages via particular media, channels or networks; in their interaction with interfaces of various kinds (exit and entry points at either end of a network by which users gain access to it); or in their encounter with a signal or message to be received and decoded by an intended recipient.

In Trotter's analysis, all three concepts converge in a ground-breaking interpretation of Mansfield's writing that argues for her 'fascination with techniques and technologies of short-range communication' (p. 237); this is evident in the different attempts at communication within her stories, which emphasise the spatial, technological and other barriers that must be negotiated in order to get the message through. Thus, Trotter discusses the various technologies that prompt scenes of signalling and communication in Mansfield's stories – the ring of a doorbell in 'Psychology'; the telephone bell in 'Revelations'; or the lift-call bell in 'The Man Without a Temperament'. Elsewhere, he demonstrates the ways in which forms of (tele)communication are required as characters move between public and private spaces in Mansfield's work. So, for example, in 'Bliss', Bertha Young's misplaced key means that she must rattle her house's letter-box in order to gain entry; later, Pearl Fulton's 'signal' to her prompts a move from the dining room at the front of the house to the more private space of the drawing room, and with it the subsequent series of communications and miscommunications that forces the story to a climax. The chapter on Mansfield culminates in an insightful reading of 'The Stranger' as enacting a form of 'media theory', initially triggered by Mr Hammond's attempts at signalling from Wellington harbour, an exit and entry point that forms part of a global, imperial telecommunications network. Trotter considers Hammond's attempts at identifying and controlling a clear channel of communication with his wife that will cut out all distractions and interference, and his eventual inability to do so. Ultimately, Trotter suggests that 'the problem in Mansfield's stories is that *all* communication is telecommunication', which requires the negotiation of a medium, interface and signal in order to function; her characters 'know that they have no choice but to communicate with each other at a distance, or through a barrier, created by habits, attitudes, and anxieties that are at once personal and political. But they don't know how' (p. 141).

Trotter's insistence that '*all* communication is telecommunication' for Mansfield brings us full circle, back to her own persistence in forging links and maintaining communication 'at a distance' in her personal correspondence. As Davison and Kimber note in their introduction to the Edinburgh Edition of the letters, throughout her life Mansfield produced an entire 'network of letters that [. . .] made their way across Britain, across Europe and even across the globe [. . .], fuelled by thriving rail and steamship connections and not yet under serious threat from the telephone' (p. 5). As such, they provide further evidence of Mansfield's location and participation within an increasingly expanding, interconnected, global system of (tele)communication. These impulses to seek connection have particular resonance at the time of writing, during a pandemic in which the world has become simultaneously more expansive and condensed, linked by video calls yet divided by local and national lockdowns. A century ago, at the end of another global pandemic that was prompted by the outbreak of influenza in 1918, Mansfield's *Bliss and Other Stories* was published, gathering together several stories in which characters sought to 'get the message through', as Trotter puts it (p. 236) – 'Bliss'; 'Psychology'; 'Je ne parle pas français', with its 'paradox of an announcement, in French, that someone doesn't speak French' ('Signes of Spring', p. 11). Again and again, in these stories and elsewhere, Mansfield's writing attests to the importance of these attempts at communication, so that what Ali Smith terms '[t]he casual, demanding, vital, dialogic attempt at getting to meaning' ('Signes of Spring', p. 11) recurs throughout her writing as a whole. On the evidence of the material under review here, this determination to 'get to meaning' continues to generate exciting new connections, new readings and new directions for Katherine Mansfield studies.

Notes on Contributors

Erika Baldt is Associate Professor at Rowan College at Burlington County, a community college in New Jersey, where she teaches composition and literature. Her research interests include Anglo-American modernism and cosmopolitanism, and she has published several essays on Katherine Mansfield and her contemporaries.

Martin Griffiths is a cello teacher, examiner for the New Zealand Music Education Board and principal cellist of Opus Orchestra (NZ), as well as guest performer with Vox Baroque and NZ Barok. He performed 'Katherine Mansfield, Cellist' at the 2019 Katherine Mansfield Society conference in Krakow, Poland. Martin is editor of the KMS Newsletter and has published in the journals *Tinakori* and *Crescendo*, as well as in Katherine Mansfield Studies.

Michael Hoover earned his undergraduate degree studying psychology and education. He then proceeded to open a business in a completely unrelated field. He is an avid reader and finally convinced himself to give writing a try.

Daniel Humberd is a journeyman sawyer and aspiring fiction writer living at the foot of the Great Smoky Mountains in the United States. He holds an MA in Communication.

Kathleen Jones is a poet, biographer and novelist whose subjects include Katherine Mansfield, Norman Nicholson, Catherine Cookson, Christina Rossetti and the women of the Wordsworth and Coleridge families. She worked in broadcast journalism and is the author of two novels and four collections of poetry. She is currently a Royal Literary Fund Fellow.

Janka Kascakova is Associate Professor in English at the Catholic University in Ružomberok, Slovakia, and Palacký University Olomouc, the Czech Republic. She is the Vice-President of the Katherine Mansfield Society and the author of numerous articles, book chapters and a monograph on Katherine Mansfield (2015), as well as a translator of Mansfield's short stories into Slovak (2013).

Gerri Kimber, Visiting Professor at the University of Northampton, is co-editor of Katherine Mansfield Studies and was Chair of the Katherine Mansfield Society for ten years. She is the deviser and Series Editor of the four-volume *Edinburgh Edition of the Collected Works of Katherine Mansfield* (2012–16) and, together with Claire Davison, is currently preparing a new four-volume edition of Mansfield's letters, also for Edinburgh University Press.

Monica Macansantos earned her MFA in Writing as a James A. Michener Fellow from the University of Texas at Austin, and her PhD in Creative Writing from the Victoria University of Wellington. Her work has recently appeared or is forthcoming in the *Colorado Review*, *Anomaly*, the *Pantograph Punch* and elsewhere.

Jenny McDonnell lectures at the Institute of Art, Design, and Technology (IADT) in Dún Laoghaire. She has published widely on the work of Katherine Mansfield, including the monograph *Katherine Mansfield and the Modernist Marketplace* (2010), as well as essays on material cultures in Robert Louis Stevenson's ghost stories, and New Zealand Mean Time in Samuel Butler's *Erewhon.*

Ann Herndon Marshall writes about the intersection of modernism and feminism, and especially about Katherine Mansfield, Elizabeth von Arnim and Vita Sackville-West. She holds a PhD from the University of Virginia and taught for twenty-five years at The Hill School in Pottstown, Pennsylvania. She now lives in Charlottesville, Virginia, with her husband, Richard Cappuccio.

Todd Martin is Professor of English at Huntington University and President of the Katherine Mansfield Society. He has published articles on John Barth, E. E. Cummings, Clyde Edgerton, Julia Alvarez, Edwidge Danticat, Sherwood Anderson and Katherine Mansfield. He is the co-editor of Katherine Mansfield Studies, and editor of *Katherine Mansfield and the Bloomsbury Group* (2017) and *The Bloomsbury Handbook to Katherine Mansfield* (2020).

Tracy Miao (Miao Miao) is a lecturer in English at Xi'an International Studies University in China, where she teaches literature and language courses. She has published essays and book chapters on Katherine Mansfield. Her recent work is an essay included in *The Bloomsbury Handbook to Katherine Mansfield* (2020).

J. Lawrence ('Larry') Mitchell is a book collector and Professor Emeritus at Texas A&M University, where he served as Head of English (1989–2004) and Director of the Cushing Memorial Library (2011–14). He has contributed to *The Edinburgh Edition of the Collected Letters of Katherine Mansfield* and his articles have appeared in a wide variety of journals.

Imola Nagy-Seres taught at the University of Exeter before undertaking a postdoctoral fellowship at the University of Tokyo. Her articles and reviews have been published in the *Elizabeth Bowen Review*, the *Journal of Modern Literature* and the *Modern Language Review*. Her current research focuses on the material culture of play in Victorian and modernist literature.

Oliver Stead is Curator of Drawings, Paintings, and Prints at the Alexander Turnbull Library, Wellington, New Zealand. Oliver undertook his doctoral research on the New Zealand-born art dealer and collector, Sir Rex Nan Kivell (1898–1977). He lives in Karori.

Index

Also available in the series:

Katherine Mansfield and Continental Europe
Edited by Delia da Sousa Correa and Gerri Kimber
Katherine Mansfield Studies, Volume 1

Katherine Mansfield and Modernism
Edited by Delia da Sousa Correa, Gerri Kimber and Susan Reid
Katherine Mansfield Studies, Volume 2

Katherine Mansfield and the Arts
Edited by Delia da Sousa Correa, Gerri Kimber and Susan Reid
Katherine Mansfield Studies, Volume 3

Katherine Mansfield and the Fantastic
Edited by Delia da Sousa Correa, Gerri Kimber, Susan Reid and Gina Wisker
Katherine Mansfield Studies, Volume 4

Katherine Mansfield and the (Post)colonial
Edited by Janet Wilson, Gerri Kimber and Delia da Sousa Correa
Katherine Mansfield Studies, Volume 5

Katherine Mansfield and World War One
Edited by Gerri Kimber, Todd Martin, Delia da Sousa Correa, Isobel Maddison and Alice Kelly
Katherine Mansfield Studies, Volume 6

Katherine Mansfield and Translation
Edited by Claire Davison, Gerri Kimber and Todd Martin
Katherine Mansfield Studies, Volume 7

Katherine Mansfield and Psychology
Edited by Clare Hanson, Gerri Kimber and Todd Martin
Katherine Mansfield Studies, Volume 8

Katherine Mansfield and Russia
Edited by Galya Diment, Gerri Kimber and Todd Martin
Katherine Mansfield Studies, Volume 9

Katherine Mansfield and Virginia Woolf
Edited by Christine Froula, Gerri Kimber and Todd Martin
Katherine Mansfield Studies, Volume 10

Katherine Mansfield and Elizabeth von Arnim
Edited by Gerri Kimber, Isobel Maddison and Todd Martin
Katherine Mansfield Studies, Volume 11

Katherine Mansfield and Bliss and Other Stories
Edited by Enda Duffy, Gerri Kimber and Todd Martin
Katherine Mansfield Studies, Volume 12

Katherine Mansfield and Children
Edited by Gerri Kimber and Todd Martin
Katherine Mansfield Studies, Volume 13

www.edinburghuniversitypress.com/series/KMSJ

EU representative:
Easy Access System Europe
Mustamäe tee 50, 10621 Tallinn, Estonia
Gpsr.requests@easproject.com

www.ingramcontent.com/pod-product-compliance
Lightning Source LLC
Chambersburg PA
CBHW070222030726
47505CB00006B/1785

* 9 7 8 1 4 7 4 4 9 1 9 1 4 *